VIVIAN AWAKENED

A COUPLES NARRATIVE OF A HOUSEWIFE'S EVOLUTION TO EMPOWERED HOTWIFE

SEBASTIAN WOLFE

© **Copyright 2025 Sebastian Wolfe - All rights reserved.**

The content contained within this book may not be reproduced, duplicated or transmitted without direct written permission from the author or the publisher.

Under no circumstances will any blame or legal responsibility be held against the publisher, or author, for any damages, reparation, or monetary loss due to the information contained within this book, either directly or indirectly.

Legal Notice:

This book is copyright protected. It is only for personal use. You cannot amend, distribute, sell, use, quote or paraphrase any part, or the content within this book, without the consent of the author or publisher.

Disclaimer Notice:

Please note the information contained within this document is for educational and entertainment purposes only. All effort has been executed to present accurate, up to date, reliable, complete information. No warranties of any kind are declared or implied. Readers acknowledge that the author is not engaged in the rendering of legal, financial, medical or professional advice. The content within this book has been derived from various sources. Please consult a licensed professional before attempting any techniques outlined in this book.

By reading this document, the reader agrees that under no circumstances is the author responsible for any losses, direct or indirect, that are incurred as a result of the use of the information contained within this document, including, but not limited to, errors, omissions, or inaccuracies.

This book could not have been written, or been made possible, without the love and support of two extremely important women in my life.

To my wife Vivian, thank you so much for being the inspiration to this story. Thank you for trusting in me to even make this adventure a reality in our lives and thank you for trusting me to share this story with the world. I know it may not be easy sharing our personal trials and tribulations out in the open and for that I am eternally grateful. This book would not have been a possibility without you and your support.

To my partner Lacey, I thank you so much for your unwavering support throughout the entirety of this writing process. You have been there for me from the start with the first keystroke made until the last keystroke of this dedication. I could not have dreamed that you would bring so much excitement and support to a book about our story. You have gone above and beyond with reading, editing, and providing me feedback on this book, and I am not sure I would have had the motivation to push through without you and your support. I hope you are ready for the next one!

CONTENTS

Prologue ... 7
Introduction ... 11

1. THE WHISPERS OF DESIRE ... 19
   Life in Predictable Patterns ... 21
   The Initial Spark ... 28
   Restless Whispers ... 34

   Interlude: Shane ... 39

2. DEFINING HOTWIFE: BEYOND THE EROTICA ... 43
   The Origin of Hotwifing ... 44
   The Emotional Spectrum for Her ... 52
   The Allure of a New World ... 56

   Interlude: Sebastian ... 61

3. CONVERSATIONS, CONCERNS, AND COURAGE ... 63
   Conversations, Dream, and Signs ... 64
   The Eye-Opening Revelation ... 72
   Bridging the Gap ... 78

   Interlude: Martin ... 87

4. AN OFFER SHE CAN'T REFUSE...RIGHT? ... 91
   The Choice ... 92
   The Emotions ... 94
   The 'No' ... 98

   Interlude: Vivian ... 101

5. THE EVOLUTION BEGINS ... 105
   The Catalyst ... 106
   Embracing Change ... 117
   Alternate Means ... 130

   Interlude: Nate, Jennifer & Christian ... 153

6. VIVIAN AWAKENED 161
   The Dance of Seduction 162
   The Awakening 178
   Navigating New Waters 190

   Interlude: Dante, Paulina & The Hot Tub 211

7. THE GOOD, THE BAD, AND THE UGLY 219
   The Downward Spiral 222
   The Line Crossed 243
   Exploring Boundaries Together 263

   Interlude: Wolves and Sheep 297

8. VIVIAN'S EMPOWERMENT 299
   The New Vivian - Reclaiming Sexuality 301
   Vivian's Empowerment 308
   Unexpected Endeavors 314

   Conclusion 359
   About the Author 365
   References 367

PROLOGUE

> "We must be willing to let go of the life we planned so as to have the life that is waiting for us."
>
> — JOSEPH CAMPBELL

I have shared this story numerous times with select individuals over the past few years, and the feedback has been nothing but consistent. *"What an amazing story! There are many couples out there dealing with similar situations that could benefit from you guys. I hope one day, my wife and I can reach the same level that you both have reached. You should write a book!"*.

Truth be told, the entire journey has never actually been told to just one person. Sure, some have heard fragments. Most have heard the beginning. Others know some of the parts in the middle. But no one, and I mean no one, has had the opportunity to hear the entirety of it until this very moment. You might even consider yourself privileged. Sharing the complete package has been an insurmountable task up until this point in time. It is just too grand of a narrative to tell verbally and would take far too many days. One main reason is that this magnificent story is a collection of minor occurrences, stepping stones if you will, that my wife and I have experienced over a nine-year timeframe. These small occurrences have compiled together to create this incredible journey that we have endured together. The most phenomenal part of this tale is that there is no ending yet. The future has yet to be decided.

Our true journey is just beginning, and that is the most exhilarating aspect of all of this. By now, you are asking yourself, who are we, and what is this story I keep rambling on about? We are Sebastian and Vivian Wolfe. We are a married couple madly in love after 22 years of marriage. This story is about transformation. This story is about personal growth. This story is about a scary journey down an uncharted, bumpy road that neither of us ever imagined in our wildest dreams. This story is about hope and inspiration. This story entails raw emotions. It involves desire, urges, courage, anxiety, trust, self-confidence, and communication (both good and bad). This story is about making mistakes, granting forgiveness, having patience, showing perseverance, and displaying love.

This story is about a highly fortunate man who is tremendously grateful to have the love of his beautiful and unique wife, yet just insane enough to risk potentially losing her to newfound sexual desires. It is about a devoted wife's self-growth and her ever-developing self-confidence. It is a story about her exploration of her own sexual desires and needs. The names and events have been changed to protect the innocent (and maybe not so innocent), but the occurrences and emotions that will unfold on the pages ahead are all filled with truth, heartache, and happiness. It's about a wife's internal transformation, her sexual exploration, and her newly found self-empowerment. This story is about Vivian and her awakening.

INTRODUCTION

> "To burn with desire and keep quiet about it is the greatest punishment we can bring on ourselves."
>
> — FEDERICO GARCÍA LORCA

There you are, standing in front of the mirror. You gaze at yourself and realize that your bow tie is just a bit crooked. You adjust it ever so perfectly and check one more time to ensure your tuxedo fits perfectly. You look fabulous! You finish washing and drying your hands, and you step out into the grand ballroom. Your eyes begin to shift as you scan the elegant crowd anxiously. So many shimmering gowns surround you. Beautiful women and handsome men everywhere. You head back to your table, but she isn't there. Her wine glass is there with her red lipstick marks around the rim of the glass. You notice her handbag there, with her phone, so she can't be far. Just then, your gaze focuses on another glass next to hers. There is an empty whiskey glass nestled right up against her wine glass. Your pulse immediately begins to increase.

You begin to scan the other tables, frantically searching for her golden locks trickling down her open-backed dress. She is nowhere in sight. Your heart rate quickens as you turn to your left and set your sites on the dance floor. The two of you have fantasized about this exact situation before, but never in your wildest dreams could you have imagined that she would engage in it! That's when it happens. You hear her laughter. Her infectious laughter. Her amazing and captivating, infectious laughter. Your eyes lock on her. There she is, but she is not out on that dance floor alone. Her arms are wrapped around another man's neck. Who the hell is this guy embracing your wife? Your adrenaline begins to cause your body to tremble at the site of his arms caressing her. Deep down inside, you wanted this, you remind yourself as you focus on them intently. You are just in shock that she is going through with it.

You notice one of his hands is around her neck, and it appears that he is stroking her soft hair while the other hand is gripping her around the small part of her back. Your pulse slows down a bit as you notice their hips are moving together in unison, grinding against each other. Why has your adrenaline failed you suddenly? Why are you not shaking and convulsing in anger, teeth grinding down to the bone, fists clenched so tight you hear your knuckles crack, with thoughts of his blood all over your split knuckles and tuxedo?

Why do you suddenly feel calm and observe them with intrigue? You inhale deeply as the slow and seductive song comes to an end. It's over. You will talk to your wife about this on the way home, and it will be…..hold on one minute. Why is she slowly raising her head and beaming at him? He says something to her, but it seems like a whisper that was only intended for her ears. He tilts his head while leaning down to her. This can't be! He begins gently kissing your wife. She hesitates a bit at first, but you are relieved that she is withstanding his charm. But simultaneously, you witness her weakening and giving in to him. Their lips and tongues are dancing in rhythm. You are frozen—a statue. You have never felt like this in your entire life. You are confused. Society has taught you that you should be absolutely furious with her, furious with them both, but you are not for some bizarre reason beyond comprehension. You are instead feeling mesmerized by the scene that has unfolded before your eyes. You are fixated on this embrace, lost in this kiss, taken aback by the passion and pleasure that this handsome stranger is causing her.

As he kisses her hand, he turns to walk away. She turns simultaneously and you notice her eyes are frantically scanning the dance floor. That's when it happens. Her eyes lock onto yours. There is a new look in her eyes. One that you do not recognize. There is something primal about her gaze. She begins to walk towards you with the slightest smirk forming from the corners of her perfect mouth that transitions into a pleased grin. Your heart pulses, but it feels different than it did just mere moments ago. You glance down at your pleated pants and notice that your excitement is on full display for all to see through the ultra-thin fabric. You look up, and there she is, standing in front of you with a yearning in her eyes that you have never borne witness to in your 20 years of marriage. You want her badly. Right there on the dance floor. It is inexplicable, and by all means, you should be livid with her, but the smile that she delivers tells you that everything is going to be just fine as she kisses you. Welcome to my life.

I am willing to wager that you are thinking one of two thoughts after you just read that scenario. There is a chance that you are likely appalled by the entire situation and would have been furious with your partner and her gentleman friend. On the flip side, there is a chance that you find yourself slightly intrigued about what transpired, and perhaps you were thinking that sounds kind of hot. What would your reaction be in this scenario? Would you be filled with hate and disgust, or would you be filled with passion and love? I suspect you might be the latter since you decided to read this book in the first place.

Truth be told, we live in a monogamy-driven society where the predominant thought process is that the scenario is inherently wrong. It is considered taboo. If a woman were to act as she did in that example, she would be unethical, deceptive, deceitful, and a downright unfaithful cheater. Many people will resonate with that way of thinking because that is the society in which we were born and raised. This book was not written for those people. This book was written for you.

This book was written for individuals who are not afraid to think outside the box. This book was written for the loving couples in the world that are interested in exploring boundaries and new dimensions together. It was written for the modern woman who is seeking her own discovery and

INTRODUCTION | 15

empowerment and is excited to hear the true story of another woman's transformation and self-discovery. It was written for the modern man who is comfortable with who he is and what he desires and wants nothing more than to guide his partner to a world of sexual freedom, autonomy, and empowerment. It was written for the curious reader who has an open mind and an open heart and who is perhaps interested in learning about the phenomenon that is the hotwife lifestyle.

At its core, *Vivian Awakened* is about my dear wife and her transformation from a devoted housewife to a vivacious hotwife, but that is not what led me to the realization that this story must be told. That is far too simplistic. Our story has many underlying themes and far more profound meanings than that, thus leading me to the conclusion that this story must be told to serve as encouragement and inspiration to others. What is our story truly about, then?

- It is about gaining a better understanding of societal molds and how they interact with alternative relationship dynamics.
- It is about defining personal growth and daring to push boundaries.
- It is about facing the challenges of change within love.
- It is about the importance of choice and autonomy.
- It is about the awakening of a woman who was suppressing her feelings deep inside and freeing herself from fear and judgment.
- It is about the hope, determination, and perseverance of a husband whose love for his wife knows no bounds.

Married life can be challenging. I don't think anyone can argue with that. Sometimes, within the complexities of married life (careers, children, car payments, mortgages, etc.), the urge for novelty can develop. Once the urge is recognized, it can smolder and start to burn hotter until it develops into a desire. When we admit that we have a smoldering desire inside of us, we are faced with deciding how best to act on this desire. We have the option of putting that fire out instantly and burying the desire in the ashes of our urge, or we have the option of fanning the flames with a bit of oxygen until the desire is raging wild and burning almost out of control.

As you read through the pages of this book and learn of our trials and tribulations, we urge you to keep an open mind. We are certainly not perfect, and we have absolutely made our share of mistakes along the way, but we have learned and grown together. We hope others will learn from us and avoid making the same mistakes that we have made. Try to relate your own experiences to our personal stories and attempt to relate to both sides with reflective empathy. We hope that this story will awaken love, trust, and potential for change within all of you.

1

THE WHISPERS OF DESIRE

> *"The desire to live within our comfort zone and to be in control all the time is a denier of a fulfilling life that excites. Let go."*
>
> — ASSEGID HABTEWOLD

It was twenty-two years ago that my entire life was destined to change forever. I did not think I was capable of falling in love again. My shields were up. I was on the defensive. I was in my mid-twenties, and I was guarding my heart from another invasion by one more unfaithful lover. It must be me, I would think to myself. I considered myself unlovable. I had spent that past year and a half mourning the death of my four-year relationship with a girl who decided it was more fun to cheat on me with a married man. I should rephrase that. I had spent half a year mourning the death of my four-year relationship, and I had spent the last year drinking, clubbing, and sleeping with every girl I could find who was interested in me. It was an exhilarating year for sure, but its allure and luster quickly ran its course. I found myself at the point where I wanted to settle down soon with the girl of my dreams if I could find her. If, I could trust her.

It was a Saturday night when I was invited to go out to dinner and a concert with my very good friend Damien and his girlfriend, Brigitte. Brigitte was a beautiful and sweet girl who always tried to hook me up with her cute friends, but it never quite seemed to work out. On that given Saturday evening, she told me that I had to attend because she had some gorgeous friends coming and insisted that I would not want to miss out on meeting them.

I suppose it was divine timing that caused a flat tire for me that night and made it so that I arrived at the restaurant just a smidge late. I was rushing in from the parking garage at that point. I despise being late. I scurried into the restaurant and saw my friend waving to me from his table, so I hurried in that direction. That is when time stopped. Ok, it did not stop, but it slowed down considerably. I felt as if I was in a movie scene with the main character walking in slow motion for the dramatic effect as I made my way to the only empty chair at their crowded table. As I approached the chair, I thought to myself; I must be the luckiest man alive because right in the chair next to mine was the most stunning girl I had ever laid my eyes on. She was absolutely lovely. Her blond hair almost reached her shoulders, and she had a sexy, messy look that drives me wild to this day. I already loved the way she tucked it behind one ear as she engaged in conversation. She had the greenest eyes I had ever seen in my life. It was like looking into the Caribbean Ocean when she turned her head to gaze at me as I started to round the corner of the table, slowly approaching the vacant seat next to her. She had the most endearing little dimples that lit up her face when she smiled at me as I sat down and slid my chair in next to hers. "Hello. My name is Vivian". Checkmate!

LIFE IN PREDICTABLE PATTERNS

To say it was love at first sight would not only be the use of a sappy and overworked cliché, but it also doesn't do any justice at all to how we truly felt. The phrase feels a bit inadequate if I am being truthful. I should rephrase for clarity's sake. It was love at first sight for me. She was terrific in every sense of the word. Her infectious laugh, her sexy Central European accent, her warm and endearing smile, and her magnetic personality all draw you in within a nanosecond of meeting her. I was fascinated by her. She thought I was cute, but she was also guarded, having been recently single from the most toxic relationship to human trash that you can imagine. She thought I looked like a "bad boy" type, which had always attracted her, so she was intrigued by me. She had been enjoying her newfound freedom from the biggest scum on the earth when her friend Brigitte invited her to a concert with dinner beforehand. She decided to accept the invitation and showed up a bit late. Thank you universe for saving her a seat next to the last open chair at the table.

The Love Story

My persistence, "bad boy" looks, and witty charm won her over in almost no time at all. It was not long before we were entirely in bliss. We were engaged a short time after meeting and married even a shorter time after that. Marriage suited us just fine. We were madly in love, and our sex life was great. It was not what it is now in the present time, mind you. We have indeed evolved, but we will get to that a bit later! When we first got married, we both thought we had fantastic sex, but looking back now, we realized that perhaps we were both holding back. I was very shy, and I am still very introverted, but I had developed very low self-confidence over my body. I was not comfortable being seen naked over my not-so-toned abs and my average, to below-average, sized manhood. I was sure that I could not make a woman happy with my length or girth. I had convinced myself that this was why my previous girlfriends had cheated on me. I was positive I was not enough for them and that they needed a bigger guy to make them happy. Vivian seemed quite satisfied with my size from day one, so I must have been doing something right!

As I mentioned before, Vivian is an extremely beautiful woman. She always had been, even when she was a young teen. Her biggest roadblock was that she did not know it or believe it. Despite my comparison of her to a mix between Cameron Diaz and Scarlett Johanson, she had very low self-esteem and low self-confidence in her body. She said she always felt like a teenage boy with no boobs and no ass. Vivian grew up in a relatively small town in Central Europe, and she was the prettiest girl around. She disagrees with this statement, but that's just one of her roadblocks. Despite her self-described "teenage boy body", Vivian was extremely popular with the boys. She had so many guy friends because she got along with guys much better than she did with girls. Her biggest problem was that she was very hot, and guys would like her "too much", or even fall in love with her, causing her to get scared and avoid them with all her might. She could not have them fall in love with her. It terrified her.

Later in her teens, she kissed a good number of guys and even performed oral sex on a few of them, but when it came to intercourse, she was too fearful and would push them away. She wanted to lose her virginity badly, and the day finally came when she would give in and face her fears. Unfortunately for her, the guy's package was so big that it hurt her, and she had to make him stop immediately. The experience traumatized her for a long time before she finally decided to try again. At that point, she had so much anxiety about sex that the second guy was beginning to enter her when she again made him stop. She was so worried about sex that she would push any guy away who got too close to her, even though she wanted it. At the age of nineteen, Vivian was strong enough to go for it, and she gave her virginity to her boyfriend, to whom she would stay faithful for the next two years despite his cheating, manipulation, and toxic presence.

As their relationship collapsed before her, she was presented with the opportunity of a lifetime to become an au pair and move across the world to the United States. Vivian made the most significant decision she would ever make in her life when she packed up her belongings and left everything behind. She came to America with the mindset that it would be a temporary move to gain new experiences and improve her understanding of the English language. It was only for a one-year contract, but it would put her in the position to return to her homeland and make much more money in the capital if she were fully bilingual. While Vivian was doing her best to integrate into her new country, she was trying to maintain a long-distance relationship with her boyfriend back home for reasons that neither of us could explain. Vivian remained faithful and celibate for an entire year. The woman was a saint.

Vivian made new friends, of course, but with people from her own country, so her English was not improving much since they spoke their own language predominately. She loved going to bars and dance clubs and loved flirting with guys, but the language barrier always crept up as a bit of an issue when it came to having any real conversation and connection. After almost a year apart, she decided to plan a trip for her and her boyfriend to New York City to try and rekindle their relationship before her triumphant return home. They had their issues, and he was hurting her constantly, but she loved him and very much wanted it to work out with him. After a year of celibacy, she was very excited to be together when she boarded her plane and flew to New York City to meet him. She waited for him at the arrival terminal that day, but he never walked through that gate. Vivian never heard from him ever again.

Devastation, self-loathing, and anger overtook her emotions. She was faithful to him for an entire year, even while feeling nearly certain that he was cheating on her the whole time, yet there she was, waiting for him so that they could revive whatever spark they once had between them. She paid for his plane ticket and managed the whole trip for him, but he never got on the flight. Vivian did the only logical thing there was to do in that situation. She went out that night, met a guy at a club, and went back to his room to engage in primal sex that she desperately needed, and then she was gone. Vivian fought her way through the breakup for many months until the fateful night that I sat in the empty chair next to her. She was deeply hurt, and I am more than grateful that she even gave me a chance to love her.

Vivian and Sebastian – *The Early Years*

Shortly after we married, I discovered that Vivian had only those two sexual partners and that she did not have much sexual experience at all. My mind was blown! She told me that, looking back, she really loved the idea of sex and wished she was not scared of it when she was a teenager. She also found that she would get bored with one guy after too long and would create a reason to move on from them. She admitted that she wished she had engaged in more sex with other guys before getting married to have that experience and that fun. In the next breath, however, she said it's a good thing she lost her virginity at such a late age. She told me, "If I had lost my virginity at a younger age, I probably would have become a whore with all the guys that wanted me." You can be certain I took a mental note of that comment.

With all that being said, due to both of our self-confidence issues with our bodies, we made love in complete darkness for many years. We were both very quiet during sex, almost afraid to show our pleasure and show how much we enjoyed each other. There was no dirty talk, there were no spankings, and most nights, it was just missionary sex because that was what felt most comfortable for both of us. I enjoyed other positions immensely, but we could not find the comfort level to make the positions pleasing for both of us.

We both can agree that our sex life, while very satisfying to each other, was also very conventional. Conventional sex, which is also sometimes known as vanilla sex, is regular sex that doesn't include kinks, toys, or fetishes. You could have put our picture next to the phrase in the dictionary. But we were immensely happy, and that is all that really mattered. We were so happy that we decided to start a family. Something funny happens after you start a family. As almost every married couple can attest, you can easily slip into the mundane daily routines and tasks, which can lead to you losing sight of each other in the process.

Daily Routines and Tasks

In the absolute blink of an eye, twelve years can disappear with the snap of your fingers. There is no warning. There is no goodbye. They are just gone. Vanished into thin air without a trace. Our lives were very different twelve years later. We had belly-flopped into the deep end of married life and parenting, but luckily, we were still treading water. We swiftly became the All-American mom and dad. Both Vivian and I had full-time professional careers that were demanding of us, to say the least. We had both just spent the last ten years slowly working on our degrees so that we could improve our financial situation and live more comfortably. We had two small children between the ages of ten and two. For all the married couples out there, I do not have to tell you what careers, classes, small children, a mortgage, two-car payments, student loans, and tons of credit card debt can do to your sex life with your spouse. Oh, I forgot to mention that I worked overnights, so I was only home two to three nights a week; therefore, any time we could enjoy each other needed to be scheduled in advance. So much for spontaneity.

Our days were full of stressful work, crying kids, boogers, poopy diapers, rushed dinners, baths, and temper tantrums. Unfortunately, these daily routines and tasks can suck the life out of a marriage and drain it dry of lust and desire. We had our arguments and disappointing nights because of sex, or the lack thereof, but at the end of the day, we had a typical loving and normal marriage that utilized love, trust, and stability as the foundation on which we were based. I never considered myself to be an abnormal husband. I made love to my wife once or twice a week and satiated the rest of my needs with pornography and masturbation when I could not be with her. It was an arrangement that was working for us just perfectly. No need to rock the boat. Well, have you ever experienced one small and insignificant event that caused you to spiral out of control and alter everything you thought you knew or felt? Hold my beer.

THE INITIAL SPARK

It was a hot summer night; fortunately, the sun had finally started embarking on its descent behind the tall oak trees. The shade of dusk had been most welcoming. We had been tailgating for two hours in the blistering sun with a large group of our friends, eating smoked barbeque and drinking cold beers while we anticipated entering the music festival. I was on grill duty, which I do not wish upon anyone. Not in that heat and not for that amount of people. I was grateful that the beer was ice cold and that Vivian was having a great time. She was in her element! She was laughing, smiling, and genuinely enjoying herself. I loved seeing her that happy. Vivian also enjoyed the ice-cold beer, and I could see her letting go a little more with each sip. Most of the people that we were tailgating with were coworkers of hers. She started a new job about a year prior, and she really immersed herself with her new friends wonderfully. I could tell she was not as happy as she used to be. We had moved to a state far from home very recently, and she seemed to be struggling with the change of scenery. She was getting agitated at home more quickly than I was used to witnessing, and she openly complained that she was tired of only being around kids all day. She needed adults in her life. This new job was what she needed. She was alive again.

The Spark of Dormant Desire

Over the past year, we had gone out with most of her new friend's multiple times, and I was very aware that there was a slight shift in her when she was with them. Vivian was always entertaining when she was drinking, but more recently, she would become very flirty with her female friends. It was nothing too over the top, but lots of touching, lots of dirty talk filled with sexual innuendos, and lots of jokes or comments riddled with sexual undertones. It was a new version of Vivian that I really enjoyed. I could not tell if she was changing and becoming more open or if this was always her, and she was finally comfortable with being her true self in front of me after thirteen years. Either way, it did not matter. I enjoyed the spark that had ignited inside of her.

I had just finished cooking all the food and grabbed another beer out of the cooler when I noticed Vivian was chatting awfully close to her coworker, Shane. I had met Shane a few times before that day, and I sure did hear a lot about him at home. It was not long after Vivian started her job that she came home telling me stories about him. She told me how nice he was. She told me how funny he was. She told me how smart he was. She told me how well-endowed he was. How would she know that you ask? It was rumored that Shane was sleeping with another one of Vivian's coworkers, Natalie. It quietly spread through their office like wildfire, and it quickly spread inside my home as well. Vivian told me about the rumored sexual relationship in the workplace and happened to mention the potential size of his tool. She and I made some jokes about her coworker needing "the monster" inside of her, and I do not use that term in a derogatory way toward anyone who is exceptionally well-endowed. I will trade places with you in a heartbeat, but I digress.

Inside the festival, I bought another drink for me and Vivian, and we made our way to the lawn section with our group. I was standing there, involved in conversation and having a great time, when my previously alluded to small and insignificant moment occurred right before my eyes. Vivian and Shane were talking to each other, but that time was different. That time, there was this undeniable connection between them that towered over the previous minor flirtations that I had seen. There was this aura of sexual energy being transferred between them. They were standing side by side but wrapped in a one-armed embrace. Their bodies faced the festival stage with Vivian's right arm wrapped around Shane's back. Shane draped his left arm over my wife's shoulder, around her neck, and down her other shoulder with his left hand close to her breast. Their heads were turned towards each other as they continued their quiet conversation.

My initial emotion was instant jealousy and confusion. What the hell is my wife doing? Is there something going on between them also? Is she so drunk that she forgets that I am here, or worse yet, does not care that I am here? She has made it super obvious that she likes him, but to what level? These random thoughts all sped through my brain at the speed of sound and all at the same exact time. I was not angry, which surprised me. I was more confused. I was in shock. I decided I needed to get closer to investigate better. Their situation was not improving with every slow step I took to get closer. It was actually getting worse. I could then see their faces.

They were staring at each other very intently, almost gazing into each other's eyes, as they drunkenly carried on with their conversation. Shane's face filled with lust and desire, looking into my wife's eyes as if he was getting ready to press his lips on hers. Vivian's face moved closer towards his with an expression that is best described as "take me eyes" that I knew rather well. I stopped maybe six feet behind them in astonishment. I started to get a little upset. Their facial expressions gave away what they were feeling, and Vivian now had her face about three inches from his. It appeared as if an inevitable kiss was about to occur at any moment. I then made a split-second decision that I would break it up peacefully before it was taken too far. For whatever reason, before I made my move to breakup whatever this was, I took out my phone, and I snapped a picture of them.

"What's going on ever here, you two?" I interrupted playfully while sliding my phone back into my pocket.

"Hey, baby!!" Vivian drunkenly yelled out, but I could tell she was not rattled about what I had just interrupted. She was genuinely happy to see me.

"Sebastiannnnnn!!" Shane loudly proclaimed as he wrapped his arm around my neck now. He was also not rattled.

Just then, another girl from our group came into our little trio with her phone in her hand and suggested that the four of us take a selfie together. We jumped into a quick pose with Shane in the middle, me on his right, Vivian on his left, and the selfie girl squatted low in front of Shane. "Cheeeeeeese!!!" We all smiled at the camera. Well, almost all of us.

Sebastian's Awakening

Sunday morning arrived, and my hangover was not very kind to me, but we sure did have a fun time the night before. The image of Vivian and Shane flashed in my mind. I had a lot of fun with Shane at the festival, but was he someone I should be worried about? I was not sure if asking her outright about the moment they shared was the best idea. It was really hard to deny the look they had for each other, though. I opened my phone and looked at the picture again. Damn, they really looked like they were going to kiss. I stared at the picture, contemplating if I had been overthinking it and fabricated a soon-to-be affair in my head or not. I was a bit confused about how I felt, if I am being totally honest. The picture was just seductive enough to make your typical jealous husband go bonkers, yet I felt something else entirely.

Later that day, the selfie girl sent a bunch of pictures to all of us in a group message. As I scrolled, I began to notice a theme from these pictures that I had not quite seen in person. Vivian was in most of the photographs in some capacity. However, she was very flirty or devious-looking in almost all of them. I went back through the rotation one more time just to be sure.

- There was a picture of her leaning over to the camera while squeezing her cleavage together with a big smile on her face. *Swipe.*
- Her bending over with a sticker on her ass that read "Spank Me I've Been Naughty." *Swipe.*
- Another identical picture with a girl spanking her while her own hand is over her mouth playfully. *Swipe.*
- Vivian sitting on the lap of the selfie girl, laughing. *Swipe.*
- Sitting on the same selfie girl, but the girl's face was in Vivian's cleavage, and the girl was pretending to lick her boobs. Wow. Was this my wife? *Swipe.*
- And there was the last picture in the thread. The selfie of the four of us, all smiling for the camera. Except for Vivian. Oh, she is smiling for sure! It's just this one tiny detail. Her head was turned directly, and she was staring at Shane!

I closed the thread and dropped my phone on the bed. Well, that was it. That was all the proof I needed. If Shane was not already sleeping with my wife, I was sure that he would be soon. I opened my phone and returned to my picture of the two of them. I stared at it as my brain was suddenly filled with lots of emotions. I was convinced my wife was enjoying his rumored monster package or that she really wanted it and would be on it soon. I did not recognize how that thought made me feel inside. It was foreign. There was an initial feeling of sadness that engulfed me at the thought of that possibility. She was the love of my life and the mother of my children. How could I have let that happen? I imagined her kissing him in a loving embrace like the ones we shared.

Anger began to creep in next. I imagined her on her knees, with her eyes staring up at him, and her mouth stretched around him as he filled her throat.

My wavering thoughts transitioned to her long, gorgeous legs locked around his waist with her arms wrapped around his neck as he pounded and thrust deep inside of her while she moaned and shook with ecstasy like never before in her life. It was at this moment that everything transformed suddenly. Something so highly profound yet so decidedly terrifying transpired inside of me. I felt this undeniable and unexplainable feeling of being turned on. Vivian's body in multiple positions coursed through my brain. I peered at the picture once again. My imagination had them kissing right there in front of me, tongues swirling, his hands ravaging her body. I was so turned on unexpectedly with the thought of seeing my wife with another guy right in front of me. This felt like madness. This felt like the most unnatural and dangerous feeling that I had ever experienced. Little did I know, a desire that lay dormant deep inside of me, down at the deepest corners of my subconscious and being, had been sparked.

RESTLESS WHISPERS

After I had to take care of myself and had a tremendously strong and intense orgasm, I decided that it was in my best interest not to bring the picture up to Vivian quite yet. I needed time to digest the situation appropriately. I needed time to figure out this monumental transformation that I was going through. I had always been a somewhat jealous and protective type of husband with Vivian up until that point, so having that feeling of almost wanting her to have this connection with Shane and imagining them kissing and pleasing each other was just too intense for me to comprehend. It did not make sense to me whatsoever. I decided to block it out and move on with my life. Forget all about my newfound desires and pray that Vivian was not having an affair. Questioning her would likely lead to a huge fight due to her history of being defensive when questioned about things like this. I put it to rest. That is when the dreams started happening. I began having very intense dreams about Vivian having sex with other men or multiple men, and most of them ended the same exact way. I would come home some night from work and find her in a sexual act, but with her behaving like everything was fine and she had done no wrong. Like she was innocent, and what she was doing was actually no big deal at all.

Daydreams and Fantasies

These dreams spilled over into daydreams, which, of course, rapidly morphed into fantasies. My mind began to run wild. I was at the point where I could not even pleasure myself without imagining Shane coming over to visit. Oh, this was my favorite fantasy by far. He would sit on the couch with us, her in the middle, of course, and she would turn to me and ask me if she could see his package. I, being the loving husband that I am, would say yes, of course. She would take it out, play with it, stroke it, and comment on how big it was before turning to me one more time to tell me she had never sucked one that big before. She would then ask me if she could put it in her mouth. You can imagine how this continued. Am I normal? That was the question I would ask myself many times over.

I began to feel that there must be something wrong with me to have let those feelings go that far. What husband in his right mind fantasizes about his beautiful wife being in numerous sexual encounters with her co-worker? I became scared and started to freak out a little bit because I felt that my thoughts had begun to spin out of control, and it felt as if I was losing my mind. I had just turned thirty-seven at that point. Was it a midlife crisis of some sort? Was I the only one that happens to? Did my friends think of their wives that way? Could I talk to them about it? I decided it was time to investigate, so I sprung onto my computer, and in the search bar, I typed, "Is it normal to want your wife to have sex with other men?" I am not sure what shook me more, the extent of my strange sexual fantasies that revolved around my pure angel spouse or the answer that was about to hit me square in the face on my computer screen.

World of Hotwifing

One hundred and three million. Such a large number. Is it not? One hundred and three million results when I typed that question into my search engine just now as I write this. I am not aware how many results appeared when I did just that almost eleven years ago, but nevertheless, you can appreciate the fact that those numbers are staggering. With that amount of information readily available at the click of a mouse, I was more than relieved to discover that I was not alone in these thoughts. Links to all sorts of articles appeared before me to ease my worried mind.

- *What Secret Male Sexual Fantasy is Surprisingly Common?*
- *Why Would Any Man Want to Watch His Wife With Another Man?*
- *How To Encourage My Wife To Have Sex With Other Men*
- *Wife Sharing: Why Does My Husband Want To Share Me?*

I am not alone. A calming wave of relief flushed over me as I repeated those four words to myself. I was not alone. For a hundred and three million search results to come up from such a question, there had to be millions of other men who felt the way I did, if not billions. I felt liberated and exhilarated all at once! There was so much information available, and I had no idea where to even begin. I knew one thing for sure. My perverse thoughts finally had a name. Wife sharing. Wife sharing sounded so delightful and fun. I scrolled and clicked. Scrolled and clicked. There were articles, blogs, communities, stories, and websites. My mind was opened to a whole new world that I never knew even existed. I came across the term "Alternative Lifestyles". I needed to explore that more, but just before I clicked that link, there was a new term that caught my attention just a bit more. Hotwife! *Click.*

Ok, so if I have a wife that is hot, then that means I have a hotwife correct? Not so fast. I quickly found out what the difference was between having a hot wife and having a hotwife. A hotwife is a married woman who has sexual encounters with other men with the consent and knowledge of her husband (www.dictionary.com, 2018). These were my people. Husbands who loved showing off and sharing their beautiful, hot wives actually existed! Married wives who were happy to agree to meet other men and enjoyed having sex with them actually existed! I read so many articles and stories that day that my mind was overloaded. I discovered clarity that day in my wants and desires. I discovered what I wanted my marriage to develop into, but I had no idea how we were going to get there. I had discovered that all I wanted was for Vivian to become a hotwife, and I was determined that I was going to do all I could to help her evolve into just that. Vivian, my little hotwife! I needed more research to make that happen. *Scroll and click.*

INTERLUDE: SHANE

When Sebastian asked me to move very far away from the home that we were building, I was not sure about it. After moving to this country, it took many years of school and many years of studying English to finally start my career in an Industry I was great at. For the first time in forever, I was not watching children. I was not a nanny anymore. Believe it or not, I truly loved that I could go to my job, be relied on by adults, and have adult conversations while not being surrounded by crying children all day.

I loved Sebastian and I trusted him that this move across the country would be the best for our family. I left my job that I loved. I didn't really have enough experience yet to be considered for a new job for relocation. We decided we would wait to get established in the area before we searched for me, so after the move, you guessed it, I went back to watching kids. It wasn't bad at first, but after spending all my days with five screaming kids for an entire year, I was starting to go a little bit crazy. I was feeling very depressed. I needed more adult contact in my life. We had no *friends where we moved to. All I had was Sebastian. I love him dearly, but with him not being home many nights a week, I felt so alone.*

As you can imagine, through this period of my life, I wasn't feeling very sexually excited. It's hard to feel sexy and good about yourself when you are sad or disappointed and feeling isolated. I tried to keep these feelings to myself the best I could, but I wasn't doing such a great job. On the nights that Sebastian was home from work, of course, he wanted to have sex with me, but I struggled with desire. There were many nights that he was thinking that we would make love, but I just wanted to put my pajamas on and go to sleep. I would explain to him that I wasn't in the mood and was tired and would ask if we could wait until the next night, or I would just go through with it, but then he could tell I wasn't fully present with him. Our diminishing sex life had started to cause many arguments and problems between us.

We had many discussions about this, and he knew I needed a change to start to feel happy again, so finally, after a year, I was able to get a job in my industry! I was so excited to be working with adults again; you have no idea. This is where I established myself in with my new friends at work. I felt so happy to have them in my life. It was so fun to go out after work, have some drinks, and enjoy a little freedom. Very quickly, I became friends with my coworker Shane. He was awesome. He was this funny guy that was so cool and smart. Shane and I had lunch together a lot at work, and it was so nice to just talk to him about all sorts of things. We talked about our families, our childhood, our parents, and our experiences in the world in general. It is true I developed a strong closeness with Shane, but it was never on the sexual level that Sebastian thinks. I always described us like we were brother and sister.

I was excited for Sebastian to meet Shane, and they did hit it off nicely. I was worried because Sebastian could sometimes be a little jealous, but Shane was so easy to like. The few times we all partied together with my new group of coworkers, Sebastian and Shane were great together. This made me very happy. Then, one night, we all went to a concert, and I guess lots of things changed for Sebastian after that night. My husband is correct. I was changing a bit. I had this new group of friends that was very funny and maybe a little inappropriate at times, but they fit my style that I missed from when I was a teenager. I always enjoyed people just laughing, making jokes, and being free to say what was on their mind. Not to be scared. I started to open up a bit out of my shell, and yes, even in front of Sebastian. I think where we lived before, with our old group of friends, I was not able to be myself. Here, I felt more free, and Sebastian seemed to be ok with it. So, I continued. At the concert, I had a little too much to drink, I think. There are pieces I remembered and some I didn't. Yes, I was talking closely with Shane at the concert, but again, it was more as very great friends. There was not the sexual desire that Sebastian thought or that he sees when he looks at that picture of us. It truly was innocent.

2

DEFINING HOTWIFE: BEYOND THE EROTICA

> "She's a summer love in the spring, fall, and winter. She can make happy any man alive."
>
> — GRATEFUL DEAD

There were several studies conducted back in 2019 that were researching the topic of Consensual Non-Monogamy (CNM), also known as Ethical Non-Monogamy (ENM), or more commonly known as open relationships, among young adults in North America. The results may shock you and I am confident the numbers have increased since then. The data concluded that approximately 4% of adults admitted to having sexual relations with others with permission granted, had engaged in swapping sexual partners, were practicing polyamory, and were committed to more than one person. Now, 4% does not sound like a huge number, but according to (Castleman, 2019), "it means one couple in 25. If you know two dozen couples, chances are one participates in consensual non-monogamy (CNM), also known as "open" relationships. Put another way, 4 percent means some 2.8 million U.S. couples."

Castleman (2019) went on to say that several studies show that swinger couples, in comparison to monogamous couples, typically report the following:

- Appear to be in happier marriages
- Express more affection to their spouse
- Find their sex to be more gratifying
- Engage in more robust communication in the marriage
- Have praise for their spouse more often
- Display less jealousy

Ok, so one out of every twenty-five couples, on average, explores alternative lifestyles, enjoys swapping sexual partners, and practices consensual non-monogamy. This data was alarming to me, without a doubt, but this didn't tell me much more about the hotwife lifestyle. I was not interested in swapping sexual partners whatsoever. My primary fantasy was sharing my wife with other men only. I needed to find more answers about the hotwife lifestyle. Next, we will explore the origin of hotwifing and unpack the term on a deeper level.

THE ORIGIN OF HOTWIFING

The term hotwife became mainstream in 1997 when horny husbands like me started personal ads because they wanted to show off their hot wives to other men. It eventually transformed into what it is today. Here is what I discovered:

- **Hotwife:** A hotwife is a woman who is married and has sexual relationships with other men, all with her husband's consent. The husband does not have any affairs of his own.
- **Hotwifing:** Conducting the prearrangement of the wife-sharing event and engaging in sexual affairs.

Hotwifing vs. Cuckolding

The pertinent question here is how many men actually fantasize about their wives having sexual relations with other men? Get ready for it, people. Men, you are not alone in your feelings; half your friends feel the same as you but will not admit it. Ladies, there is a 50/50 chance your husband wants you to sleep with other men, so if you have an interest in becoming a hotwife, then go on and ask him if you can. Research back in 2018 showed that 45 percent of men had sexual fantasies about seeing their female partners engaged in sexual activity with other men (Lehmiller, 2018). This data coincides with pornography research that suggests that pornography searches related to cuckolding have increased yearly, are becoming more widespread, and have become very popular.

You may be asking yourself right now, what is a cuckold, and how does it differentiate from the world of hotwifing? That is a fantastic question! Let's dive deeper, shall we? The major factor that distinguishes cuckolding from hotwifing comes down to the level of participation by the husband. The husband's involvement depends entirely on the couple's prior agreement and comfort level. In a hotwife scenario, the husband may not be involved at all. The wife may partake in her affairs on her own and go on dates independently, leaving her husband at home. When the wife returns home, the husband may want to hear about her date to arouse him. In some scenarios, the fortunate husband is allowed to watch the sexual encounter between his wife and the other man occur before his eyes.

With cuckolding, there is still another man pleasuring your partner in front of you, but the husband often plays a more interactive yet submissive role to the other man, and sometimes humiliation can play a part. Research has found that with either option a couple chooses, there is no substantial difference between them and monogamous people. They are still normal and healthy people who are playing out their sexual desires and staring down shame and taboo right in the face. I needed to find some answers as to who initiates cuckolding and hotwifing in a relationship and how I could attempt to get this conversation started with Vivian. I found the following quote, "When I investigated cuckolding and hotwifing, this was a practice almost universally introduced by the husbands to their wives. I heard only rarely, if ever, about women who chose to seek this out themselves, or introduced it independently, for their own interests. It was almost always something that occurred in relationships that had been stable and lasting, and had started monogamously." (Ley, 2022). Ok, that was great news! I was not the only one who had these thoughts, and in these proven scenarios, the man typically introduced it to their wives. And it worked!

The Psychology Behind the Lifestyle

If I was going to bring this up to Vivian, I needed to have some solid evidence backing me up to show her that this would be a good idea for us to pursue. I knew that I was not alone in having those feelings, but admittedly, I still had not grasped what really changed in my mind to cause them. Witnessing Vivian and Shane in their intimate moment certainly was a trigger, but where did I get it from initially? There are many psychological factors that can motivate a man to want to chase the hotwife lifestyle for his spouse. For some people, it's the pure allure of engaging in something that is highly taboo and embracing the feeling that they are doing something that is considered by most to be shameful or even immoral. Others have said that they had been cheated on in the past, and they are now turned on by their current wife doing that to them. I can assure you that my memories of being cheated on did not play a role in the desires that I had so strongly.

That's when I stumbled upon another group of people, and I knew in a heartbeat that this was the category where I fit in perfectly. For this group of people, there is a very high level of arousal that is experienced when they see their partner being satisfied sexually. Knowing that other people find their partner attractive is their ultimate high. Sharing these intense and magical moments of trust and love is a feeling like no other. Understanding that their partner will still be theirs and be home with them at the end of the day fills them with tremendous levels of confidence, joy, and happiness. This was me essentially, but I came to the stark realization that my motivation had a tiny different flavor to it. My passion was fueled by compersion.

I did not know what compersion was until I conducted my research on wife sharing. I also knew that I had not fully experienced compersion up to that point, perhaps a very small dose of it, with my happy feeling that Shane may be attracted to my wife. One thing was for sure. I wanted it. I needed to experiment more to increase my compersion for Vivian. In its simplest form, compersion just means a form of joy in other people. You typically feel joy for your child when they learn to walk, learn to ride a bike, get accepted into college, etc. You feel 100% pure joy and happiness for that child. I discovered that people living in the CNM lifestyle have a different interpretation of the word.

Per (MasterClass, 2023), "In the world of consensually non-monogamous relationships, it more specifically relates to the happiness someone finds in their partner seeking out and enjoying sexual and romantic intimacy with other people." What I found astonishingly fascinating was that compersion is essentially the opposite of jealousy. A person who is immersed in compersion does not feel jealous or possessive toward their partner for experiencing this joy and sexual satisfaction with someone else; rather, they are there side by side to embrace and celebrate their experiences right with them (MasterClass, 2018). I knew I had the chance at reaching compersion if we were to venture down this road, and I discovered I had more reasons than I thought.

Let me start off by saying that since the day we met, I have felt that I did not deserve Vivian. I have felt that she was meant to have been with someone better than me. I felt that she was so far above me that I counted my blessings each day that I was with her because I knew that she could be with anyone that she chose to be with. I still feel this way about her today, and she knows that. She calls me silly when I say things like this and reassures me that she loves me very much, but it is how I feel. I have always put her very high on a pedestal. You may be thinking right now, Sebastian, why on earth would you be willing to push her into the beds of other men when you hold her in such high regard and risk losing her? Oh, it comes with its risks, do not get me wrong, and we will get to that in the next section. However, I desired this so intensely and was potentially willing to risk our marriage for the following reasons:

1. **We Had a Very Strong Marriage:** Let me start this off by stating that if you are not in a strong, loving, and, yes, committed marriage, then you absolutely should not attempt CNM, hotwifing, or cuckolding. If you are getting into these lifestyles for the wrong reasons, like forcing your wife to sleep with other men just so you can sleep with other women, the percentage of relationship failure is exceptionally high. We were in a loving and strong marriage, and I

knew in my heart that it would always be me and her until the end. Even with my own issues over self-worth, I trusted her profoundly and had faith in our marriage and relationship.

2. **Unconditional Love for Her:** I loved her so much that all I ever wanted was her happiness. This is where compersion came into play. All I wanted was for her to live the exciting life that she had missed out on when she was younger. From my mental notes of when we first got married, I knew that she wished she had been with more men. I knew she would have likely been with many guys if she had not been so afraid. I now wanted her to experience all the power and self-expression in her ability and to date and sleep with whoever she wanted as long as they made her happy.

3. **She Was Too Amazing Not to Share with the World:** There she was, as high up as she could be, up on her pedestal of gold for which I had placed her. She was my everything. Conventional wisdom says that I should have wanted to protect her at all costs, hoard her all to myself, and keep all testosterone-bursting men with their throbbing slabs of meat away from her precious vagina. Who believes in conventional wisdom anyhow? I adored her so much, and held her in such high regard, that I began to feel that Vivian was too special to keep tied down with just one man. She was simply too beautiful and amazing to not share with the world. I felt that I was not special enough to have her all to myself, and to keep her for only my love and satisfaction was just plain selfish. I decided that she deserved to be

satisfied by other men, and other men deserved to feel her love, her exuberance, her passion, her magnetism, and her zest for life. I was genuinely happy for her when I had these thoughts. I was also genuinely happy for the potential other men when I thought about how lucky they would be and how fulfilled their lives would be when they got to experience my wife.

I was sure that was the compersion that I was feeling, and I knew I was ready to take this enormous step in our life and in our marriage, but first, I needed to muster up the courage to approach Vivian with this unbelievable proposal. Before I did that, I needed to consider all the risks and benefits that existed when opening a marriage up like this and consider all that it would expose us to.

Risks and Benefits

When you close your eyes and envision your wife sleeping with another man, primarily dark and negative thoughts can fill your mind in an instant. These thoughts end up resulting in your head being flooded with every single risk that comes with this hotwife decision. Here are a few that I had to consider with great care.

Risks:

- Negative emotions
- Jealousy
- Insecurity
- Sexually Transmitted Infections (STI's)

- End of the relationship; break-up or divorce

Ok, so the risks are high. I understood that. Was trying to instill this lifestyle for kink and pleasure worth potentially losing my marriage and losing my dear Vivian to someone else? I was not so sure at that point. I needed to understand the benefits and see if they would outweigh the risks or not.

Benefits:

- Improved Relationships
- Increased physical and emotional intimacy
- Increased sex and more adventurous sex
- Boost in self-confidence for the hotwife
- Extreme increase in self-esteem for the hotwife

The benefits sounded quite compelling, and they started to make me consider the risks involved a lot less. Hotwifing sounded like perhaps what we both needed. In fact, studies have shown that many people who act on these hotwife fantasies report being more satisfied and happier in their relationships, and it has improved their relationship overall. Getting in touch with our sexual fantasies, sharing those desires with our partner, and potentially acting on them when it is mutually agreed upon is something that can benefit all relationships in a lot of ways (Kort, 2019).

THE EMOTIONAL SPECTRUM FOR HER

Through all my excitement and imagination that was igniting, I knew that the bottom line was that Vivian's happiness and well-being were the most important things to me. I had a small hope inside of me that Vivian would listen to my hotwife plea and that she would jump into bed with glee, excited for her new and thrilling life to begin. I had already discovered many wonderful benefits that people had experienced engaging in the hotwife lifestyle. It was time to fully understand why some women do agree to this lifestyle in the first place and what is truly in it for them besides a lot more sex.

Empowerment, Control, and Confidence

A major aspect of the hotwife lifestyle for her is the focus on female pleasure, empowerment, and sexual exploration. A woman who is engaging in the hotwife lifestyle can feel in complete control and in charge of her own sexual exploration. This is her opportunity to fully dive into her sensuality while pushing her limits and realizing her new desires with a lover who is not her husband nor the father of her children. Most hotwife's take advantage of this to the fullest. They play out their fantasies, experiment with new fetishes, and push their own personal boundaries further than they ever could have imagined in their wildest dreams.

The hotwife is in a unique situation because she not only can fulfill her own sexual fantasies and desires, but she is also in the position to fulfill her husband's sexual fantasies and desires, too, which is a very empowering position to be in. She is in control of the entire situation. She chooses who her lovers are. She decides what she does. A very positive consequence for her is the increased level of self-awareness and self-confidence that is typically gained. Not only can this increase in sexual desire and empowerment lead to more excitement within the couple, but she now feels wanted and desired by other people, all while the husband wants her to be desired by multiple people. It's a win-win situation for both! It can deliver a ridiculous boost of self-confidence in her that she perhaps has never felt before ever in her life.

The Thrill of the New

Novelty is nothing new. We all like shiny new things. For most of us, it is exciting to move into a new house and start decorating from scratch, drive around in a new car with that new car smell, or take a trip and explore a new country we have never been to before. Now imagine jumping into bed and exploring someone new whenever you want! That is just one perk for a woman in the hotwife lifestyle. Yes, she loves her man, but after many years together, sex can lose some of its excitement. There are many examples of how couples can look to instill some novelty into their relationships. There is pornography, toys, fetishes, role play, and kinks, to name just a few. Those things can be fine and dandy, but they often offer a temporary fix to a more profound need. With hotwifing, both partners get to experience the thrill of the new almost equally and get to experience it whenever they choose to.

DEFINING HOTWIFE: BEYOND THE EROTICA | 55

It can be exhilarating for the hotwife to be with a new man for obvious reasons. Just dating and getting to know someone new can be exciting. Particularly in long-standing marriages, the idea of just meeting another man for drinks and conversation is enough to make most wives raise their hands to volunteer. But with the bonus that she is allowed to go and have sex with him too? Research indicates that this may be very beneficial indeed.

According to Amy Muise, assistant professor of psychology at York University in Toronto, Canada, "In a relationship, often there is a discrepancy between both partners' interests. However, people with multiple partnerships might be more fulfilled overall. If you have the interest in being sexual with other people, it can be healthy to explore that." (Park, 2020). One study, in particular, questioned people who were curious about this lifestyle but had yet to approach their partners about it. The questions they asked were geared toward their relationship and their sexual satisfaction. They were then questioned again sometime later about their satisfaction with their romantic lives and whether they had opened up their relationships or not. "For the people who wanted to open their relationship and who did end up doing it, their satisfaction was significantly higher," says Samantha Joel, assistant professor of social psychology at Western University in London, Canada. "Meanwhile, for the people who thought about it but didn't, their satisfaction dipped, but barely significantly." (Park, 2020).

Samantha Joel hypothesizes that the increase in satisfaction among couples who switch to open relationships may be the result of something called the dragging effect. According to Park, 2020, "A better quality of sex life with a secondary partner drags up satisfaction with the primary partner because suddenly the pressure of one person having to provide all of their enjoyment is removed." To me, this sounded like a no-brainer. Vivian's empowerment and self-confidence will increase because she is wanted and desired by other men. She can experience lovemaking by someone new other than me, and I have the thrill of knowing, and potentially seeing, that she is being fulfilled by another man. This all sounded way too good to be true.

THE ALLURE OF A NEW WORLD

My extensive hotwife research had come to an end, and after much deliberation, I concluded that this was the journey for me and my wife to embark on. What I had not expected was that my eyes would be opened to a whole new world that I never knew existed. I had discovered that there were many different variations of the CNM lifestyle to choose from.

CNM is not a one-size-fits-all lifestyle. As previously mentioned, I found out so much more about hotwifing, cuckolding, swinging, and polyamory, just to name a few. I found that there are many websites, online communities, and forums that all cater to the CNM lifestyles. I discovered there were swingers' clubs and things called hotel takeovers, where an entire hotel is booked out for a weekend by people in the lifestyle, and they meet each other, party, and have fun together. I also was able to learn from other couples who shared their experiences.

Online Communities and Forums

When I first conducted this search, there most definitely was not the amount of information and support that there is today. Here are a few resources for couples that may be looking to expand their horizons:

- https://www.wifewantstoplay.com/ - *Wife Wants to Play* is a hotwife/cuckold community for members to explore and share the lifestyle. It is a forum with a discussion thread in various categories where members can post topics and questions, share pictures, and get to know one another. The site has 133,020 members.
- https://hotwifecommunity.com/sessions/new - *Hotwife Community* is a hotwife/cuckold community for members also, but you can also purchase tickets to lifestyle events such as swinger's cruises, topless resorts, swinger's clubs, and island parties.
- https://blog.swingtowns.com/hotwife-bull/ - *Swing Towns* is a great site with tons of information about swingers, hotwifes, cuckolds, polyamorists, etc. Not only is there information, but you can also create a profile and search for other members that are in each category.
- https://compersionclub.com/ - *Compersion Club* is a website that is devoted to connecting couples in the wife-sharing lifestyle with their ideal play partners. It offers a new opportunity for hotwifing and cuckolding couples to seek vetted and verified bulls on the platform. Oh yeah, for those who do not know what a bull is, the term "bull" refers to an attractive and physically fit man who displays confidence and is typically very well-endowed. The bull is experienced in hotwife and cuckold gatherings. All hotwives should have a bull, in my opinion.
- https://adultfriendfinder.com/ - *Adult Friend Finder* is almost like a dating site where you can make a

profile to meet other members in your area. There are single men, single women, and couples on there looking to feed all kinds of sexual appetites.
- https://www.tumblr.com/ - *Tumbler* is a blog community with tons of regular profiles and blogs of people posting pictures of animals and nature. I quickly discovered there is a dark side of Tumbler with an extensive wife-sharing community.

Another Couples Shared Experience

After scanning people's hotwife profiles and reading all about bulls and hotwives, was I ready to become a cuckold? Was I prepared to open up my innocent wife and expose her to a world of gratifying sex with other men? Thankfully, the internet has many successful first-experience stories from other couples who have pioneered this trail before me. One example is from a guy named Rick and his wife, Laurie. Rick and Laurie had spent many nights discussing her going on dates with other men. Rick loved this fantasy and had tried to convince Laurie that it would be exciting for them both. Laurie was not a fan of the idea from the start, but she could see how excited Rick was when they talked about it, so she agreed to give it a shot just for him. They did not know how to find a guy for her first time, so they decided to reach out to an old friend of hers that she had kept in touch with.

Rick and Laurie clearly discussed their personal ground rules and decided that Laurie would meet her old friend while Rick was out of town. Laurie booked a hotel room and arrived early. She then waited for her friend to call. They were both nervous that he would change his mind and cancel, but Rick was relieved when Laurie texted him that her friend was on his way. Rick was out of town with his friends and could barely maintain his excitement level from the thoughts of his wife's sexy body being ravaged by another man. The idea of her releasing with a stranger was a massive turn-on for Rick. When Laurie was finished with her very first date, she texted Rick some pictures of her adventure and filled him in on the details. The date went so well that they made plans to meet again the very next night. Rick loved how empowered Laurie felt by being desired by multiple partners, and he said the reclaim sex after she came home was quite erotic, just to top it off!

A case study like that was all I needed to hear. My mind was made up. This is the life I so badly wanted for me and Vivian. I not only wanted her to experience this fantastic sex life that I felt she deserved, but I also wanted us to grow even closer and enhance our marriage as it did for Rick and Laurie and countless others. I knew the first step to attain this lofty goal started with opening the lines of communication between us, but how?

INTERLUDE: SEBASTIAN

After we went to the music festival, something had changed inside of Sebastian, but I could not quite put my finger on it. It almost felt like something had awakened inside of him. He seemed a bit different. As previously mentioned, our sex life took a hit due to my unhappiness with my life watching those kids, but we started to slowly recover after I started my new job. Then, out of nowhere, our sex exploded and started to get a bit more exciting and intense. Sebastian was becoming a bit more aggressive in bed, and I did not mind that at all. It was a very welcomed change. I didn't really notice it at the time, but thinking back on it, Sebastian started talking about other guys a lot. He started off by talking about celebrities. He began asking innocent questions as to who I thought was sexy or playful comments like "I bet you would like one night alone with him". He was always a little jealous in the past, so I enjoyed this different side of him. I will admit I was cautious as to how much I was willing to confess at first because of his past jealousy. I would tell him he was a silly boy and laugh it off.

Then he started to say more things, such as that he knew the type of man I was physically attracted to. He would describe my ideal sexual partner to me, and damn, he was not wrong! He would say things like, "I bet you wouldn't kick him out of your bed," so I became braver and would respond with "Nope" or "Of course not." My favorite was to pretend I was thinking, and I would say, "Um, no!" in a playful and sarcastic manner. This would usually lead to him lightly spanking my butt. But the truth is that it also led to me thinking about other men in a more sexual manner.

Again, looking back, I can see that he started to talk about Shane a lot more also, but not in a bad way. He seemed very interested in asking me more questions and talking about the potential sexual relationship that Shane was having with Natalie, which I didn't mind talking about. It was nice that he was interested in my work and my coworkers more. What I do remember most, however, is that my sexual drive was increasing, and our sex and passion were increasing, so I wasn't complaining. It had become clearer to me that Sebastian seemed to get turned on more when talking to me about men that might be interested in me or ones that I might be interested in. It seemed meaningless and just fun, and I didn't think much more about it. I was just enjoying this new little spark with my husband.

CONVERSATIONS, CONCERNS, AND COURAGE

> *"Vulnerability is the key that unlocks the door to growth and fulfillment."*
>
> — TONY ROBINS

It was nearly Halloween, and a few months had passed since I became determined to share my wife, yet my desires remained hidden in silence. My online research had provided me with a wealth of new information and opened my mind to an entirely new world of alternative lifestyles that I could not have dreamed existed previously. I had learned so much about it all that my imagination was on information overload. The potential possibilities were limitless. The most crucial aspect that I was able to take away from it all was just how critical open communication between partners becomes no matter which variation of the lifestyle you fancy. Dozens of examples were given where the relationships involved failed due to the lack of pure and honest open communication. Vivian and I did not have any open lines established when it came to this subject matter. I now knew what it was that I wanted, and it was time for me to figure out how to engage in this exciting yet frightful conversation with the absolute love of my life.

CONVERSATIONS, DREAM, AND SIGNS

I came across a few websites and forums that I particularly enjoyed immersing myself in that made me feel like I was already part of the hotwife community. One of the first things I did back then was go to Craigslist. For those of you who are not aware, Craigslist was once upon a time the hottest hookup site that existed until it canceled its classified ads. I suppose it was the equivalent of Tinder in the early 2000's. Anyone could create a Craigslist account, check out the ads from other members, and create posts looking for hookups in their area. The site was filled with lots of people searching for lots of different satisfactions, and that is where I first discovered the section called MF4M. This section was for male and female couples who were looking for another male partner to join them for sexual gratification. It was here that I learned the term "bull" and would get extremely excited at the thought of Vivian becoming a bull rider. Most of the posts would feature sexy pictures of their hotwife, either posing in lingerie, nude, or in action with other men if she was an experienced bull rider. It was very entertaining indeed. I dreamed of the day I might be able to create a post for Vivian and me to find her bull.

There was also a section called M4MF, which was single men who were strictly looking for couples to meet up with to make their fantasies come true. I knew that Craigslist was where we would start when we were ready to find her a man. Somewhere along the way, I discovered the previously mentioned blog site, Tumbler. I really enjoyed going on Tumbler. Once you had created an account, you could search for blogs in the wife-sharing category. You could follow bloggers and click like on their pictures and posts; it was truly amazing. Tumbler is where I first learned the term "hotwife" by clicking on hundreds of memes with women in lingerie asking their husbands if they were ready for what their bull was about to do to her.

You could also re-share memes on Tumbler as you can on Facebook, so I would see pictures, memes, or blog entries that I liked, and I would share them on my blog. I started gaining a lot of followers quickly because they loved the content that I would share. Throughout this process, I had conversations over the Tumbler messenger with a few other guys who were just like me. They would send me a message about pictures I shared and how much they wished their wives would partake in the lifestyle. It was like a little fraternity of brothers all living the same dream with the same ultimate goal in mind: being lucky enough to see our wives taken by another man.

Innocent Conversations

Day by day, I carried on suppressing this secret need for my wife, and I had developed my daily routine of going on Tumbler to let my imagination run wild. It was my outlet. Every picture, meme, or story that passed in front of my eyes had Vivian in it. I saw her in each image of a blonde, sexy woman being satisfied by some well-endowed bull, and I imagined her in each story about a reluctant wife looking at her husband as her lover mounted her from behind. Perhaps I was ultra-sensitive or hyper-aware of anything that remotely involved this topic. Still, I had begun to notice a slight shift in Vivian's personality that could not be denied.

She started to go out a little more with her coworkers after work for drinks. As I mentioned earlier, they were a fun group of people with dirty jokes and sexual implications, and she was beginning to fit in quite nicely. I remember she started saying little innocent comments out of nowhere, like letting me know when there was a man that she found herself attracted to. She started saying things like, "Damn, he is hot!" or "I wouldn't kick him out of my bed." She became more vocal with her opinions and claims because she could see that I was more than ok with it. I was influencing her and supporting her. We had our little jokes and comments about the type of man she could not resist and would "not say no to," and all of it drove me absolutely wild. She went out for drinks with the crew one night after work and came home very eager to discuss Shane and Natalie with me.

"Shane and Natalie were so obvious tonight; I think she is definitely riding that monster", is how she started it off.

I loved it when she talked about his package as it told me that it was on her mind. Vivian proceeded to tell me about the drinks and shots that they all had and how Natalie was getting just a tiny bit too cozy in a booth with Shane. She even noticed Natalie's hand was a bit busy under the table in front of everyone, which absolutely shocked her. I agreed with her that I could not believe Natalie had her hand full in front of everyone, and her joking reply was, "Yeah, it was fucked up, and I do not even know if it is that big. I am just going by what I heard. I kind of want to see it now to see if it's true!" I made a Mental note.

Sending Mixed Signals

As the weeks passed, Vivian and Shane were becoming a bit closer at work. She had not really noticed it at all, but she was coming home and talking about him more than a regular husband might have tolerated. Natalie began to display some jealous tendencies toward Vivian. She told me many stories about how she and Shane would be talking, and Natalie would come running over and interrupt and ask them rudely what they were talking about. Discussions about Shane and his manhood would pop up every so often between us. Vivian would make cute jokes like "I still haven't seen it yet, damn it," or "I'm still waiting for when it is my turn to see it."

Of course, I was instigating 100% of the time. I remember telling her that perhaps she just needed to ask if she could see it or maybe just lick it once. She would laugh, and I would go on Tumbler and tell my pen pals. They were so happy for me that my wife was even talking about another guy's manhood with me. It was a huge step, they felt. I could not disagree. It felt like a discussion between us about her sleeping with Shane and being a hotwife was fast approaching with these signals she was sending me. How could I indeed be sure when the time was right? My dearest Vivian forced my hand the day she came home and was visibly upset about something, which led to our first mini-conversation that I was not at all prepared to have.

When she walked through the door, it was easy to see that she was rattled over something. I was doing the dishes when she came over to give me a kiss.

"Hey baby, how was your day?" I asked, delighted to see her.

"So, you'll never guess what happened almost right before I left. I am still upset about it", was her reply.

"Oh no. What Happened?" I asked, concerned.

"Natalie asked to talk to me and pulled me out into the hallway. She seemed very upset and asked me straight if I was sleeping with Shane! I know he and I are friends, but can you believe she is so jealous that she accused me of sleeping with him?" Vivian said, perplexed. I only had a split second to reply to that question. I decided to take my shot.

"Yes, I actually can believe it," I said as I turned the hot water off and spun my body around slowly to face her. The look on her face had me rethinking this decision almost immediately.

"I hope you are joking right now," she said as she glared at me.

"Not really!" I quickly blurted. What the hell was I thinking?

"Why on earth would you say that??" she questioned me as her eyes began to well up.

I was going to come clean about all my thoughts, the picture of their embrace, their almost kiss in front of my eyes, but in a split second, I changed my mind. It did not serve me well to play that card at this moment. I cautiously began to tell her that I could see why Natalie might think that she had been sleeping with him. Her glare did not soften. I proceeded to tell her that both Natalie and I have witnessed her and Shane being very close to each other at concerts. Lots of arms around each other and close talking conversations. I told her that she does talk about him an awful lot, and from what she has told me, they are very tight at work. Lots of lunches together, lots of private conversations with Natalie interrupting them constantly.

"I can't believe you are saying this to me right now. You really think I am cheating on you and having sex with Shane?" she said incredulously.

"That is not what I said", I quickly fired back.

"Please do not twist my words here. You asked me if I could believe that Natalie would think you guys are banging. I said yes, I can believe that she would think that. I did not say I think that. I can just understand why she might." A white lie, perhaps.

"Well, if I am going to be accused of something, I might as well be doing it. I guess I should have sex with him since everyone thinks I am already!" she shouted as she began to leave the room to end that conversation.

"I guess you should, Vivian. You might as well enjoy the monster if you are going to be blamed for it already", I said playfully.

"I know, right?" as her voice faded up the staircase.

Fear of Judgement

Vivian cooled off rather quickly that night. Partly because who really cared what Natalie thought, but I think partly because she realized that we just had a "discussion" about her being so close to another man at work that his potential work hookup was jealous enough to question her about it. Yet, I did not get mad or upset with her over it. In fact, I did the opposite by telling her I could see why the suspected lover would think that and telling her that maybe she should be doing it. She did not question me as to my motives or reactions to this incident, which was a great sign to me. Had I shown her how I handled that situation enough to get her mind turned on? Was this her cracking the door open for me to push it wide open? Part of me was ready to seize this moment and take the opportunity she had given me. I mean, why did she come home and tell me that Natalie thought she was sleeping with Shane in the first place? Would not any other wife keep that one to themselves? How exactly did she expect me to react? How did she think that conversation was going to go? Was she testing me?

I thought I was ready to take the leap of faith, but there was also a massive part of me that was fearful of her judgment upon me. I still was not entirely sure that bringing this up to Vivian was a great idea in the first place, as one study I found concluded that 67% of female participants reported that they would leave their partners if the partner admitted that they would like to have an open relationship (Zuckerman, 2020). That was an extremely high percentage that scared the daylights out of me. Fear of rejection was tolerable, and I knew that I would get past that. I would feel sorry if she rejected this idea. I would feel sorry for her for passing up the opportunity to experience more love and satisfaction than she could hope for, but it would be alright.

Fear of judgment did not make me feel warm and fuzzy inside. We already had a nearly perfect marriage, so why should I jeopardize that? What would happen to our relationship if she not only told me that she did not want this in our lives but then cast judgment on me on top of that? What if she began to feel that I was not the man she thought I was? What would happen if she started to feel I was a terrible pervert or something, and it began to tarnish our sex life together?

Then, there was the worst fear imaginable to me that caused me physical pain in my gut. What if she was one of the 67% that would end our marriage over this proposition of giving her the sexual freedom that I so very much desired for her? Was our marriage not as strong as I thought? Could we survive if I was to tell her that I want this for her? Could she throw away our twelve years together, take my children, and leave me alone and heartbroken? I absolutely would not have been able to live with myself if I destroyed the excellent and loving marriage that we had already established. I was almost certain that she had unlocked the door and opened it a crack for me, yet I chose to close it and walk away.

THE EYE-OPENING REVELATION

Days passed by, and I felt a bit sorry for myself. I was down in the dumps, I guess you could say. I could not help this terrible feeling that I potentially missed my only opportunity to broach this subject with Vivian. I could not shake this sadness that my wife might have been sending me signals this entire time, indications of her being open to experiencing another man that she had a deep connection with, feeling that I wanted it for her, and all I had to do was ask her. It was too late now. The moment had passed. Vivian was not talking about Shane as much anymore, if at all, and I was not bringing up his package to her anymore. I was confident that I had closed the door in front of me, and Vivian had turned the deadbolt and turned off the light.

An Unexpected Source of Inspiration

It was Thanksgiving morning, and the mouthwatering aroma of our thyme and sage-rubbed turkey filled the entire house. I could not wait to sink my teeth into that bird. Vivian and I had completed most of the meal prep together. Working with her in such close proximity in our tiny kitchen always turned me on. We had amazing sex the night before, so we were both still basking in the afterglow. Vivian was wearing the shortest little black booty shorts with a super tight pink tank top that you could see her nipples through, especially when they were hard. It was my favorite sleeping attire that she wore. I kept getting distracted by slapping her on the butt and rubbing her breasts from behind her. Concentrating on stuffing the bird was tough when I really wanted to be stuffing her again. Somehow, we behaved just enough, and we accomplished getting the food all prepared so that we were only waiting on the turkey now.

I was at the sink washing dishes, and Vivian was in the living room vacuuming the carpet. I decided to go upstairs and update the kids on when dinner would be ready. Walking past the living room, I could not help but notice Vivian bent over with those cheeks calling to me, so of course I had to go over and spank her again. She turned off the vacuum.

"That's my bum", she said smiling.

"No, it's mine!" and I spanked her again. "Tonight, you're getting dick, so that you know", I warned her as I started back to the kitchen.

"I'm getting dicks tonight? Score!" she said playfully. I stopped dead in my tracks. Choose your following words very carefully was all that jolted through my brain in a nanosecond.

"Ohhh is that what you want, babe, multiple dicks in our bed?" was the best I could muster under such a pressurized time constraint. I could feel the pounding of my heart in its ribcage as I awaited her response.

"I mean, it sounds good to me", she replied enthusiastically.

"Oh, ok!" I laughed while feeling instant hardness underneath my shorts. I could not leave it at this. Not again. This was it. This was my shot. She needed to hear how I truly felt about these joking comments. I must not ignore this moment. I turned around, took a slow, deep breath, and confidently marched back to the living room and got up close to her. My left hand gently rubbed circles on her right butt cheek.

"I thought you should know that you just made me instantly hard talking about two dicks in our bed", I said quietly in a shy and gentle manner. Her eyes drifted downward to the prominent bulge that I was packing. Her hand followed her eyes, and she got a pleasant grip on me through my shorts.

"I can see that baby. That made you excited?" she asked matching my volume and tone. Looking down at the floor and still playing the shy role, I nodded only.

"Well damn. Let's do it then!" she answered back in her lively tone, then laughed and started to wrap the vacuum cleaner cord.

Actions Speak Louder Than Words

The fleeting but monumental Thanksgiving conversation propelled me into another stratosphere of optimism and wonder. I could not believe her responses to me after a simple mistake of her mishearing me. I was on cloud nine, but I was trying not to get too excited about the big reveal. To me, the facts were all there. She now knew that having another man in our bed with us excited me very quickly, and she had me feeling that if I was excited by it, she might be open to trying it. There was one sticking point, however, that remained, and that was the fact that I didn't know how to bring it up again. I decided to leave it alone for a couple of days so as not to come off as pushy or eager, but I lost my momentum and panicked anytime I thought about bringing it up to her again. They say sometimes actions speak louder than words. I felt like Vivian had already given me the words I needed to hear, and I yet again let it slip out of my grasp. It appeared that Vivian was trying to use actions to show me what I needed to see, but it is hard to tell what is real and what is imagination sometimes.

I had recently made friends with a guy from work named Martin, who I found out was a tremendous international soccer fan like me. I invited Martin over to the house one Saturday afternoon to watch a match and drink some beers with me. When I introduced him to Vivian, I really didn't think that much of it, to be honest, because he really was not her type of guy. I take that back. He had one characteristic that she is very attracted to, and that was his humor. Martin was hilarious, witty, and sarcastic, so I should have categorized him as a "triple threat guy" in Vivian's eyes. She is highly attracted to a man who can make her laugh, and low and behold, Martin did not waste much time before having her in tears.

I was just enjoying the soccer game and my beer without a care in the world until Vivian entered the room with a drink in her hand. Martin and I were sitting on a smaller three-person sofa that faced the television. There was a much more oversized five-person couch adjacent to us, but Vivian decided she wanted to be sandwiched in between me and Martin. She squeezed in between us, and Martin even commented that he would try to move over more to give her room. They talked, joked, and laughed through almost the entire game. I would have had to be blind not to see that there was a definite chemistry between them. I could not help but peek out of the corner of my eye and see how close she was to him. Their legs were touching each other, her arm almost touching his, and yet there was some space between me and her.

I tried really hard to focus on the game, but damn it, this woman had my mind and heart racing. Was she really flirting like this in front of me with my friend? They just kept talking and laughing, and both enjoyed each other's very sarcastic humor. She was extremely happy at this moment, and I could not help but love seeing her like this. I got up to use the bathroom, which happened to be right around the corner, and while I was in there, I noticed that they were suddenly very hushed. There was no laughing. No joking. Just silence. Deafening silence other than the quiet buzz of the crowd and the call of the announcers on the television. I was sure in my mind that they were taking this opportunity to start kissing passionately after my departure. I washed my hands as quickly and quietly as I could. I exited the bathroom as silently as I could. Was there a chance I might walk around the corner to find their tongues twirling on my couch with his hands all over her body? I turned the corner in anticipation. There they both sat, legs still touching while staring at the television in silence.

Allure of Her Empowerment

I never uttered a word to her about any of it after Martin left. I did not want to question her about their chemistry, why she sat between me and him, why her leg was touching his, or why they got so silent when I left the room. I did not want to scare her. I did not want to ruin whatever that was and whatever she was showing me. As a few weeks had passed, the same flirty behavior continued between her and Martin. He suddenly wanted to come over to watch soccer games every Saturday, and every Saturday, Vivian would squeeze in between me and him on that three-person couch. One Saturday afternoon, an epiphany came to me while the three of us snuggled up on that sofa. As small and innocent as this all might have been, it felt like Vivian was feeling a level of empowerment. To me, it seemed like she was beginning to feel her empowerment and that she could do almost whatever she pleased. My darling wife tested the limits with me that first time Martin came over. She didn't have to sit that close to him. She could have sat closer to me. It almost appeared as if she was feeling her own limits, testing them, and enjoying it all simultaneously. Truth be told, I was drawn to it. Was she drawn to it as well? Had she started to realize that she was gaining the power of freedom, the control of choice, and the autonomy of expression?

In the blink of an eye, Vivian didn't seem like your average housewife to me anymore. She had an aura about her. She was more than aware that both Martin and Shane wanted her. That was obvious. She knew I was also aware of that, yet I had not addressed it with her. Why had I not? That was not as obvious. By then, she must have wanted to ask me that exact question, but I am sure she was too afraid to bring up the subject. I know how that feels. I could see how her demeanor changed around both Shane and Martin. I could see her face and smile light up when she joked with them. I could see her body language shift as she invited more physical contact with them, whether by hugs, touching an arm while she spoke, or sitting so close that their legs touched and neither one moved them in discomfort. I could see that it was time to ask my wife if we could talk.

BRIDGING THE GAP

There was a giant gap between where I wanted our marriage to go and where it was, and even though I could feel it shrinking by the day, I did not know how to bridge the gap entirely. I was much too afraid. I could feel it in my soul that the time was now. I had reached the point of no return. I had made my final decision that I wanted this too severely for Vivian to ignore it any longer. It had been nearly six months of living with this fascination alone, and I realized that I simply could not stand it anymore. Especially with what I perceived to be Vivian's attraction to Martin, which was clambering my brain. I suppose I was willing to risk it all for what I believed to be happiness on a new plane of existence that most cannot comprehend. All that was left was to identify the perfect moment for me and Vivian to engage in this conversation and for me to decide what the fuck I was actually going to say!

Choosing the Right Moment

Choosing the right moment was of the utmost importance for that situation. I could not be too hasty. I had shown myself such great restraint over the past six months, and I was not about to blow it by opening up my mouth and just spewing my desires all over my wife. The scene needed to be flawless. The mood had to be perfect. The execution required ultimate precision. Coming up with the right moment proved to be more complicated than I thought. I started by eliminating the wrong moments. It was evident that I should steer clear of starting this dialogue with her before work, right after work, or right after the joyous occasion of putting our children to bed.

Perhaps during a date night while we enjoyed each other's company over a glass of wine? I did not love that idea. I envisioned the conversation going badly and ruining the rest of our evening. Some prevailing thought and popular opinion from my brethren on Tumbler was to bring it up during sex. Some had experienced luck mentioning the thought of another man with their wives right at that moment and then gauged how turned-on she would get from that. I did not love that idea either for two reasons: 1) See ruining the rest of the night mentioned previously, and 2) Some had said their wives had reacted well to it, but they later dismissed it as fun pillow talk with no real substance at all. This approach typically resulted in a "No" answer.

My last two options were to target when she would be the most relaxed and happy, which was either right before having sex or directly after having sex. Again, let me reference the previously mentioned "ruining the rest of the night" fear that made those both seem less than ideal to me. I think I was starting to overthink this.

Framing The Conversation

It was apparent that I had a lot more decision-making to accomplish in order to find my absolute perfect moment. It was fine. I wasn't in a rush. I spent so much time racking my brain for the right moment that I hadn't really considered what I was going to say or how I was going to say it. Shit. This was perhaps way more important than defining the right moment. The message I was going to convey required finesse. How I was going to frame it demanded tact. If I chose the right words, it could lead to glory and bliss. If I chose the incorrect words, it could lead to a tremendous fight. Or worse.

I was not even sure as to how I would start this chat. Would I confess to Vivian that I had a picture of her and Shane and inform her how much it turned me on? Should I express my feelings for her and Martin and their obvious closeness on the couch right in front of me? I did not hate these ideas entirely, but I was concerned that either approach could put her on the defensive. They could make her feel like she was being attacked and judged by me. I could see her shutting down quickly, and the conversation would be ruined forever. I remember feeling that I had started to overthink the situation, but the reality was that I had begun to rethink the situation entirely.

Revealing Hidden Desires

It was a Friday night, and the teenage babysitter had just arrived. The kids loved her. The smell of hot pepperoni pizza just delivered made me hungry, but I was taking Vivian to our favorite Hibachi place for our date night. You know, the place where you sit at a table shaped like a "U", and you watch the cook clang his utensils down on the sizzling stove and make fire volcanoes out of freshly cut onion slices? It was our favorite spot for date nights. We had a few drinks with our dinner and had a boundless night of conversation. We arrived home, and the children were already fast asleep. I paid the babysitter a little extra for that. They were not easy to get to bed, so she earned it.

I was in the shower waiting for Vivian to join me as she typically did each night. She was taking off her makeup in the mirror, brushing her teeth, etc., when she complained that her stomach was hurting. She said it started hurting her on the ride home, and she was hoping it would go away soon, but it felt a little worse now. She asked if we could skip "having fun" tonight and push it to the next night instead. I told her, of course, I did not want her trying to have fun in pain. We would see how she felt the next night. I said let's just go to sleep. That is when it occurred to me. The realization that this was the right moment had hit me square in the face. Despite her stomach pain, which did not seem bad enough to at least talk, this appeared to be the perfect moment. It was an excellent date night, a couple of drinks, relaxed with no putting kids to bed and no sex to ruin.

My adrenaline engaged. My heart started beating faster and I started to tremble a bit from fear of the unknown. I still did not know what I was going to say, but I knew I needed to say it right now. Part of me did not want to say it with her in the shower looking at me. I felt safe with the thin and opaque shower curtain between us. It was like an invisible cloak protecting me. I opened my mouth, but no words came out. Say something, damn it! Anything to buy you a few seconds.

"Hey, so I wanted to ask you something." I barely got out while praying she couldn't hear the indecisive fear in my voice.

"What did you say, honey?" she asked, buying me more time.

"I said, I wanted to ask you something. *(dramatic pause)* I've wanted to ask you for a while now, but I wasn't really sure how to say it", I answered with a little more confidence that came back to my voice.

"Okayyyyyy. What is it?" she replied with a hint of apprehension.

What is it, Sebastian? Think man! She is waiting! Thanksgiving popped into my head. You got this!

"So, do you remember a while back when we joked about you having two dicks in our bed, and you said something like let's do it, baby?" I questioned, then awaited her answer.

"Wait, what? I have no clue what you are talking about", she said, confused.

She was either playing dumb or that conversation meant so little to her that it did not even register on her radar. Fuck. I took a deep breath.

"Do you remember when you thought I said you were getting dicks that night, and you pretended you were excited, and I got super hard from it? I came over and showed you that I got so hard from you, saying you were excited about two dicks in our bed. You said to me, ok, let's do it, baby!" I repeated slower, grasping at the hope that she remembered that interaction but realizing that she likely did not mean it at the same time.

"Ohhhhh. Yeah, I remember that vaguely. Why?" she responded, sounding more perplexed.

"Well, I just wanted to say that if you were serious about that and wanted two dicks, I want to make that happen for you", I retorted.

There were no words spoken for what felt like a twenty-second pause. I actually had to peek out the shower curtain to confirm that she was still there.

"I hope you're joking right now?" was the answer that I suspected and most expected.

"Well, no, I am not. I showed you that day that the comment turned me on, so if you were serious about it at all, I would like to make that happen for you", I said in the most loving tone I could muster.

There was yet another long pause. Perhaps she did not know how to admit that she did want it. However, it felt that this was not going well at all.

"Wow. I said that stuff as a joke. We always joke like that. I am a little surprised right now that you are saying this to me. You would really want me to do this? To fuck some other guy?" she reacted with what sounded like either intrigue or disgust. I was having a tough time deciphering.

"It got me really excited when you said it. I showed you how hard it got me. And I thought that excited you when you saw that. I have been thinking a lot about it since then, and it turns me on a lot to picture seeing you with another man. I love you so much and want to see you happy and be pleasured. It's not a big deal if you don't want it. I just thought maybe you wanted to try it is all, and we could find someone for you", I said with my final shot. This felt like a sinking ship.

"So even if I said yes, who would it be? You would find me some guy?" she asked. I found that question extremely promising, and it was a 180-degree turn from where this was going.

"Well, you seem to have a connection with Shane or Martin. I was thinking maybe one of them?" I countered.

"What the hell? Why would you say those two?" She was not happy.

"I have noticed a lot of chemistry between you and them. I know you like them both, so I would be ok if you wanted to have sex with one of them", I responded.

"They are our friends and co-workers. That is not happening, ever!" she snapped.

"Ok, well, we could easily find a guy on Craigslist", I slightly snapped back.

She asked what Craigslist was, so I explained everything to her about how we could find a stranger on there to join us.

"Absolutely not! We are not having some disgusting stranger with diseases in our bed. If I ever agreed to this, which I wouldn't, it would never be with friends or co-workers, and not some gross stranger on a website!" That seemed to be her final answer.

"Well, that doesn't leave anyone else, Vivian!" was my final answer.

"Well then, I guess it's not happening!" She fell silent.

She finally entered the shower with me, and I could see she was not pleased. The night was ruined. We did not speak. I had finished washing after that long exchange, so I exited the shower rather quickly. I put on shorts, and I figured that I would not be able to sleep after that back-and-forth exchange. I decided to let her go to bed upset with me, and I would drink some beers and play video games. She got out of the shower and was drying her body with a towel as I approached her to say goodnight and tell her I would play football for a while. I gave her a kiss and told her I loved her. I turned to leave the bathroom when she started to speak.

"I want to say thank you for telling me how you feel about this. I am still in shock and don't know how to take any of this, but I am sorry if I was mean. Can I have some time to process all of this, and we can talk about it later?" she asked, almost dazed.

INTERLUDE: MARTIN

Conversations between me and Sebastian continued to get more and more risqué as the weeks and months passed. Sebastian was encouraging me to be myself and say what was on my mind without the fear that I would be in trouble. The one day that actually worried me was when I came home and told him that Natalie had spread the word around the office that Shane was packing a large member in his pants. I remember my mind telling me that I was making a huge mistake for telling my husband that we talk about my coworker's dick size, as the words were coming out of my mouth. But he didn't get upset; instead, he smiled and asked me questions. That is why I had no problem coming home and telling him that Natalie was rubbing it at a restaurant under the table. However, I did have that same moment of regret when I said to him that I kind of wanted to see his dick. Damn vodka.

The truth is that I was a little bit intrigued and wouldn't have minded seeing it, but I think the real reason I said it was because I knew the reaction I would get from Sebastian. He again encouraged me. It was a whole new level of closeness and intimacy that we were embarking on, and I was enjoying it. I felt like I had this new freedom of speech with my husband, and it was so refreshing, yet I still felt I had to be careful how far I could take it. I didn't want to cross boundaries and upset him. Then, the day came when Sebastian introduced me to Martin, and I threw caution into the wind.

When I met Martin over eleven years ago, I was not the same woman that I am now, or this story would have ended up very different. I wouldn't say there was a spark or chemistry when I first met him, but he had won me over within the first hour he was in my house. One of my biggest weaknesses is that I am so attracted to a man that can make me laugh, is sarcastic, and has a dry sense of humor. I could tell that Martin had all those qualities very quickly when I said, "Hi Martin, I am Vivian. It's nice to meet you", and he turned to Sebastian in front of me and asked him what I said because he didn't understand a word with my accent. He made me laugh immediately, and, in that instant, I was inexplicably drawn to him.

Yet again, I didn't really know I was drawn to him. I do not remember having thoughts about him, but there was something about him that I was magnetized to. Yes, the boys went to the living room to watch the soccer game. Yes, I went to the kitchen to make myself a drink. And yes, something made me decide to squeeze right in between them on that loveseat, yet I am not sure why. One thing is for sure: I was very comfortable on that loveseat in between my husband and this other man.

Martin joked with me most of the game and made me laugh so hard I thought I would pee my pants. I got up and made a few drinks for myself but came back to my tight spot in the middle of those boys on my loveseat each time. I really do not know what was *controlling me. It felt like I was a different person all of a sudden. My leg was touching Martin's leg, and I looked at Sebastian out of the corner of my eye to see his reaction. Was he witnessing this chemistry I had with his friend right in front of him? It didn't appear so. If he did, he was playing it cool I thought. He was very quiet and attentive to the game, so I do not think he noticed that my arm was practically resting on Martin's arm.*

When Sebastian got up to use the bathroom, it was a very intense few minutes with no words spoken but so much tension you could feel it. I sat staring at the television with my hand and arm touching this man, but neither of us moved. I did not slide over and give him room. Deep down, I think I liked his touch. I wish I knew what was going on in his head at that moment. He just stared at the television also, sipping his beer, probably terrified of what mistake he might make in his new friend's house with his wife. When Sebastian came out of the bathroom and turned the corner, he looked right at us. I tried not to look directly at him, but could feel his gaze. He knew exactly what was happening here. I got scared at the intense feelings that were flowing through me, so I decided it was time to get up and start dinner.

Martin came over many times to watch games over the next few weeks, and each time, it was the same scenario being played out. He would joke with me and make me laugh, I would squeeze in between them, and we would watch the game together. It was our tradition. Our routine. I noticed that Sebastian would almost act as if everything was normal, and he didn't want to draw attention to the closeness that I was sharing with Martin. He would just watch his game, drink his beer, and be happy. I was worried that he was going to say something to me and be upset, especially after the first time, but he never did. I almost felt empowered, and it was awesome!

One night, Martin came over for a firepit outside in our backyard, and something came over me that even surprised me. I went inside the house to get another drink, and when I came back out to join the boys, I went over to Martin's chair and sat on his lap. I put my arm around his neck and over his shoulders as I sat sideways on him. I felt Martin touch my back with his arm to support me, but in the dark behind me, he gently rubbed my back with his thumb only. I think he was a bit uncomfortable with this new boundary I pushed in front of Sebastian, so he covered his comfort level with humor. He immediately started making jokes that I was trying to get him in trouble with Sebastian. He said to Sebastian that I was out of control and that he needed to control me and keep me on a leash.

Sebastian laughed, looked at me, and said, "She is a big girl and is allowed to do whatever she wants." I decided maybe I should get up and go sit in my chair, but as I started to get up, Martin pulled me back down on his lap and said, "Well then hell, stay right here on me, Vivian, and keep me warm." We all laughed, and I stayed on his lap for a while longer. I felt this thrill inside that excited me. I had this freedom of flirtation that I enjoyed. I knew it would never go any further than this because I was a married woman, and Martin understood that.

Again, I was worried that Sebastian was going to say something to me after Martin left, but all that happened that night was he took me upstairs, and he pounded the hell out of me, if you know what I mean.

4

AN OFFER SHE CAN'T REFUSE... RIGHT?

> "Some of our important choices have a timeline. If we delay a decision, the opportunity is gone forever. Sometimes our doubts keep us from making a choice that involves change. Thus, an opportunity may be missed."
>
> — JAMES E. FAUST

It was a short, frustrating, and agitated kiss goodnight. Vivian's reaction, while expected, was disheartening still. Her last statement gave me the tiniest bit of hope and promise, but I was not filled with much optimism overall. Her initial reaction had confused me, to say the least. Had I misread our little jokes and comments over the past six months? Had I really been this mistaken, or should I have taken them for what they really were, perhaps? Just little jokes and comments. I had started to think I had overanalyzed her responses, but how could I have overanalyzed what I saw with my own two eyes? When I looked at her around

Shane or Martin, I saw a strong woman who knew what she wanted and was not afraid to show it. I saw a woman who appeared to be ready to be sexually liberated from the shackles of a monogamous marriage. In our discussions, I heard a wife who was not afraid to say the dirty things on her mind in front of her husband. What a fantastic freedom that is in itself! Most wives do not get to experience that autonomy. She knew she had the liberty to say sexy things to her husband about other men. She knew she had the independence to say sexy things to other men and flirt lightly with them in front of her husband. She was already freed in her mind, and she loved that she could share those moments with me. Had I taken it all just a bit too far, and would this cause her to shut down on me? I prayed not and pleaded with the universe that I had not made a colossal mistake. Only time would tell.

THE CHOICE

It was a Friday night, and I had just stepped out of the shower. It had felt like six months had passed since I opened my heart to her while hiding behind that floral shower curtain. It had only been fourteen days. I dried off with a towel as Vivian entered the bathroom, and she was completely naked. She pulled back the shower curtain to feel if I had left the running water too cold for her. I bent down and bit her ass cheek as I walked by her to leave the bathroom. Lying in bed, I was already hard and excited from the anticipation of her joining me. I heard her shut the shower off, pull back the curtain, and remove the towel from the towel rack. After drying off her naked body, I heard her turn the faucet on and begin to brush her teeth. The faucet turned off, and a few seconds later, the bathroom door opened. She stepped into our bedroom with the towel wrapped around her, hair brushed straight but still visibly wet, but with what appeared to be a nervous look on her face.

"Hey, hon, I wanted to talk to you about this whole thing with you wanting me to have sex with other people", she said with a look in her eyes that told me all I needed to know.

"Sure, babe", I replied, sitting myself up in the bed.

"Well, I wanted to say first thank you for talking to me and telling me how you feel about this. I know it wasn't easy. I have thought a lot about what you said the other night, and it really disturbs me that you would be ok with letting me have sex with another man. It makes me feel sad and so low about myself that I am not good enough, and I do not excite you enough that you need this from me to excite you. I am sorry, I am a boring person, and you can just divorce me and find some other girl that will make you happy", she said in a quivering voice while fighting back the tears.

She turned, returned to the bathroom, and shut the door behind her. I heard the sound of her hair dryer being turned on.

THE EMOTIONS

With the sound of her hair dryer blowing in the bathroom, I sat there in utter disbelief. I could not comprehend how bad that just went. If that was a contest for a situation taking a wrong turn, then where was my gold medal? I could not believe the things that she just said to me. I could not believe the feelings that she portrayed to me. I could not believe the thoughts that gushed through her mind. I could not believe how badly she was hurting. I fucked up big time. I felt terrible, not for me, but for her. My heart ached for my poor wife, who right now was so confused about her marriage, a marriage that felt like it was just turned upside down on her by her ridiculous husband. I had to fix us.

The hair dryer shut off, and the bathroom door opened. Vivian came into the bedroom with a distraught feel about her. She walked over to our bed without saying a word. She had that look on her face that a woman gets when she is trying so hard not to look in your general direction. Therefore, she is focusing intensely on whatever silly task she is doing at that moment. This moment was her plugging her phone in and setting in on what time her alarm should go off in the morning, followed by rubbing lotion on her hands methodically. She turned off the lamp on her nightstand and crept into the bed next to me as meek and timid as a lamb. I wasted no time.

"Come here, my love", I said to her as I moved my body across the sheets and pulled her head into my chest. She began to sob.

"I am so sorry, hon. I had no idea that you would feel this way about all of this. I started having these thoughts, and it felt like we were on the same page, but I can see that I was wrong." I apologized to her with the utmost sincerity.

"I just can't believe you feel this way, and you want this from me", she sniffled through her congestion from crying.

She continued, "I get it that we like to joke sometimes, and we say things that are funny, but I had no idea that you were thinking about me this way with some other guys. It's very disturbing to me. What does that mean anyway? Don't tell me that you are gay and you want some man in our bed so you can be with him too. Or, that you are wanting to be with some girl so that you hope I am with some man so that it will be ok for you to fuck some girl!"

She was rambling on while tossing false accusations into the darkness of our bedroom. I needed to fix this. Vivian was broken. I needed to set her mind at ease. No more secrets. No more joking.

I proceeded to tell her everything. I went way back to the start of all this mess. I went back to that fateful night at the concert. I filled her in about her hanging all over Shane. She heard about the embrace I witnessed and the photo I took of them gazing at each other like they wanted to kiss passionately right in front of me. She did not believe me and denied the entire occurrence, which angered me a bit, so I decided it was time for her to see the picture with her own eyes. As they say, a picture is worth a thousand words, and this digital victory piece was all I needed—this captured moment told the entire story. She flipped it around on me big time. She was appalled that I even took that picture in the first place! Forget about the fact that I still had it on my phone, admitted to looking at it frequently, and yet kept it from her for six months. This was not going as I had planned!

I explained to her that I was a little bit pissed when I saw this embrace in real life, but it had suddenly turned into me being excited by it instead. I told her how the talks and jokes about her being intrigued by Shane's massiveness had put many thoughts inside my head. I enlightened her on the attraction that I felt between her and Martin and all the reasons why her interactions with him had made me feel the way that I did. I emphasized to her that I was not upset with her about any of this; it was quite the contrary; all of it delighted me, filled me with excitement, and made me come to the realization that I wanted to share her with other men. I wanted her to become my hotwife.

Naturally, she did not know what the term "hotwife" meant, so I had to explain it all to her. It was important for her to understand that this was a real thing, with many people interested in it, and that it was not just me being weird for wanting to share her like this. It made her feel better when she understood that there were other wives who had sex with other men, and it made their husbands elated. As I talked, she listened, only interrupting a few times to clarify, "And you want this for me?" She could not believe that there were more people out there in the world who were into this hotwife lifestyle. She was perplexed as to why a husband would want to let his wife have sex with other men or even watch her do it to be more accurate. She could not fathom why her husband of twelve years dreamed of having this for her. It did not make sense. She was filled with initial shock and denial. She began to ask questions like, was she not enough for me? Was she uninteresting? Then her questioning became a bit more thought-provoking, such as, if she agreed to this, would she be able to choose someone she wanted, or would I choose? Would she have sex alone with him, or did I have to be there to watch? That was not the turn I had anticipated. It was roughly 3 a.m. when Vivian had decided the conversation had run its course. With her beautiful green eyes closed and her voice trailing off to la-la land, she whispered, "Thank you for explaining this to me more. I need to think about what all this means, and I need sleep. Good night, baby. I love you."

THE 'NO'

It was a Friday. Fourteen days after the last Friday that we spoke about this topic. She again waited until shower time to broach the subject. This appeared to be our routine, so it seemed. She informed me that she had thought about everything I had said two weeks ago. She said that she honestly considered it, but only to make me happy. However, the whole idea still freaked her out. The more she thought about it, the more it gave her anxiety. She said she had not been able to sleep well. She could not stop crying all the time. She said if I really wanted this in my life, I could divorce her and find someone else who could make me happy. She said she truly wanted me to be happy and knew she was boring and not an exciting girl for me. With tears in her eyes, she pleaded with me to never mention this to her ever again. So, there it was. She made her final decision. Her answer was no.

I was in shock. How could I have been so wrong? Her rejection and harsh criticism really blindsided me. I have seen her flirtatious ways. I listened to all her questions two weeks ago about if she could choose her own man. None of this made any sense. Her reactions were so far off base and not in line with the behaviors she displayed, but the answer was final. I had to respect the no.

I fully understood the weight of this decision that I had placed on her, as I had that weight on me not so long ago. The weight almost suffocated me. Perhaps that was unfair of me. I nearly did not bring this to her because the weight was so significant. Our entire family was at stake. I took a risk bringing this to Vivian, and her going through with it was not a risk she was willing to take. I tried talking to her a little bit more, mainly to tame her wild thoughts of her not being good enough and me requiring divorce, but I was well aware of the danger of pushing her boundaries too much, so I did not put pressure on her whatsoever. I fully understood the gravity of the situation.

No, was her final answer and I was more than ok with that. She meant more to me than any of this silly sex stuff, so I knew it was time to do my best and try to suppress my desires on my own. For the past six months, I had let my desires and imagination run rampant, and now was the time to squash them because the life I envisioned us living was not a reality.

I still felt that she was suppressing somewhat. Something was off, and it did not make sense. I could not let her reaction dispel everything I had witnessed these past six months. Her reaction was just that. She reacted. Sure, she took some time to think, but it was all a reaction. A reaction of fear. A reaction of loss. A societal reaction, perhaps. I reacted by dropping it entirely. I decided not to bring this up to her, possibly ever again. That is what she pleaded with me for, was it not? To never mention this to her ever again? I understood the importance of patience; if this was meant to be, then it was meant to be. I was not willing to risk my marriage to continue any further if she was not one hundred percent on board. It was over in my mind. I had started the process of moving on and suppressing my desires, and Vivian carried on with just being a loving housewife and mother. Unbeknownst to us both, the seed of curiosity had been planted regardless.

INTERLUDE: VIVIAN

I could not actually believe what Sebastian had asked me. Sure, our marriage had blossomed right in front of our eyes, and yes, I loved this new freedom we shared together to say some of the dirtier things that were on our minds, but he really wanted me to have sex with another man??!! Joking and making sexy comments were one thing, but having sex with other men who were not my husband crossed so many lines. This request was against everything that our society stands for. It was against everything I was taught and how I was raised. I was in shock, I was scared, I was worried and sad. I did not handle it well at all. I felt a tiny bit bad because here Sebastian was, showing his courage to tell me exactly how he felt. I could not help but admire how brave he was to say to this me. I know it was not easy. I also could not help the sick and nauseous feeling I had in my stomach, the panic attacks that caused my chest to tighten so that I couldn't breathe, or the constant stream of tears that flowed down my cheeks. Was my marriage over?

I know we had our issues a few months ago, but all marriages go through those bumps in the road, right? Things were getting so much better; how did it turn into this? I love Sebastian so much. How could he even consider allowing me to have sex with another man? The thought of him with another woman ripped my heart out. He had always been jealous. I know he has been changing and saying more sexy things, but I never thought he would take it to this level. Who is he? I am not sure I know this man anymore. I couldn't believe he mentioned Shane and Martin! First of all, why Shane? We are very great friends and coworkers. Why would he think I want to have sex with Shane? Because of a silly hug at a music festival? So, this is why he changed suddenly and became more sexual? He mentioned Martin. Damn it, he saw the attraction I had with Martin and took it to a whole new level. Flirting, legs touching legs, and sitting on his lap is not having sex.

I was freaked out that Sebastian had been hiding all these secrets from me for months. I was not happy that he took a picture of Shane and me and that he had been looking at it repeatedly over many weeks. It really creeped me out, and I told him that. Then he said this word "hotwife" to me also and tried to explain what it is. It made me want to puke. What happened to my fucking normal marriage???!!!!

I tried very hard to consider this hotwife concept for him and accept it only for him; after all, sex with other men wasn't the worst thing in the world. All I could do was panic and cry. I wasn't sleeping well because of this, either. I was a mess. I understood that I had changed a lot recently, and I became much more relaxed with joking or even flirting with other guys because Sebastian made me feel safe that I could. I loved the attention I was getting from Shane and Martin. It made me feel wanted, and I loved being wanted. It is also how I was as a teenager. I loved being wanted by guys, but then, when it got real, I got scared, and I was done with them. This was the same situation. I was just having my fun and enjoying being wanted, but Sebastian made it real, and I got scared immediately. Scared is not the correct word. I was terrified. Sebastian put me in this horrible position, and I wasn't sure I could ever forgive him for that.

The way I saw it was that I had two choices that led to two outcomes. The first outcome was that I agree to this. I lower myself, degrade myself, and sleep with someone that I do not love while my husband watches me do it. The thought of Sebastian watching me have sex with a man caused my panic attacks to become more severe. Let's face it: I am sure jealousy will take over at some point, and our marriage will be over.

The second outcome was I stand up for myself and stand up to Sebastian. I defend my body, and I refuse to do this. I worried that Sebastian might resent me. He will think I am not exciting enough. He will start searching for another woman who will do this for him, and our marriage will be over. Either way I chose, I saw constant fighting in our future and our marriage failing. All I could do was cry. I knew what my answer was going to be the second the situation was presented to me. I waited a few weeks because I was petrified to bring this subject up again with him. Deep breath, Vivian. You got this girl. The look on his face broke my heart when I told him that I couldn't do this for him and then begged him to never bring this up to me ever again.

5

THE EVOLUTION BEGINS

> "This life was never meant to be permanent. It is an opportunity to grow and be yourself so I hope you don't continue to exist like its spectator. Live. Dream. Hurt. Forgive. Heal. Evolve. Try."
>
> — REENA DOSS

Four years can be a relatively long time, especially if there is something exciting waiting at the end of that duration. We must wait four years for a leap year to bring us February 29th, which is a long time to wait if you celebrate a birthday. Soccer fans need to endure four long and excruciating years for another World Cup tournament to commence and fill us with joy, excitement, hope, and disappointment. College students need to wait four long years to graduate with their bachelor's degree and embark on their journey to their professional lives. Four years had passed since Vivian pleaded with me to never ask her about being a hotwife ever again. It did not seem long because I did exactly as she asked.

I withdrew the indecent proposal entirely. I mentioned nothing of it ever again. There was nothing exciting waiting at the end of the duration. It was just another four years gone.

THE CATALYST

After Vivian and I had our final discussion on the topic of her being shared, life went on for us both. There was no resentment on my part. How could I resent her for refusing to partake in such an outlandish request? I was just thankful to the universe that she did not resent me for bringing it all up in the first place and making her feel so terrible. I understood her feelings and accepted her answer, but something deep inside me did not buy it. My gut told me that I should not give up hope of her ever becoming my hotwife because I knew to my core that it was what she needed. She just did not know it yet. So, I decided to honor her feelings and drop the subject, but I could not drop my desire. I could not give up on her.

At first, I continued going on Tumbler frequently and fantasizing with my friend from California, but it started to feel empty because all momentum had died at home. Eventually, I stopped logging in because I had no new information to share with him. We were stagnant. Our marriage had regressed as far as our openness was concerned. All sexy comments about other men or other dicks, had ceased. There was no way that we could go back to that now. Vivian completely stopped talking to me about Shane unless she was talking professionally only. The day came when Shane left her company, and we never saw him again. Martin also changed jobs, and we never saw him again either. Everything had fallen apart. I had made things very awkward between us. I regretted it deeply and did not see any possibility of returning us to where we were four years ago.

New Friends

It was a Saturday night, and Vivian and I were invited to a party at our new friend's house. We had only met them maybe a month before they had invited us to their home. Being a somewhat antisocial guy, of course, I had zero interest in attending this festive gathering. The thought of being surrounded by a group of people I did not know sounded worse than getting a root canal. Vivian was persistent and pleaded with me that we needed to make new friends. Plus, she really liked these people. Begrudgingly, I agreed to attend with her, and for most of the evening, I had wished I was not there. It wasn't until approximately the last hour or so that I noticed a very attractive woman talking to Vivian. I tried to act as if I was not watching them when they both started to head in my direction. I grabbed a tortilla chip from the bowl and ran it through the seven-layer bean dip as Vivian put her hand on my arm.

"Sebastian, I want to introduce you to my new best friend, Jennifer. Jennifer, this is my husband, Sebastian!" Excitement resounded out of Vivian's voice.

I was mesmerized by her new best friend within an instant. Jennifer was as cute as a button. She had bright blue eyes that gazed at you as she spoke, long brown hair that was riddled with wavy curls, and a sweet southern accent that just made you want to listen to her keep talking no matter what she was rambling on about at that moment. The two of us exchanged pleasantries that ordinary people do when first meeting at a party, but there was something different about her energy that I did not recognize. She turned to her right and waved someone over to her as a man made his way to the kitchen where we stood. He was a very good-looking man with blue eyes that matched his wife's.

"Vivian and Sebastian, this is my husband, Nate", Jennifer introduced us in her twang.

The four of us talked for about thirty minutes until the party began winding down. Damn it, I didn't want to go home now. The friendly couple asked us for our last names and immediately sent us Facebook friend requests. On the way home, Vivian could not stop talking about Nate and Jennifer. We were both delighted to have met them. They were both hilarious, super nice, and extremely outgoing. They were the perfect ying to our shy and quiet yang. They were very good friends with our new friends, so we figured we would see them again sometime at another party over the course of the year.

The following Thursday, I received a Facebook message from Nate, a mere five days since the party. He and Jennifer were going out for dinner and drinks that night and wanted to see if Vivian and I were available to join them. Vivian's eyes widened with excitement when I told her of the invitation that we had received. She was in disbelief. We still did not have many friends due to our busy family life and shy demeanor. She could not imagine these super fun people had invited us for dinner and drinks after meeting them only five days before. We were astonished that they actually wanted to hang out with us! We had just finished eating dinner, but without hesitation, we decided that we needed to meet them for drinks at least. There was a sudden desperation in how fast we cleaned the dishes, took showers, and got the kids situated for the night before bounding out the door to meet our new best friends.

Evolving Desires

Over the next six months, our friendship with Nate and Jennifer blossomed. Nate worked a similar overnight schedule as me, so we often texted late at night, strengthening our bond. Almost every other week, Vivian and I would receive a text asking to meet for dinner and drinks, and each time, we would drop all that we had going on to join them. They were intoxicating to us. Their humor and banter between each other were entertaining enough, but there was a sexual tone in their personalities that we both recognized and enjoyed being around. They did not hide who they were. They were refreshing. On our first night meeting them for drinks six months ago, they told us a story about how they were in a pool in Las Vegas and how they were both making out with four girls at the same time. They were not your typical married husband and wife. I knew what we were getting into from the very first date, yet we were drawn to them.

It was a chilly Thursday night in April that changed our lives' trajectory forever. We met Nate and Jennifer at our favorite spot for dinner and drinks, which was relatively close to our house. It was around 10 p.m. when we were about to head home for the night. Vivian had to work early in the morning and was already yawning. Earlier during dinner, we told them about the hot tub that we had just got at our house, and they also had a hot tub, so it was a good flowing conversation. We have a tiny hot tub. The manual calls it a four-person hot tub, but the truth is that one seat is a chaise lounge; therefore, it only fits three people comfortably. Four, if you did not mind being in extremely close contact with the other three people.

"I think we really need to go back to your house and go in the hot tub", Jennifer said with a big grin on her face.

"It is getting late, but I guess we could for maybe one hour. Then I need to go sleep. But you guys don't have bathing suits", Vivan said hesitantly.

"We don't need suits, silly. We can go in our underwear, and all I need is a T-shirt from Sebastian, and I will be fine", Jennifer responded.

"Perfect, let's go then", I chimed in.

THE EVOLUTION BEGINS | 111

We got home, and I made another drink for everyone. I will admit I was a bit nervous about what we were going to do. Vivian and I had been the only two in this small hot tub, and now we would somehow squeeze another couple in there with us? It might get interesting. Into the hot water, we all enfolded. It was very tight proximity, but we were all just drunk enough that we did not mind. There is something about hot, steamy water that makes a lot of things okay. I was sitting on the one lone seat on the left side of the hot tub that was facing toward the other three seats. Nate was perched to my left, facing me on the chaise lounge that was a bit raised out of the water. Directly in front of me, to his right, were the ladies, with Vivian sitting in the seat next to him and Jennifer all cozy on her lap. Jennifer had to put her legs on my lap. Again, this tub truly was not meant for four adults.

The instruction manual says that due to health concerns, you should not be in a hot tub for more than thirty minutes, and you should not drink alcohol in a hot tub, so we broke all the rules that evening. We did not care. Three hours and three trips to the house for more drinks had passed. That is when it happened. It was after 1 a.m. when Jennifer decided to flip over and was now straddling and facing Vivian. Jennifer started telling Vivian how beautiful she was, and Vivian giggled with nervous tension. That is when Nate interjected that they were both so hot and suggested that they should just make out with each other. Vivian again giggled and laughed while Jennifer told him how stupid he was.

I could tell what was going on here. I could see the cat-and-mouse game that Nate and Jennifer were trying to play. He suggested three more times over the next twenty minutes that they should make out with each other. Each time Vivian would laugh and shake her head with a big grin on her face, Jennifer would assess her laughter and tell him to shut up and stop being stupid. At this point, Jennifer was laying on Vivian with her legs on both Vivian's legs and mine, with her thong underwear sticking out of the water and in my face. She started to slowly slide down Vivian's body, putting her ass just mere inches from my face. She then would deliberately glide back up toward Vivian, putting her face very close to hers. She performed this maneuver a few times, with no words being spoken by any of us. We just watched her with eager anticipation. As Nate said one final time that somebody needed to make a move, she began sliding up toward Vivian and stopped again. That's when I took charge. I put both my hands on Jennifer's ass and pushed her slowly all the way up to Vivian's face. My harmless wife did the rest. I watched as Vivian's hand came up out of the water and grabbed Jennifer's head. She pulled Jennifer up close to her, and simultaneously, one of her long, sexy legs came up out of the water and wrapped around Jennifer's back, as their mouths connected and their tongues swirled with passion. I said not a word as I silently watched my wife kissing a woman. It was pure bliss.

Craving More

The next morning came unforgiving and fast. Vivian struggled at work all day due to being both tired and hungover. She was not accustomed to drinking vodka and going to bed at 2 a.m. on a work night. When I woke up in the afternoon, I immediately checked my phone, and I had the following text from her:

I was on cloud nine with this conversation between us. When Vivian got home from work that evening, I gave her a big hug as she walked through the door. After a few moments, I asked her how kissing a woman was and if she enjoyed it. She said, "Yeahhhh, it was pretty good. I am not making a habit of this, so don't think that will ever happen again. It happened once, and it was good, but I am all set; I like men". We shall see about that Vivian, I remember thinking.

While at work that night, I took my phone out of my pocket and started to text Nate. I wanted to thank them both for a fabulous night and chat with him about how hot it was watching the girls kiss each other for more than twenty minutes. He asked me if Vivian had ever kissed another woman before, and I told him no, that it was her first time. He was surprised by that. Jennifer told him that she had kissed amazingly and that she was very aggressive with her. He asked how she was and if she was ok with what had happened. I told him that she did enjoy it, and she joked with me that it was a one-time thing because she likes men. He mentioned that Jennifer felt a little guilty about it and didn't want the kiss to ruin our friendship. I assured him that we were both more than ok with what transpired and that it was me, in fact, that put my hands on Jennifer's ass and pushed her up to Vivian's face. He said he saw that but still wanted to be sure we were good.

Two weeks had passed, and there was not a second that had gone by that I did not see the visual replaying in my head of Jennifer and Vivian passionately kissing in that hot tub. Any guy who has witnessed this event for the first time knows exactly what I am talking about. However, I had a cautious excitement inside of me because I did not want a repeat of what happened four years ago to transpire again. This felt different, however. We were both four years older and four years more mature. Vivian had just turned thirty-eight and perhaps was hitting her sexual prime. Cautious excitement, I know. She had just come home from work and was stressed from a very long day. I kissed her, hugged her tight, and told her she was about to have a lovely, relaxing evening with a glass of wine and her soulmate. As she was agreeing that this was precisely what she needed, the ding of a text message alert echoed out through the air from my phone. It was Nate.

Driving to their house, Vivian reminded me that she would only have a few drinks with the dinner they were cooking for us because she did not want to be up late. Nate told us to bring our bathing suits, and she reminded me that she would set a timer for no longer than one hour in the hot tub so we could leave. I agreed with all the stipulations that she made in order to approve of us going to their house on yet another Thursday night. They greeted us at the door with warm and inviting hugs when we arrived. My mind was racing in overdrive as I hugged Jennifer while watching Vivian in an embrace with Nate.

As requested, we changed into our bathing suits after dinner. Vivian handed me her glass and asked me to make her a third drink but asked that I not make it too strong. She was getting a little "fucked up", as she said. We removed our towels, and the four of us climbed into their enormous ten-person hot tub. My first thought was that this tub was way too big for any close contact and potential kissing from the ladies again. We all sat rather spread out while chatting about the beautiful evening, the moon, and the stars. It was a fantastic night to relax in a hot tub with amazing people, I thought while looking up at the stars. As I lowered my head back down to reality, I saw Vivian sitting on Jennifer's lap with her legs turned sideways and on Nate's lap under the water. Nate's hands just happened to be rubbing Vivian's legs slowly.

The erection in my bathing suit told me all I needed to know about how I felt in this current situation. Was Vivian really pursuing them this time? Jennifer was hot from the water, so she asked Vivian to shift so she could get up and sit on the tub's edge. Jennifer did not seem to be in the same mood that she was in at our house two weeks ago, but she looked absolutely gorgeous sitting on the edge of that tub in the moonlight. Vivian must have thought so as well because she stood up from the water in her wet and tight bikini in the blink of an eye and made her way to Jennifer. Vivian was on the prowl. She had this look of hunger on her face for more of what she got two weeks ago, and she would not be satisfied until she got it. She wanted to kiss Jennifer deeply again. She wanted her lips on hers. She wanted to feel wet skin on skin with her again. It was obvious.

Vivian wrapped her arms around Jennifer's neck and complimented her on how amazing her boobs looked. Jennifer thanked her and returned the compliment, but there was a glaringly obvious feeling in the air this evening. Jennifer was not engaging sexually with Vivian. She seemed distant, cautious and guarded, but Vivian had just enough drinks to miss the signs. Vivian leaned in for a kiss, but Jennifer turned her head at the last moment, forcing the kiss to land square on her cheek. Jennifer had rejected Vivian's advancement, and I could see the soul of my love crush instantly. It hurt me inside to see the look on Vivian's face and witness her reaction as she attempted to play it cool. I was confused by this turn of events. Was it because of my comment to Nate about Vivian saying that she was all set with any future engagement? Or was it Jennifer feeling guilty over last week's misbehavior? It was not long before we all decided to call it a night, and Vivian and I headed out on our journey home. She talked for a good portion of the ride about how confused she was and how rejected she felt being denied by Jennifer, but one thing was sure: my wife was craving more.

EMBRACING CHANGE

It was 6 a.m., and a startled Vivian awoke in a heart-pounding panic as the alarm sent her into a frenzy far too early in the morning. She was intensely adamant about leaving their house by 10 p.m. the night before, but time flies when you are having fun in a hot tub, and unfortunately, 2 a.m. arrives in a flash and conversely becomes your reality. The morning was hectic. Breakfast, lunches, arguing with children about clothes, and crying about hair not doing what it is supposed to do was a typical morning for Vivian. That morning, however, it all consumed her. She finally got both kids on the school bus before she hurried off to work on her four hours of sleep yet again. Two weeks ago, it had totally been worth it since, much to her surprise, she spent most of the evening making out with a woman, and she was riding high on excitement all day. However, that hellish morning, there was no value in her sleep-deprived hangover. It was all for nothing. When I woke up in the afternoon, I texted her to check how she was doing.

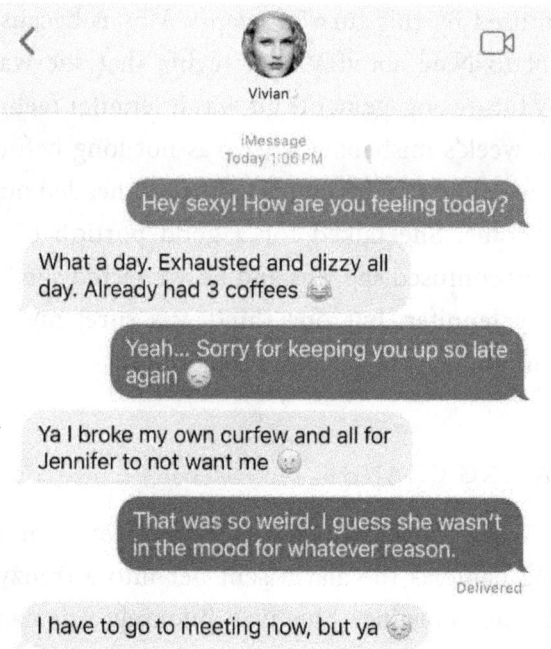

Facing Her Demons

When Vivian came home that evening, there was not much time to talk about what had transpired the night before. We were thrust into family life with homework, dinner, dishes, baths, and bedtime stories, so you can imagine my excitement when our youngest child was finally in bed. Vivian suggested that we relax in the hot tub with a drink. This evening started a chain reaction of many more nights of Vivian and I having naked conversations in the hot tub.

"I'm sorry Jennifer didn't want you last night, baby", I said to her shortly after we sat down in the water.

"I'm so confused. Two weeks ago, she was all over me, jamming her tongue down my throat, literally, and then last night, wanted nothing to do with me. It's weird".

"I know. I was very confused, too. I was surprised at first when I realized that you were trying with her because you said that was a one-time thing only, but it was awesome that you tried. I actually felt really bad for you when she turned her head. I could not believe that she did that", I said sympathetically.

"Yeah, well, I know I said that it wouldn't happen again, and the truth is that I don't want it to, and I don't care if it doesn't. It doesn't mean anything to me. I don't sit and think about wanting to kiss a girl or anything, but since I did it once, I guess it wasn't that bad. So, I got a little drunk and decided to make you all happy last night because I know that's what you all wanted to happen, well, you and Nate, that is. But she rejected me, and now I am done. She made my confidence so low. I don't think I can forget that, and she can find some other girl to make out with now. I am done".

That was that. Vivian was done with Jennifer and her on-again/off-again antics. I was in solace that I got to see my wife kiss another woman at least once during our marriage. Many men would absolutely kill for that opportunity, and I had the fantastic memory of her night of hot female passion. I was honored that she let me witness that once, but she was done now, and I was at peace with it.

So, I hope you can understand the level of my utter surprise when, a little over one month later, there Vivian was in the hot tub again with her long, sexy legs wrapped around Jennifer's waist, her arms wrapped around her neck, pulling her into her bosom, as they slowly kissed passionately through the steam of a chilly evening. To be fair, it was not Vivian's fault at all. Jennifer was very good at batting an eyelash and using her charm to instigate and manipulate any situation she wanted to. Vivian did not appear to be "done" with Jennifer from my vantage point; it was quite the opposite, in fact. From where I sat in that hot tub that night, I equated her to a timid rose bud that was just starting to bloom.

Growing Confidence and Self-Awareness

Over the course of the next year and a half, no, that was not a typo; this roller coaster ride of sexual tension between us, Nate, and Jennifer rumbled on. So many things had changed in our life together over that year and a half, and Vivian had really embraced all of the changes gracefully. It was funny to think that almost six years ago, I had desired nothing more than to share my Vivian with other men and watch her enjoy her pleasure immensely. It did not appear that my past desire would ever come to fruition. Still, the universe had brought us something equally amazing: Vivian was perfectly fine with her female exploration with Jennifer in front of me and Nate. Things had progressed up to that point where they were comfortable taking each other's bikini tops off and even kissing and licking each other's nipples. I never thought I would see the day that Vivian had a boob in her mouth, and it was better than I could have ever imagined! Up until that point, Nate and I had been respectful of the boundaries that our women had put up. There were unspoken boundaries that the women were only interested in each other, and we were both perfectly fine with that.

There was a wonderful repercussion of Vivian's wet and wild, curious exploration, and that was the remarkable sex between us for many nights to follow. The same held true for Nate and Jennifer. Nate was not shy when it came to texting me about how hot their sex was because they would start talking about Vivian and it would explode from there. Everything was going quite amazingly for us all, but there was still one aspect, which was a bit of a dark cloud, and it was the fact that it still felt like a gigantic roller coaster ride with Jennifer. She continued to be overly concerned about ruining our marriage or our friendship, which had caused so many up-and-down occasions where the girls would not fool around. Vivian had started to recognize when Jennifer was in one of her moods and would dial it back with the sexual aggression, but I could tell it was still bothering her that all the fun revolved around Jennifer and whether she was in the mood or not.

Vivian had indeed evolved and was growing her confidence more and more every time we hung out with Jennifer and Nate. She loved the excellent nights that ended with them embracing in a kiss, and it was obvious that the inconsistent nights that did not progress that way were wearing on her. As much as she understood it was Jennifer not being in the mood, those nights made her feel less connected and even slightly rejected.

I started to develop this gut feeling that maybe Vivian was ready to branch out and begin to explore other people who might be more consistent with us, but I was very hesitant to mention anything to her. This would have to be dealt with in a highly delicate manner. I patiently waited until the night came when the two of us sat on the barstools at our kitchen island, and she started talking about Jennifer.

"We have dinner next Wednesday with Nate and Jennifer, right?" she asked.

"No, Tuesday, babe".

"Ok. I thought it was Wednesday. I guess we should bring bathing suits with us for hot tub", she enquired.

"I was thinking we should not bring them and just go in the hot tub naked!" I grinned as the words came out of my mouth.

"I am not comfortable with naked. That is never happening. I am ok to go with no top, I guess, but don't push it with me. Also, do not forget, it all depends on what Miss Jennifer is feeling that night, so naked would be too much", she reminded me starkly.

It was time for me to shoot my shot for the second time.

"Since you mentioned that, I wanted to ask you about your thoughts on us maybe trying to meet some new people. I was thinking I could make a profile on a site and see if there are any nice couples in our area that we could maybe meet and make friends with. Nate and Jennifer are great and all, but I can tell you get a little frustrated when Jennifer just decides she doesn't want anything to do with you and rejects you. I know we could meet some new people that would be much more consistent", I said willfully.

There was a longer pause than I had hoped for before she began her response.

"I had a feeling this was coming. I like hanging out with Jennifer and Nate, and I know I have been letting go a lot lately. But I have pushed myself so much already. I don't mind having a little fun, and surprisingly, I don't mind kissing Jennifer, but I do not want to do anything else more than this with anyone else. I do not want any other dicks than yours. I don't want any vaginas. All I want is you", she uttered cautiously.

"That's fine baby, and I know you have been pushing yourself a lot lately, and you have been amazing! All I am saying is that it may be nice to meet some new friends that live much closer to us, and we can just see if maybe we develop the same friendship as we have with them. Just search and see who is out there. We may meet some really great people", I responded even more cautiously.

"Ok. I am fine with that. If you want to make an account, and we can see if there are any nice people in our area that we can maybe be friends with and see what happens. I do not like pressure on me. I don't like the idea of meeting people online when they will have expectations from me. I don't mind meeting people naturally like we did with Nate and Jennifer, but I understand it is hard to meet people that way. So, I guess let's try this and see what happens", she whispered shyly.

I could barely believe my ears were hearing the words that were coming out of her mouth. Let the hunt begin!

The Thrill of the Hunt

I am a man of action, so after Vivian went to sleep, you best believe that I got my ass to work on our couple's profile on AdultFriendFinder.com. I really loved AFF for its abundance of individuals who were all looking for the same things, but I also really disliked it for the number of fake accounts and bots that sent messages to your inbox. You must be cautious in deciphering who the real people are who are looking for a fun time, from the creepy collectors who just want to get pictures of your sexy wife and then disappear. I wrote an intriguing biography for us, I put some sexy photos of us with our faces not shown for discretion, and our account went live. I reflected with amazement that Vivian had just agreed to make this account so that we could search for other couples. I could not have been prouder of her evolution up to this point, especially when hope had seemed so bleak.

I spent hours searching other couples' profiles and sending messages to those I thought would be an excellent match for Vivian. After a few days had gone by, I was a little disappointed because I did not get as many responses as I thought I would. I realized that might be attributed to one major issue: that most of the couple's profiles were for "full swap" couples. This means that they are looking to swap sexual partners fully and have full intercourse, and that is not what we were. Our profile stated that we were new to this lifestyle with a wife who was just starting to push the limits of her female curiosity, so we were looking for a couple where the women lightly play with each other only. We were not a hot commodity up to that point.

I decided I had to spice up the profile a tiny bit by adding a little white lie. I wrote that this was all for the wife and the husband would not be involved, which was true. I wrote that she was willing to explore with a woman, but then I added that if they played their cards right, she could potentially be open to exploring with both the man and the woman simultaneously. I was aware, from what she said to me about not wanting other dicks, that this was not true, but the memory of her and Martin was still somehow fresh in my brain like it was just yesterday. The truth is that in that past year and a half, she and Nate had not crossed any boundaries besides her typical joking and flirting, which I figured was actually one of Juiliana's restrictions with him. Vivian had not tested the limitations with him either, so perhaps she just needed a fresh nudge.

I awoke the next afternoon to find four messages in our inbox. To say that I was pumped is a severe understatement! Four sexy couples within fifteen miles of us, highly interested in my angelic wife, sent us messages. I was so incredibly excited to tell her about this that I could hardly contain myself. I could not wait for her to get home from work! About an hour before she came home, she texted me to say that her friend was coming over after dinner for some wine and to catch up on life. Damn it. I would have to wait until her friend went home to show her our potential new best friends and see who she might want to meet. That evening turned out to be when I would make my first of many rookie mistakes. I actually made three rookie mistakes that night, and they all nearly cost us dearly.

It was nearing 10 p.m. when Vivian said goodnight to her friend and closed and locked the front door. She turned towards me as I sat on the couch, looking at our laptop.

"Gosh, I am exhausted. I might skip shower and just go to sleep. I have to get up earlier tomorrow for a meeting. You weren't planning on any action tonight, were you?" she struggled to get out through a yawn.

"No, babe, I was thinking I will bend you over tomorrow night."

"Gooood, gooood, I like the sound of that", she replied

"I did want to show you something really quick and get your opinion on some things."

"Ok, can you show me upstairs while I brush my teeth and get ready for bed?" she requested.

I followed her upstairs, laptop in hand, excited to show her the messages and profiles from our interested couples. She grabbed her pink toothbrush, turned on the faucet, and began adding toothpaste.

"So, you know how we talked about making a profile the other night? Well, I made one for us, and we got some messages from four couples that I wanted to show you really quick and see what you thought", I said excitedly.

"Wait, you already made an account for us, and you didn't tell me?" she asserted while glaring at me in the mirror with that look I had known all too well.

"So, we talked about it a few nights ago, and you told me to make an account. I am telling you now. That is what this is. This is me telling you now", I replied with a growing agitation in my tone. I didn't want to go down this path.

"Yes, I know we talked about it, but you haven't told me anything about it since. Now you tell me you already created it and you are messaging people already? I don't even know what our profile says. You didn't show me what pictures of me you put or anything!" she now responded with her agitation level growing in her tone.

I could see where this conversation was starting to turn, and I was not a fan. It was time to try and diffuse the situation before it escalated further. I touched her shoulder gently, and I apologized for my lack of thought on this matter. I told her I was unaware that this was important to her as I was basing my decision on her telling me to make the account. I did not think she wanted to be part of the process. She clarified that she did not want to be part of the process, but she wanted to know what I was posting before posting it. It was not an unreasonable request on her part. Rookie mistake #1.

I proceeded to show her the sexy pictures of her that I had cropped. She was ok with most of them, but there were a few she was not happy that I had used, and she asked me to delete them immediately. Done. She then asked me what I wrote in our bio. I do not claim to be an intelligent man, but I knew it was time for me to bend the truth with this one. There was zero chance in hell that she was going to be peachy with me, claiming that she might ready to play with a woman and a man at the same time, so it was time to tell a white lie in reverse now. I acted as if I was reading, but I was spewing words from my memory of what I originally wrote. I read to her that we are looking for local friends, and if there is chemistry there, the wife is open to exploring her bisexual side a bit more. This did not quite fly, and she argued with me that she was not bisexual. I countered with the fact that she likes kissing Jennifer. She proclaimed that she did not mind it, but it was not what she needed. I asked her why she agreed to this profile in the first place. She came back with "just to make friends." We were talking in circles. She finally agreed that the bio could stay, and she now wanted to know what the couples wrote to us and what they looked like.

One by one, I read each message to her and showed her each picture. One by one, she became more and more mortified. The messages did not bother her all too much, to be fair. Most were filled with compliments about her and how much they would like to meet her/us. But their pictures. Their pictures were another story. To be honest, it was not just the pictures that were the issue; my excitement level and description of the photographs profoundly impacted the situation. I showed her pictures of women's boobs. I showed her pictures of women's vaginas. I showed her pictures of erect dicks and commented on how big they were. I showed her pictures of couples engaged in threesomes with men, as well as threesomes with women. I concluded my X-rated slide show with, "So what do you think? Are you interested in meeting any of them?" Rookie mistake #2.

Men. A nickel's worth of free advice, well, I guess it is not free since you purchased this book, but I digress. When you find yourself in a situation like the one I am describing, do not spew X-rated pictures all over your innocent wives! I know it sounds like common knowledge, but man, it is easy to get overly excited in these situations and fuck it all up. I have learned the better technique of showing her lovely, smiling G-rated pictures and then letting her know that there are some naked pictures, too, if she would like to see them. She used to decline constantly; however, things have changed recently, but we will get to that in the next book.

SHE. WENT. OFF. ON. ME. She reverted to the old Vivian from more than six years ago. She was appalled. She was livid that I would show her these people who posted those "disgusting pictures," as she put it. She reminded me that she did not want to see disgusting dicks, and she certainly did not want to see disgusting vaginas. She reiterated that she did not want any of that at all. She only wanted to flirt, have fun, maybe kiss, and fool around, but this was far too much, and these people would expect everything from her. This led to an argument, of course. I was so excited to show her these couples because I thought we were on the same page once again, but I was wrong.

As she crawled into bed, trying to stop herself from crying, she whispered, "I am sorry you wasted your time and money making that profile, but I am telling you now that you should just delete it because I do not want this. I do not want to meet these people online that will be putting pressure on me to fuck them. I do not want the pressure from you that I have to fuck them, or you will be disappointed in me. Just please delete the account and never show me this again. I am ok with still fooling around with Jennifer now and then, but I do not need that either. I am sorry to disappoint you once again. I am a terrible wife. And thanks for bringing this up so late tonight when I was having a good night. I told you I was tired; I told you I had to go to work early. I will not be able to go to sleep now, but you don't care, so fucking thank you!"

And that boy's and girl's was rookie mistake #3.

ALTERNATE MEANS

The week came and went, and Vivian and I had no more discussion of couples, profiles, or websites. I was shot down again and forced to shut down again. I should have known better and not pressed my luck. Things were going so well with Nate and Jennifer, and I was acting greedy. Sebastian, the asshole. Did I shut down our couple's profile on AFF? No. I probably should have listened to my wife and deleted the account; I was about to actually when Vivian asked me if we could talk.

"Sure, what's up, babe?" I answered.

"I wanted to talk about the other night and how I acted. I know I came off harsh, and I didn't mean to. I just got really freaked out by everything. It was too much for me. I know you said I send you mixed signals, and I say one thing and then act another way, but that is just me, and I don't know why I do that. I hate that I agree to things to push myself and make you happy and then get scared when it becomes real. What I want to say is that I do not want to meet anyone online that is set up because of the expectations that it puts on me, but I am ok with meeting people naturally, and if something grows and happens slowly, then I am ok with that. If that is ok with you?"

"Of course, honey, no worries, and thank you for talking with me", I said as I hugged her.

The Unicorn Hunters

I knew there was no way in hell we would ever meet anyone naturally like Vivian was suggesting that we might. Sure, we met Jennifer and Nate that way, but I mean, come on! That shit does not happen every day. People do not typically just start hitting on and hooking up with their friends, or their friends of friends, or hitting on random couples at the local steakhouse. Vivian made it clear to me that she was open to testing the waters with people in a natural and normal setting, and I knew that it was up to me to force that hand a bit. It was at that moment that I concocted a failproof plan for us to meet new friends. Vivian wanted to meet people naturally, not to be set up and bound by the expectations of such an arrangement, and that was precisely what I would deliver for her. The first step was to do what I usually do, so I returned to the computer and began sending messages to couples on AFF.

She did not want me to show her any more couple profiles, so now it was left up to me to decide who she may or may not like. Being married to her for sixteen years, I felt that I was more than qualified to determine what qualities she found most attractive in a man and now in a woman as well. One stark reality I discovered very early on is that it is tough to find two people married to each other who are both equally attractive enough to make her want to pursue them. Vivian has particular types of people to whom she is attracted, so I could not just send messages to anyone available. I identified four attractive couples that seemed like they would be an excellent fit for us. I had to choose couples that were not looking for other couples as well since I was not part of the planned playtime adventure. I needed to find couples looking for a girl only to join them. I was searching for unicorn hunters.

Now, before I take this story any further, I think it is important to define what, in fact, a unicorn is. We all know that a unicorn is a beautiful and majestic beast that is made up of folklore and does not exist, despite what my daughters used to think. There are four definitions of the word unicorn according to the Merriam-Webster dictionary, but for this topic of discussion, we will only focus on two of them. According to Merriam-Webster, a unicorn is "a mythical, usually white animal generally depicted with the body and head of a horse with long flowing mane and tail and a single often spiraled horn in the middle of the forehead." The second definition we will focus on is "something unusual, rare, or unique" (https://www.merriam-webster.com/dictionary/unicorn). Some examples of that could be a rare baseball card with a curse word written on the handle of a baseball bat that never made it to mass production or a vintage model DeLorean in mint condition with only approximately 9,000 to come off the assembly line (www.wikipedia.com).

For folks in the lifestyle (LS), the term unicorn takes on the same implication but with a twist. It is also something that is unusual, rare, or unique, yet can also be considered mythical, magical, and non-existent. To put it extremely simple, it is a woman who is interested in sexual relations with partnered couples and plays with both partners equally. So, now that you know what a unicorn is, it is pretty apparent what a unicorn hunter is. The ratio of couples seeking unicorns to actual interested unicorns is severely undistributed. I say actual unicorns because of the skewed number of fake accounts and bots. For all the couples out there searching for their unicorns, I wish you the best of luck, but they are out there. The rarest of all the unicorns is a husband who is helping his wife become a unicorn, which I am not sure there is even a term for yet. But I assure you, we do exist. I can't be the only one! I will call myself a unicorn creator until society develops a better term.

So, my unorthodox search for unicorn hunters for my wife continued with my messages to four couples. They were all very attractive couples, and I knew they were going to be excited to meet my Vivian. To save time, I copied and pasted the same message to all four couples.

"Hey guys! Just came across your profile, and you have very sexy pics! My wife and I are looking for a fun couple like yourselves to meet for drinks and see if we connect and just see where things go with no pressure. This is mainly for her. She has been recently pushing her bisexual side and is open to further exploration. The one thing I should mention is that she doesn't like arranged meetings with people online. She wants to meet couples in public naturally. Would you be interested in possibly meeting us some night at a bar and just starting up a conversation with us naturally? Hope to hear from you!"

Oh, it was going so well until the last three sentences. Two-thirds of the way through, they realized they had an unprecedented unicorn situation on their hands, and then it was ruined in the final third. Looking back, I am not sure what I was thinking. I did not know enough about the lifestyle to believe that people would find this approach unethical and just downright wrong. She had handcuffed me, and I was desperate, damn it.

All four couples responded to me over the next day or two, and I was severely disappointed with the following replies that I had received.

"If you are not being honest with her, then we want no part of this", short and to the point. That was strike one.

"That is not how this lifestyle operates. It is built on open and honest communication. Anything based on trickery and lies is not welcome", and there was strike two.

"Hey there, she is so damn sexy!! We would love to meet you guys and play with her. Can you show her our pics and make sure she is interested in us? Thanks!" They did not read my entire message clearly, or they misunderstood the point that I would not be showing her their pictures. I wrote back to them explaining this in more detail. Foul tip: I was still alive.

And last but not least, *"It's obvious she doesn't want any part of this. If you need to trick her to meet people, that is not really cool man, and your marriage is bound to fail"*, and there my friends was strike three. I was out.

I was defeated once again, and the thought of us living this lifestyle was emotionally draining at this point. I had a fleeting hope that the confused couple would answer back to me and agree to meet us "by chance" at a local wine bar, but after a week, the realization hit me that they were no longer confused, and they most likely despised me just as the other couples had. I never heard from them ever again. All the last remaining drop of hope I had was depleted from me now. The idea of deleting our account had crossed my mind on more than one occasion, and for the life of me, I am not sure what stopped each time. I stopped hunting the hunters and just logged on every few days to see any new messages we got from people I was not interested in.

Dante and Paulina

It was a hot Sunday evening, and I had just got to work after spending the afternoon at the swimming pool with Vivian. I despised working on weekends after having to leave the pool to go there, but I was especially not in a good mood on this day, thanks to Vivian. Earlier that day, we were relaxing in the water when I saw a sexy couple across the pool looking over at us. I made Vivian aware that it seemed as though they were checking us out, and I asked her what she thought about them. Her response was, "Gosh, is this what you are going to do now? You are going to be constantly checking out girls and show me couples all the time?". When I asked her what she meant by that, she clarified that suddenly, since we talked about all of this, all she noticed was me checking out girls in front of her and not even trying to hide it. She said I was too obsessed and that she did not want me to ask her about every couple I saw. Yep, she pissed me off.

So, there I sat grumpy in the break room alone when I received a message from a couple that called themselves UnicrnHuntrz.

"Hey there. The wife looks amazing and someone me and my wife could have a lot of fun with. We are in the same town so that is nice and convenient. Check out our profile and let us know if you are interested in chatting more. Dante and Paulina".

I opened their profile and inspected their profile pictures. They looked like a fun couple, for sure. I was relatively confident that Vivian would be attracted to Dante. He looked like her style of man. He had a muscular build, several tattoos on his arms and chest, and a bad-boy look to him. I was not quite sure that she would be attracted to Paulina, however, as she did not really seem to be her type of woman from what I could tell early on. On the same token, what did I know, really? So, I decided to write back to them that afternoon, but what did it matter? They would lose all interest as soon as I told them about our requirements, so it made no difference. I decided that this time, I would write back and get to know each other first before dropping the bomb on them and that I could not be upfront with her about meeting them online.

The correspondence between us that afternoon was the most I had ever communicated with someone from AFF before. I traded messages back and forth with Dante. He told me about the experiences they had in the lifestyle and how they had recently moved to the area. It just so happened that they were originally from the region from which we relocated. They did not know many people living here, having been here less than a year, so they were very open to making new friends with us, if nothing else. We had children that were similar in age, which was great to have in common, too. The conversation transitioned back to us and our experiences. He was interested in learning more about Vivian's exploration and was intrigued to learn more about why I would not be physically involved with the playtime fun.

He was very excited that he wrote to us that afternoon and was most happy that I had messaged him back. Dante informed me that he felt that we were the perfect match together. He said they only liked to play with women, hence their name, which displayed their intentions of hunting the elusive unicorn. He told me that Paulina was extremely bisexual and was not interested in playing with another man, so my being on the sidelines, coupled with Vivian being incredibly sexy, made us the perfect couple for them. I was so proud and excited all at the same time until he said that I should show my wife their pictures, and he hoped that she was very interested. That is when my excitement came to a screeching halt. Fuck, it was good while it lasted.

I told him the dilemma that he, Paulina, and I faced if we were to make this happen. I filled him in that Vivian preferred to avoid arranged meetings with people that I met online. I told him that if we were out at a bar and happened to meet them accidentally, there was a chance that she might feel a connection and we might hit it off. I told him this would not be an immediate hook-up either and would take some time, but if they were patient, it might turn out to be superb in the end. He did not respond for what felt like an eternity. It was over. We scared another lifestyle member away with our untruthful plan. And then my phone buzzed.

"It seems kinda shady what you are asking, but I also get it. If she really said that she might be down if meeting naturally, then maybe it will be fun. And no worries about being patient. It makes it so much more worth it in the end. What is important is everyone has a good time, so we don't rush people. Let me talk to Paulina and see what she thinks about this. We do love a good challenge :)"

Holy hell, I could not believe what I just read! I was beyond excited that he was still interested. I could not wait to see what Paulina would say about all this. Still, deep down, I figured there was no way in hell that a woman would agree to almost trick another woman under false pretenses, even if the other woman was practically asking for it and forcing it to be this way. I returned to work and could not stop thinking about how this might all work. How would they approach us in the bar? What would I say to initiate a conversation? Would my acting skills be strong enough in front of Vivian to pull this off? I was lost in a daydream for hours until the intense moment when I felt like I could not breathe when my phone buzzed with an email message.

"We are in. The wife is excited. She said your wife is fucking gorgeous, and she is thirsty to hunt. What is your plan, bro?"

The Rollercoaster of Emotions

The plan was in place. I was not sure if it was a solid plan, but it was a plan nonetheless. Dante and I exchanged phone numbers and had been texting nearly every day for about two weeks. I told him a lot about Vivian, and he was highly confident that he and Paulina would win her over and make her like them enough to want to see them again. I just had to get them an audience with her. Neither one of them loved the idea of faking an accidental public meeting of chance, as they preferred that I just told Vivian about them and asked her if she would like to meet them. There was no chance in hell of that being a viable option, and I explained that to them ad nauseum, so they agreed to the plan that I had concocted.

Vivian and I were going to go out to one of our favorite restaurants in town for dinner and drinks. I would wear a hat from a local sports team back home. Dante and Paulina would come to the same restaurant and spot us either at the bar or our table, depending on how busy the place was that night. If we were at the bar, they would try to sit near us or at least come next to me to order a drink. If we had a table, I would walk up to the bar to order a drink. Either way, the plan was for Dante to come up to me and make a comment on my hat. He would mention the hat, ask if we were from that area, and tell us they were from there as well. Just like that, a conversation would start. I was confident that if this all went smoothly, Vivian would enjoy drinks and conversation with our new friends, and who knows where it might blossom after that.

The stage was set. All I needed to do was to get the leading lady there, and the rest would take care of itself. I asked her about going out for dinner and drinks Friday night, and she was excited to do so, as it had been a minute since we had gone out alone. Dante and I had settled on a meeting at 7 p.m. since we had to wait for Vivian to get home from work, shower, and get dressed all sexy for our date night. I had just finished feeding the kids their dinner when she arrived home after a stressful day and week at work. She dropped her bags and gave me a big kiss.

"Baby, make me a drink! I need to get fucked up after the day I had. I need to get into the shower so we can go", she said with happiness on her face that I never got bored of seeing.

"Sure thing, sexy! Go get naked in that shower, and I will deliver it to you, my dear".

"Good, good. I like that you do what you're told", she answered. I slapped her ass hard for that comment as she grinned.

"By the way, Cassie and Rob might meet us tonight. She was asking me at work what we doing tonight, so I told her we are going out, that they should join us. She will talk to Rob when she gets home and let us know", she added while walking towards the staircase.

Cassie was a friend at Vivian's work who just happened to live in our neighborhood, but that wasn't important. What was important was that Vivian and Cassie were about to destroy my plan with Dante and Paulina. I needed to act fast.

"Oh, you invited them? I was kind of hoping I was going to just spend some time with my sexy wife tonight since it has been a minute." I slid into the conversation as she paused at the bottom of the staircase.

"Well, yeah, I didn't know that, or I wouldn't have invited them. We haven't seen them in a while too, so I thought it was a good idea. Do you want me to cancel them? There was no guarantee they were coming anyway. She needed to talk to Rob", she retorted back.

"I don't know. I was just hoping for some alone time with you", was all I could muster when she interrupted me.

"This is not a big deal. I am going in shower. We will get there around 6:30 or so. If they are coming, I am sure it will be closer to 7 or 7:30; you know how they are. We will still have alone time together so I can be with my sweet husband. Now make me that fucking drink!" she said, smiling as she disappeared up the stairs.

I immediately texted Dante to make him aware of the potential crisis situation that was unfolding before my eyes. I told him that Vivian had invited our neighbors to come with us now, and I was not sure if they were showing up or not. *"Ahhhh fucking neighbors"* was his only response. I told him that I would let him know as soon as I heard if they were coming. I told him that Vivian seemed to be in a playful and sexy mood, and I was now making her a drink for a fun evening. He finally responded that they were still getting ready, and hopefully, I know something before they left.

It was 6:35 PM when we pulled into our parking spot. The delicious wave of smoked meat hit me like a stream of pure bliss when I opened my door to get out. I was starting to stress because I knew Dante and Paulina would leave their house shortly, and we still had not heard from Cassie.

"Why do you seem tense, baby?" Vivian asked me as she intertwined her fingers into mine as we made our way to cross the busy road. Before I could make up a lie, her phone alerted her that she had a message.

"It's Cassie. They are coming and will be here around 7:30. What did I tell you? Now we have a whole hour just us, my love".

"Awesome", is all I could mutter at that moment.

As soon as humanly possible, I made a beeline for the restroom after we took our seats at the bar. *"Fucking neighbors are coming, man. I am so pissed."* I hit send. I emptied my bladder and washed my hands. Still no reply. I had an idea. *"They will not be here for another hour, though. You should still come. We can get to know you for an hour and then just introduce you to them."* Send. I ran out of the bathroom.

We ordered our favorite appetizer that we love to share, ordered our drinks, and ironically, we somehow started talking about Nate and Jennifer. Vivian felt bad we had not seen them in a few weeks and said we needed to schedule a date night with them soon. We even pulled out our phones to discuss possible nights that would work. I thought she must be missing Jennifer, and it made me happy that I was trying my best to find her someone new. My eyes darted to the door each time I heard it open. It was getting later now, and my phone was silent. The anticipation of them possibly showing up still distracted me, to say the least.

It was close to 7:15 p.m. when we ordered another drink, and as the handsome bartender was walking away from us, I heard the *"ding"* of a phone. My heart started to pound as I unlocked my screen, anticipating seeing a text that read *"We are here"*, but my notifications were nonexistent.

"Cassie and Rob are not coming now", she said, peering down at her screen. "Oh well, looks like you got your wish of a night alone with your soulmate", she joked as she raised her eyebrows at me.

"It's perfect, darling. Fuck the neighbors! Here is to Sebastian and Vivian!" as I raised my glass, we clanged them together in a toast.

I was beyond frustrated with this entire situation and could not show it whatsoever. Vivian had no idea the turmoil that was going on behind the scenes and in my head. I had to keep it together. I despised Cassie and Rob at that moment. How dare they say they are coming, ruin my plans, and then change their mind? I took three giant gulps of my beer and excused myself to the restroom again. Dante and Paulina were fifteen minutes late, and I had yet to receive a message from him. I quickly texted him the great news that the neighbors were not coming. I told him we had not eaten yet, so we had plenty of time if they still wanted to come. I even described what we wore so they could find us easier.

I slid the phone back into my pocket and hurried back to find my gorgeous wife talking and laughing with the handsome bartender. I took my seat at the bar next to her as she introduced me to him.

"Sebastian, this is Christian. Christian, this is my hubby Sebastian".

"Hey man, good to meet you. Your pretty wife was just telling me how you guys got stood up by your friends, and I told her too bad for them, and that is a win for me because now I get to make her laugh all night!" he smiled as she busted out in laughter as if this was the funniest thing she had ever heard in her life.

"See, each time is a point for me. Let me get you a beer, man!" he said, disappearing in a flash.

"Hey baby!" she said gleefully as she leaned over to kiss me but was interrupted by a beer being put down loudly on the bar.

"Wow, that was so fast! What else do you do fast?" she said to Sebastian with this different look in her eyes that I remember seeing with Shane and Martin.

"I get paid to serve beer fast, darling. That's the only thing I do fast." He winked at her and walked away. I was only in the bathroom for two minutes. What the fuck did I miss?

Vivian and I sat at that bar for a few hours. The situation came out of nowhere, and I was pleasantly surprised to see where it was progressing. I had forgotten all about Dante and Paulina at that point. Vivian was engaging with a gorgeous bartender right in front of me, and he was definitely engaging with her in return. Could he sense what I was and what I wanted for her? Christian would serve someone a drink, and then he was right back in front of my wife, gazing into her eyes while I sat back like the proud husband admiring his wife's joy. He was genuinely unphased with me at all. I could feel him wanting her, and I could feel her wanting him.

Vivian was getting a little tipsy after she had a few drinks. Every time he would leave, I would tease her and say things like, "fuck he wants you badly" while rubbing her leg with my hand. She responded, "I know he does," while her eyes watched him from across the bar. He kept coming back over to her, asking her how to say words in her language and commenting on her "amazing accent" as he worded it. At one point, he commented that he was not her type of guy because she was so beautiful, and she responded with, "Oh, you are my type". I wondered if I should sit somewhere else and leave them alone.

It had started to get late, and we decided that we should pay the bill and go home. I was sure that some fantastic sex was coming my way if she could withstand getting sick between the bar and our house. Just after Vivian left to go pee, Christian put the check down in front of me and walked away. Reaching into my back pocket for my wallet, I realized he had made a mistake and brought us the wrong check. This check was for one meal and one beer only. The bill totaled $16.35, which should have been more like $116.35 based on what we ordered. Vivian returned and asked if I had paid already. I explained that I was waiting for him to return because he mixed up our check with someone else. Just then, he appeared in front of us once more.

"Hey man, I think you gave us the wrong check. This is way less than what we had", I said, trying not to embarrass him for making such a mistake.

"Shut up", he calmly told me while staring at me with a blank look on his face. I was taken aback, which was not the first time I had been with him that night.

"Ah…I'm just…this…this isn't our check. We ordered much more than this."

"Shut up", he replied more sternly, with his unblinking eyes fixated on my face.

I looked at him, severely confused and starting to get annoyed. I could not figure out why he was telling me to shut up when it was him that clearly fucked up this bill. I opened my mouth to speak when he cut me off, smiling.

"Shut up and don't worry about it. You're welcome", he stated while scooping up our bill and my credit card and scurrying off.

"What just happened?" Vivian asked, looking just as confused as I was.

"Jesus. I think he just took away like $100 worth of food and drinks. He gave us a bill for $16.35."

"That's awesome! Why would he do that for us?" she asked, unassuming.

"Because he wants to fuck you, dear!" was the only statement that made sense to me.

"Yeah, that is clear", she slurred and giggled.

"I can't believe he did this. I feel like we need to give him a crazy tip", I proclaimed.

"Yeah, for sure", she added agreeingly.

I jotted a hefty tip down on his receipt and signed it as Vivian stood to put on her leather jacket.

"Are you leaving me?" Christian had returned with a sad look on his face.

"Yeah, we have to get home and go to bed, you know what I mean?" Vivian said with a wink and laugh. "But thank you so much for what you did. That was awesome, and we gave you a big tip", she added while pointing to the check.

What happened next is still inexplicable to me and still feels like a surreal moment that just does not happen in real life for regular, everyday married couples. Christian, a bartender that we just met a few hours prior, walked around the bar and walked right up to my wife. He opened his arms as he stepped in close to her, and she did not hesitate. She reached for him. She pressed her body close to his as they wrapped their arms around each other in a warm embrace like they had known each other for years. He hugged her close, not even looking at me once, as he began to speak to her.

"It was so nice meeting you, Vivian. I really enjoyed talking with you and getting to know you, and I really, really enjoyed making you laugh. You made my night fly by. Come back and see me anytime."

"It was so nice meeting you too, and thank you again for everything", she spoke softly to him.

As he let her go from his embrace, he turned to me and raised one hand like a wave goodbye.

"It was nice meeting you too, man; drive safe and take care. Come see me again, guys. I am here almost every night now", and he turned and was back to work.

Holding hands as we walked back to our car, I spoke first.

"Well, that was weird. I have never seen that happen before at a restaurant."

"Ummm, no! I think he wants me", she said very matter of fact.

"Oh, I think he wanted to make that very clear, darling. All I can say is wow! And I can't believe he changed our bill like that, either. It's nuts!" I reminded her in disbelief.

"You gave him a good tip for that, right?"

"Yes, I hooked him up. It was awesome that he did that", I stated as I opened her car door for her.

She was about to get into the car when my sweet Vivian changed my world forever. She paused, turned her head back to the restaurant, and looked back at me.

"I feel bad that he did that and gave us all that food and drinks for free. Should I go back and suck his dick or something?" she said quietly with a joking grin on her face.

For any man who has found themselves in my position, you know the feeling that I am going to try to describe when you hear your wife say something like this for the first time. I am not sure what the feeling is. Euphoria? Pride? Excitement? A mixture of all three and then some? All I know is that it immediately made me feel like my heart was pumping out of my chest. For any man that found themselves in my position, that has not felt this yet, I pray that you do because it is fucking glorious! While I tried to take this moment in and savor it, I knew I had to respond quickly and precisely. Christian just woke up something in Vivian that I could not believe, and he deserved her mouth around his cock.

"I think you should absolutely go back and suck his dick, baby", I said with confidence while staring her in the eyes.

"I think I should. But I don't know what to do or what to say" holy shit, Vivian was really picturing it in her head and needing a slight nudge to make this happen.

"Well, why don't you walk back in there and just go up to him and ask him what time his shift ends. Tell him you want to repay him properly for fixing our check for us."

"I don't know. Then what? What if he says in one more hour? We have to wait around here for him to get out? Then it will be weird. Just forget it."

Nope. I would not be forgetting this conversation ever. No chance in hell!

I floated the next idea to her, "Ok, how about you sit here in the car? Go in the back seat. I will go back in and tell him that you are in the car and want to talk to him real quick if he can take a five-minute break."

"No honey, that is more weird. My husband isn't going to go tell him that. I am going to do this myself. I just don't know what to say", she replied.

"Ok, well, I can stay here in the car. You go back by yourself and don't say anything. Go up to him, take him by his arm or hand, and say, "Come with me". Maybe take him into the bathroom and just undo his pants and just start sucking his dick", I advised her. My mind was racing with questions like, was this real life right now?

"Hmmm. I could do that. I don't know about bathroom, though. Where else?" Vivian asked as her mouth was watering for his dick to be inside of it.

"I don't know babe. Maybe take his hand and say take me somewhere for five minutes. It's his work, so he can take you out back to an office, maybe? Or outside behind the building? He isn't going to tell you no. Did you see how much he wants you? He is probably jerking off right now, thinking about you. Go make him cum, baby!"

"I should go make him cum!" she said, turning her head to the restaurant yet again. I could see the inner turmoil inside her head and knew I was right about her desires the whole time. This woman needed more in her life, and I was ready to give her all she needed.

"By the way, you have me hard as a fucking rock right now! Thought you might want to know that ", I added to break her trance. She returned her look back to me and smiled. She stepped towards me and started to rub my cock over my jeans.

"There's my boy! Let's just go, baby. I don't think I can do this. Not right now at least."

"Ok, love. But as long as you know that you can absolutely have these thoughts, say them out loud, and act on anything you need with me", I reiterated to her.

"You are showing me that baby, and I love it", as she began to kiss me passionately. I made sure her hungry mouth was fed on the drive home.

INTERLUDE: NATE, JENNIFER & CHRISTIAN

Four years had passed since I had begged Sebastian to never talk to me about this lifestyle ever again. He respected me and never mentioned any of this during that time. I know he was disappointed how his fantasy ended so fast, but he really didn't show it. This was very important for me to move on with my life and not really think about it anymore. He never made me feel like his desires were more important than me, my feelings, or our marriage. Then one night we met Nate and Jennifer. They were the breath of fresh air we needed in our lives at that exact moment. We both knew they were our people the first night we met them. They were like us in so many ways and they were such a good-looking couple, which was just a bonus. We felt like they were almost too cool for us, but they seemed to like us a lot for some reason. They made that clear from the first day we met. We were always so excited when they would text us to meet them for dinner that we would cancel whatever we were doing that night if we could.

I loved hanging out and laughing with them, but if I am being honest, I never felt we would be more than great friends. I was just a little naive, but it was like any other innocent friendship that was just so much more fun. Then, the night came that Jennifer wanted to go into our hot tub with us. I remember being a little uncomfortable with the four of us in it together because it was so small, but Jennifer was relentless. I was hesitant, but I agreed, and I am so glad I did. For any couples that are wondering how to get started in the lifestyle, I suggest to get a hot tub. I promise you it will be worth it.

After a few drinks, I decided to calm down and go with the flow. Jennifer was sitting on my lap, which I didn't mind. When she turned to face me, she was staring at me with her big, bright eyes, but she had a different look about her that I had not seen before. She looked at me with desire and lust. I knew she wanted me, and I kind of wanted her. Jennifer kept sliding up and down my body many times. Each time, I got a bit more anxious, and I was sort of guessing what may happen next. I kept drinking to try and get more courage in case anything happened, but her taking so long to make a move on me was driving me crazy.

Each time she moved her body on mine, I got more impatient. I remember thinking, "Is she going to make a move or not?" I wished that she would take over and take what she wanted from me. I found myself wanting her to just do it because there was no way I could make that first move on my own. She was teasing me so much. She studied my face each time she glided on me, and she knew that more and more I wanted her as well. I so badly needed her to step up rather than wait.

I was so curious at that point, and I wanted to experience this with her. Thankfully it finally happened, and she kissed me! Her lips were so soft. Her kiss was so gentle. I loved the feel of her tongue in my mouth. It was a very exciting new experience for me, and I was more than okay with this new adventure I was on. I was doing my best to block out the fact that the boys were just sitting there watching us, but I knew that we made them very happy.

I could not wait to see her again, but unfortunately, it was not exactly a hot and sexy time when we got together two weeks later. I was excited and full of confidence after our last playtime, so I was more aggressive and flirtatious with both Nate and Jennifer. I wanted to kiss her again. I thought that was what everyone wanted and what they expected of me now, but Jennifer seemed a bit off for some reason. It almost did not matter because I felt like someone else was controlling me at that moment. I couldn't stop myself when I decided to try and kiss her anyhow. That was the biggest mistake for me. When she turned her head from my kiss, I felt so low about myself.

I am not going to lie, Jennifers rejection fucked me up a little bit. It made me feel not only bad about myself, but it made me feel bad about what had happened between us the first time. I was confused inside. She made me feel unwanted and really made me think that kissing me before was a bad decision for her. All we did was make out with each other. It really was not a big deal, but she took it to another level with me and decided to push me away. I decided to put my guard up with her after that. I told Sebastian that I did not care about kissing her or doing it again. I did not care until I found myself in the hot tub with them the next time, and Jennifer decided that she wanted me again. I was not strong enough to push her away from me, and I was sucking on her tongue once again.

I started to realize what Jennifer was all about. I began to figure out that Jennifer's mood controlled the night, and I had to accept it. I liked playing with her a lot and eventually, I became more comfortable, and Jennifer became more daring with me. It was *thrilling the first time she took my bikini top off and started sucking on my hard nipples in front of our men. I was so turned on. Of course I had to return the favor, and the next thing I knew, her erect nipples were in my teeth and on my tongue. I discovered that I like kissing and playing with boobs, and I never thought that I would. I was definitely growing my confidence and my self-awareness at the same time. I was on a journey of self-discovery, all thanks to my loving Sebastian, who continued to support me.*

I loved playing with her, but I was beginning to not really enjoy how everything was dictated by her mood. Sebastian asked me if I would like to try and meet another couple from online that I could explore more with, but I did not want that. I know Sebastian wanted more for me. I know he wanted me to experience having sex with both women and other men, but I honestly only wanted to have sex with him and kiss Jennifer occasionally. I truly did not want anyone else, and I tried to tell him that. I did compromise and agree to meet new friends with similar thinking online as long as he ensured that there were no expectations put on me at all.

Since I agreed to this, Sebastian made us an account on a website of course. I figured he would. I did not think that he would do it without including me and then stop me while getting ready for bed to show me pictures of naked people that wanted to meet me. I was so angry with him that he did not show me what he wrote about me, that he did not show me what pictures of me he used to broadcast to these people online, and that he immediately showed me naked pictures. Naked pictures equal expectations in my mind. How could he be so wrong to not listen to me or understand what I was telling him?

I was more than upset with him when he read to me that he called me bisexual in our profile. I was not bisexual at all, and I made that very clear to him. I did not think about women at all. Sure, I think women are pretty and hot, but I was never sexually attracted to women like that. I told him I love dick only! I know it was confusing for him because I was comfortable kissing Jennifer or even kissing her boobs, but I did not feel that made me bisexual. Everything he wrote about me did nothing but put expectations on me after I was insistent that he did not do that. This was the last straw for me, and I had enough. I told him to delete the account and that I would never meet any of these people ever. I could see his confusion and disappointment on his face, but I was done.

I knew I hurt him yet again, and I felt like a terrible wife, but he was pushing me too far and too fast. I felt terrible about how I reacted, so I did have a talk with him about a week later. We came to an agreement that there are no more online people, but if we were ever out, and people were flirting with us, I may be open to exploring that slowly. I never really thought it would actually happen, until it did. So, here is a question for my ladies. When you tell your husband that you are open to meeting people in a natural setting to see where it goes, then you find yourself in that exact situation; you must go for it, right?

That is exactly what happened to me on the night that I met the bartender, Christian. Christian was so fucking hot that I almost couldn't stand it. He had that typical bad-boy look that drives me wild. Muscular arms and tattoos peeking past his tight, short-sleeved shirt first caught my attention. He had a closely shaved head with a neatly trimmed goatee, but the first thing I noticed was his piercing blue eyes. They captivated me. Our eyes caught each other more than once as he walked past me. One of the times, he smiled at me, and I of course, smiled back. Sebastian did not notice because he kept turning and looking at the door often. I was not sure why he was doing that.

When Sebastian got up to use the restroom, Christian wasted no time coming right over to talk to me. He asked me how we were doing and if I needed anything. Oh, the thoughts that flooded my mind. I told him I would need another drink soon, but I was not sure if I wanted the same drink I currently had or something different. I can see now that it might have had some double meaning. He asked what else I like. I told him I am a vodka girl, but I like gin too, and sometimes rum. He asked if he could make me a surprise drink that he makes for only pretty ladies. I laughed, told him I trusted him, and could not wait for his surprise. He put both hands on the bar, leaned closer to me, said he absolutely loved my laugh and accent, and asked where I was from. We told each other where we were from and exchanged names. He took my hand off the bar into his, he pulled it to his mouth, and he kissed the top of it while telling me it was so very nice to meet me. He made my panties wet almost immediately.

He then asked if we were meeting anyone else tonight because it sounded like he heard we got stood up. I laughed and asked him if he was spying on us. He laughed and said it was my fault because I caught his eye the first moment he saw me. He was charming and witty. I told him about Cassie and Rob not making it, but I also told him that it was not a big deal. He told me that this was a win for him because now he will get to make me laugh for the rest of the night. It was time for me to show him who I am a little. I replied sarcastically, "I will talk to you maybe a little, but only if I am feeling it and not bored with you." We both started laughing. He looked at me and said, "Oh, feisty and sexy. I like you, Vivian." Again, I laughed, and he chuckled as Sebastian sat back down beside me. I think this was Sebastian's dream come true, but I was unsure how he would take this. I quickly reminded myself that I was not doing anything wrong, and my husband likes it when I *flirt with men. Time to see how this goes*, I remember thinking while trying to act calm and relaxed. Damn Vodka.

I introduced my husband to my bartender immediately. They shook hands, and Christian went to get Sebastian a beer. I smiled at Sebastian and gave him a quick reassuring kiss just before Christian returned with it. I decided that I was going to enjoy this moment to the fullest. I started flirting with Christian right there in front of my husband. I smiled and made cute faces when I talked to him. I had this new, fantastic feeling of confidence that I had not felt in a while, but I could only enjoy this moment because Sebastian was pushing me in that direction for so long. It felt liberating and free that I had this incredibly handsome man that was all about me, and I was flirting back, but only because I knew I could. I will admit it was very hot that my husband was sitting right there next to me. It was like a game to me. It was ironic because being the center of attention was something I had always struggled with my entire life, but at that moment, I realized just how much I really liked it.

We sat at the bar for many hours. The surprise drink that Christian made for me was delicious, and I made sure to let him know about it. He would leave to get a drink for someone and come right back to me. He was looking into my eyes and making me laugh. I felt powerful and risk taking. The defining moment, or a point of no return for me, was basically telling another man that I want to fuck him while my husband sits next to me listening. It was a crazy moment that I will never forget.

The night was incredible, but I never expected that Christian would lower our bill for us. I could not believe it and was in shock. It was so incredible of him, but it also showed us both what this hot man was trying to do. Perhaps the real surprise came when we got up to leave and he came to give me a hug. This was not normal behavior, but at the same time, what was normal about that night? I opened my arms, and he squeezed me in tight to him. I could feel his hard chest against the side of my face, and the smell of his cologne made me want more of him. I wondered what he looked like with his shirt off. He spoke to me softly and gently as he stared at me, telling me how nice it was to meet me. At that moment, I swore he was going to kiss me, and I do not think I was going to stop him. Instead, he let me go, said goodbye to Sebastian, and walked away.

As we strolled back to the car, I was soaking wet. I was very excited about everything that happened; Christian wanting me, me wanting him, and my husband witnessing it all and loving it! Sebastian rubbing my legs and telling me how bad this man wanted me made me want to explode. I always like pushing boundaries and saying things just because, so the next thing that came out of my mouth was fun and sexy, and made a super fun night with my husband. I looked at Sebastian and jokingly asked if I should go back in to suck Christian's dick. I wanted to see his response. I wanted to see his face. The power was all in my hands at that moment. Without pausing to think, he told me that I should go back in to suck it for him. That is all I needed to hear. No, I did not go back and have another man in my mouth that night, but I made damn sure to take care of Sebastian all the way home.

6

VIVIAN AWAKENED

> "The whole art of teaching is only the art of awakening the natural curiosity of young minds for the purpose of satisfying it afterwards."
>
> — ANATOLE FRANCE

Have you ever heard the saying everyone comes into your life for a reason, a season, or a lifetime? I think each and every one of us can resonate with this statement in one form or another. As I grow older and perhaps a splash more mature, I have come to realize the truth in this saying and have come to appreciate the notion that all people enter our lives for a reason. I absolutely believe that each person that we have purposeful interactions with has been delivered to us for some cosmic higher reason, whether to teach us a quick lesson, help us through a difficult time in our lives, or perhaps push our boundaries and comfort zones to aide us in our quest for continued and exponential personal growth.

I have come to accept that some individuals can be positive while others can be negative. I have also come to accept that some will only grace us with their presence for a brief period of time, while others may be around for weeks, months, or even years. Hence, they say a reason, a season, or a lifetime. Since Vivian and I began this journey, we have encountered many such individuals who have come into our lives in divine timing. When we were stuck and not continuing to grow, they were there to give us the push we desperately needed. Many positive people have entered our lives to help us expand our boundaries and take our journey to the next level. We have had negative experiences that have taught us valuable lessons at the same time. No matter the circumstance or the duration of their impact on us, we have come to appreciate their lessons and cherish the moments we gained because of them. We call such individuals *Sex Angels*, who were delivered to us from the universe, and without them, Vivian's awakening might not have ever taken place.

THE DANCE OF SEDUCTION

I woke up in the afternoon feeling quite remarkable indeed. I was naked and alone in my bed. I turned my head to the right to see the empty sheets and blankets next to me where Vivian's warm and naked body had slept just hours before. I had exhausted her last night, and she passed out before she could even put her pajamas on. We exhausted each other, really. We both collapsed and fell asleep immediately. The thrill and passion of her flirtatious actions and words had ignited us. She had crossed some boundaries that I never dreamt she would even tiptoe on, and it catapulted us into pure ecstasy and raw sexual passion. What had Chrisitan done to us? What had he awakened in my wife? Where did he even come from? Would we see him again? He was definitely a sex angel for us, and at that point, I was hoping he would be around for a season at least.

Last night's date night had not gone as planned whatsoever, but damn, what a surprising turn of events! Vivian was sprouting right before my eyes, and I was enjoying her growth. I began reliving the moments in my head and felt myself begin to harden. The images of her flirting with Christian in front of me while she smiled or laughed captivated me. The way he looked at her when he told her how much he loved her accent and her laugh. The long embrace in his arms as they said goodnight. I stiffened in my own hand. How did this have such an effect on me? In an instant, my mind flashed to her standing in front of our car with her head turned toward him in the restaurant, joking if she should go back and take him in her mouth. It was all that I could stand, and it was time to make myself happy again. After satisfying my needs with self-pleasure, I checked my phone to see if I had a text from Dante: nothing.

A few days had passed, and there was still no word from Dante after I had jerked him and his wife around, so I assumed they were pissed and were likely all set with us after that debacle. I was debating whether or not to reach out to him when, ironically, I saw his name come across my phone.

I was a bit irritated with Dante at that point, and I think he picked up on that because he chose not to respond to me for the rest of that day. I was not sure what my neighbor's interference of our plans had anything to do with "the plan" suddenly not being good enough to reattempt. Their stance seemed abrupt and unjustified, but I was forced to wait two days until I could gain any clarification from Dante. When he decided that he wanted to reach back out to me, I asked for an explanation as to why they had changed their minds about meeting us in a natural setting and why they were forcing my hand to discuss an arranged meeting with Vivian. I did not gain such an explanation. They just changed their minds, plain and simple. They both felt that the best course of action for me was to be open and honest with Vivian. They felt that if any of this were meant to be, it would happen if I told Vivian about them and asked her if she would like to meet them. I reminded Dante that I had already exhausted those conversations with her and that taking this approach would end any prospect of us meeting them. I reiterated to him that she made it clear that she did not want me to ask her to do this ever again and that I would not have this conversation with her. Their stance was firm, and I quickly learned that Dante was one hell of a manipulator.

The Open Discussion

Vivian arrived home from work and looked like she had been through pure hell. She appeared to be beaten down and drained. I greeted her with a long hug as she sighed deeply in relief to be home.

"You look like you need a drink, baby. Let's go out tonight and see if your bartender is working", I floated the idea to her.

"My bartender?" she laughed. "Ok, sure, let me go change and make the kids some pasta before we go." Thankfully for us, pasta was our kid's favorite meal.

Looking around the bar, we could both see that Christian was not there that evening. I was a bit disappointed that he was not working, but I knew that I had the opportunity to talk to her about Dante and Paulina now. I could not believe that I had let Dante talk me into opening up this can of worms with her one more time. I must have been out of my mind. After we ordered our second drink, I decided to dive headfirst into what felt like a lost-cause conversation.

"So, love, I wanted to talk to you about some people that want to meet us, but I don't want it to upset you or start a fight or anything over it. It's really not worth it", I lead off as she just looked at me and said nothing.

"I know you told me to delete the account that I made, and I am going to, but I just haven't yet since it was already pre-paid for two more months. I also know that you said you didn't want to meet anyone from there, but I wanted to tell you about this husband and wife that reached out to us".

"Ok", was all she replied.

"They sent us a message saying they would love to meet us, and I replied back to them, telling them that you were not ready for any of this and that I was canceling the account soon. They said they fully understood that and wondered if we still wanted to meet them just to make new friends. They just moved to this area rather recently like us, and they do not have many friends, also like us. They seem cool, and they said if you would like to meet them, with no sexual pressure at all, to let them know", I concluded as our drinks arrived.

"I am okay with making new friends if that's all that they really want from me. Do you have pictures of them?" she asked me after our server walked away.

I opened my phone and handed it to her. She scrolled emotionlessly and handed my phone back to me when she was through with it.

"They seem nice. Sure, we can meet them, but I am not doing anything with anyone." she responded prior to sipping her drink. I could not believe my ears!

The Hunt

We drove up to the restaurant, and I found a place to park under a giant oak tree. I turned the key to the off position and checked my hair in the rearview mirror. I did not intend to, and I certainly instantly regretted the moment that I took a deep breath and let out a large sigh that told Vivian all that she needed to know. I was nervous. I am sure in her eyes, there was nothing for me to be nervous about. We were only meeting some new people for dinner and drinks. The issue was that this was not just meeting some new people for dinner and drinks. Dante and Paulina were elated that I came clean to Vivian about how we met and that she agreed to have dinner with them. They were going to be normal and respectful, but there were no doubts that they intended to get what they wanted. They wanted to claim Vivian as their prize at some point down the road, and they made that known. For tonight, Dante assured me that their main goal was for her to like them and want to hang out with them again. So yes, I was nervous. I was nervous that she might not like them and that the night might be awkward. I was nervous that they might come off as too strong after she made it clear that she was not interested in more than friendship. I was nervous that we would not have much to talk about since she was not interested in the lifestyle aspect of their dynamic, which is what they seemed to be mainly about.

I received a text from Dante as we strolled into the restaurant hand in hand. I was praying that he was not canceling.

"They will be here in about ten minutes", I muttered.

"Good! I need a drink or two before they get here", she admitted.

"Me too!" I admitted right back.

Thankfully, getting two drinks did not take too long, so we had enough time to chug half of them before I saw them walking toward our table. It took about half a second for the nausea to set in as Vivian and I stood from our chairs to shake hands and exchange pleasantries. I watched Vivian intently through this interaction and immediately could tell that there seemed to be an attraction between her and Dante. That was a great sign! It did not take long for my nerves to subside because Dante and Paulina were simply incredible. They were both super friendly and inviting, making Vivian and I feel incredibly comfortable from the beginning. We covered various topics such as jobs, kids, relocations, and sports, and through it all, Dante had Vivian continuously laughing with a witty and sarcastic sense of humor. The conversation flowed, and we enjoyed getting to know our new friends when Vivian flipped the script on us all out of nowhere.

"So, you guys have an account online and are meeting other couples? Have you had much luck so far?" she asked them both. Dante smiled at her, and his glance shifted back to me with a look of confusion on his face. No one sitting at this high-top table was expecting her to ask a question like that since we all figured this conversation was off-limits so as not to pressure her in any way. Paulina nervously shifted in her chair.

"We have not been on there very long, but we also have not had any luck yet. You two are the first people we have actually met", Dante said as he smiled at Vivian.

"And, we haven't been really looking to meet couples either. We are really only interested in meeting girls, to be honest", Paulina chimed in.

"Oh really?" Vivian asked intriguingly.

"So, before we moved here, we had a girl for a few years that we played with all the time. Unfortunately, we had to leave her behind, which sucked. We realized that we miss having someone like her in our life, so we have been searching for a fun girl to join us occasionally", Dante informed her.

"We have never been with other couples or other men up to this point. I am not saying it will never happen, but as for right now, we are not really interested in men joining us", Paulina quipped. Vivian nodded at her comment.

"Well, since you brought it up, pretty lady, how about you two? Sebastian says there have been some couples interested, but they have not really worked out for you guys?" Paulina fired back.

Vivian took a deep breath, looked up at the ceiling, and paused before she chose her following words.

"Well, I don't know what this guy is doing on these websites", she glanced at me. "This guy doesn't tell me anything. He just makes these profiles, puts my pictures on there, and shows me naked pictures of people who, I guess, want to fuck me?"

Fuck, she was derailing in front of them. Dante glanced at me, and I stared back at him with what felt like an "I told you so" expression on my face.

"Yet here you are having dinner with us because we honestly need some fucking friends", Paulina said charmingly.

"Here we are! To new friends!" Dante toasted. Vivian laughed as she raised her hand to clink glasses with them and me. Dante was smooth. He roped her in almost effortlessly.

"Well, Sebastian was telling Dante that you have some friends that you have not exactly been an innocent angel with?" Paulina prodded almost aggressively with a devilish smile. Vivian covered her mouth and leaned back in her chair as she laughed hysterically.

"Oh, I am an innocent angel", Vivian teased with a very blank expression on her face.

"That's not what I have heard, girl; now I want details!" Paulina bantered back to her.

"Alright, alright", Vivian said shyly with a massive grin on her face. "We have some friends that are a married couple that we have been friends with for maybe two years now. Sometimes when I am drunk, typically, we like to kiss and touch and stuff, but it is not a big deal really", Vivian admitted.

"So, you haven't gone down on each other yet?" asked Paulina.

"Oh gosh, no! That is gross. I am all set. I let men to do that to me only thank you", Vivian said matter of fact while making a disgusted face.

"Ok, Vivian. Let's see about that. I would rock your world, is all I am saying", Paulina added with a sinister smile.

"Oh gosh, stop scaring me!" Vivian kidded while holding her hand to her chest and pretending she was out of breath.

Dante intelligently turned the conversation back to a more vanilla topic so that Vivian would remain comfortable and likely to think favorably of them. We hugged, told each other how nice it was to meet, and stated that we hoped to hang out again soon as we walked to our cars. I started the car and began the short drive home while Vivian silently checked her social media apps.

"So, what did you think baby? They seemed nice and funny, and it seemed like we had a very comfortable conversation with them", I asked her apprehensively.

"Yes, I liked them. I would like to hang out with them again." I took a relaxing breath.

The Pursuit

My eyes slowly opened to the view of the late morning sun peering in at me from between a small opening of the two maroon curtains that hung in my bedroom. The sole purpose of these curtains was to try and keep the room as dark as can possibly be. That day, the sun won. I quickly rolled over in bed to grab my phone. I was filled with anticipation to see if I got a text from Dante yet. There was nothing. I decided to text him first today.

Dante and Paulina were having a small gathering of friends and family for a cookout at their house the following Saturday, and they invited us to stop over. I was apprehensive because we just met them and did not know them that well at all. Dante did not want to hear my concerns when I told him I was unsure we would be comfortable with attending his gracious invitation. He only wanted me to tell my wife that we were going, and he wanted me to let him know that she said yes. It sounded so simple, but I knew what she was going to say. There was no chance in hell Vivian would be comfortable seeing them this soon, or going to their house this rapidly, or meeting their children and friends. Zero chance.

"Sure, let's go! We can bring Violet since you said their kids will be there?" Vivian said with a smile that sent waves of shock and disbelief coursing through me.

"Wait a minute. You actually want to go? I assumed there was no chance that you would want to do this", I clarified with disbelief.

"I mean, why not? I thought we were making friends with them. Then, we need to get out of our comfort zone and meet our friends. I don't want to leave Violet all day with a sitter, so if we can bring her, then I say yeah, let's do it", she said with a touch of eagerness in her voice. I reluctantly agreed with her that we would go. I decided to text Dante and spread the good news. He was thrilled.

We arrived at their house nearly thirty minutes late because I refused to be the first of their guests to arrive. I was a nervous mess, which did not come as much of a surprise, but Vivian's demeanor appeared to be as calm as a cucumber. She even had me take a picture of her posing with their pineapple décor that hung from their front door while taking a swig of her beer. I felt like I was just starting to get to know this new version of her, and I freaking loved it! The party itself was relatively uneventful and was not a really influential moment in our story to communicate in great detail. Still, it did serve two significant purposes, so I felt it was at least worthy of an honorable mention.

Dante and Paulina were both delighted to see us when we arrived. Dante whispered to me that they had bets on whether we were actually going to show up or not. He had won that bet. He gave a nice, long hug to Vivian. They were excellent hosts. They showed us around their home while introducing us to everyone, and everyone was so very interested in learning how they knew us and how we met. Luckily, Dante had a foolproof plan in his back pocket that we never put into action, and he used it as our story. They saw us at a bar wearing a hat from our old favorite sports team, and a conversation stirred. I knew it was a great plan because they all bought it. The kids even got along. It was a fine day.

Now, our attendance at this party of theirs was necessary for a few reasons. Firstly, it showed Vivian that they, in fact, were not monsters. They were just ordinary people with nice friends who knew how to function in society as normal adults and normal human beings. I say this with tongue in cheek because I think before that, she had an idea in her head that couples on the internet were just sex-crazed nympho aliens from Venus that were looking to exploit her vagina at all costs. She talked with them both, and she laughed with them both. She had a great time and did not want to go home. We were only supposed to stay for two hours and ended up staying for over six hours. The second reason that this was important was that Dante made damn sure to schedule our next date for the following weekend. Vivian had already accepted this next date with them. The wheels were in motion.

The long work week came and went, and the following weekend had finally arrived. It was date night with our new friends, and I was excited, but more importantly, it felt like Vivian was too. This was a big week for us and our progression. Dante and I texted multiple times a day. Mostly it was him telling me how bad he wanted to fuck my wife, but the rest was him telling me his and Paulina's plan to win Vivian over and help her cross over the threshold from "friends" to "friends with benefits". I had told Dante many stories of Vivian playing in the hot tub with Jennifer and how she lets her inhibitions go when she is in that hot and steamy water. He was determined to get her in there. He told me that it was my assignment to ensure she was comfortable enough to go in there with us three. I was optimistic but unsure at the same time.

Vivian was not having it. Each time we talked about what to do Saturday night, her version of the night ended so terribly that I was worried she was going to become a nun.

"Why don't we just go out for some drinks for a few hours, and then they go home?" she mentioned in a serious manner.

I was really pressing for them to come back to our house after to enjoy a nice fire in our yard accompanied by some more drinks. She said she was unsure that she wanted them to come over after but gave no reason as to why she had chosen this stance. I decided to let it be. I chose my own new stance of let us see where the night takes us and what is meant to be will be. She could not argue with that. We were almost ready to leave to meet them at a local wine bar to wet our pallets when Dante texted asking for our address because they got a new and exciting vehicle, and they wanted to pick us up in it.

We had a fabulous time at the wine bar. It is an older establishment with a speakeasy vibe, a dark ambiance, and soft leather couches everywhere to get cozy. It was the perfect venue for couples like us. Vivian was having a great time with them again. She enjoyed her wine, she laughed, and she told stories. She was happy, and I loved seeing her like that. I left the three of them together and went to the bar to order more wine for us all. I really liked Dante and Paulina, but at that moment, I looked down at them where they sat and saw Dante had moved to the other side of Vivian. This maneuver had put her directly in between them on that couch. A stark realization crashed over me that none of this was for me at all. It was all for her. She was the superstar prize that they both coveted. I was just there. I was insignificant. I felt a little like a pawn on the chess board as the King and his Bishop enclosed on my Queen. I quickly wondered if I was I making the right decisions? Was I putting my vulnerable wife out into the pasture to be slaughtered by wolves?

I returned down the stairs with four filled glasses of wine and got a rush of excitement the moment I saw how close the three of them were all sitting. I could not believe my eyes. Vivian was nestled right up against Paulina, almost touching shoulder to shoulder with her. Paulina had one arm up on the couch that was around Vivian's head. Vivian was slouching down, making it appear Paulina had her arm around her. Their legs touched skin to skin. Dante was on the other side of my wife and was almost as close to her as his wife was. Their legs also nearly touched, but his arm was touching Vivian's.

"Well. Don't you look cozy, darling?" I said as I passed the glass of red wine to her.

"Yaaaaaaaaaa", she said with an opened mouth grin. She was genuinely enjoying this! Dante smiled at me. I sat on the chair across from them and watched them work their magic on her. She seemed very comfortable in her new surroundings.

As the last drops of red wine stained our lips, we discussed what was next on the agenda. Vivian, all snuggled up between the two, mentioned coming back to our house and that I would start a fire for them. They both agreed they could stop by for a little while, but they did not want to be out too late. I decided this was as good of time as any to mention the hot tub to get Vivian thinking about it.

"Too bad you guys do not have bathing suits. We could have shown you our little hot tub", I teased.

"We do not need bathing suits; we have underwear", Dante joked innocently. Vivian laughed.

"Maybe next time we will be more prepared, and it will not be so late", Paulina answered back, smiling while slapping her hand on Vivian's leg.

When we arrived back at our house, I lit the propane fire pit on the patio while Vivian made our guests drinks. The four of us cozied up around the flickering flames under the full moon's light while getting to know each other just a bit more to the sounds of the crickets and spring peepers in the backdrop. Things were progressing very nicely, and there was a feeling in the air that it was only a matter of time before things were going to explode. However, we had yet to learn just how soon that explosion would detonate.

THE AWAKENING

There was something different about Vivian, but I could not quite put my finger on what it was. Over the last two-plus years, she had grown very comfortable with her occasional yet sexy-as-hell hot tub smooching of Jennifer, and she even seemed to enjoy kissing boobs now too. I never saw that coming. Then there was Christian, our sex angel bartender, who swooped down into our lives for only an instant seemingly. He touched Vivian's life for only a few hours, but his profound impact on us both was immeasurable. He showed her how amazing it felt to be wanted by another man in front of her husband and how freeing it felt to show her husband that she potentially wanted another man. Sadly, we only saw him one more time after that night but we were a large group of friends so there was no chance for any real interaction.

Only a short time after meeting Christian, we find Vivian snuggled in between Dante and Paulina on a couch in a wine bar with a giant smile on her face that could light up the world. This was her awakening. This was her liberation, so to speak. This was her true inner being coming to life. An inner being that had been lying dormant her entire life, with whom she was just starting to become acquainted. She was beginning to test what she truly desired. She was beginning to challenge the societal norms that oppress and shackle so many men and women and keep them from becoming who they were justly meant to be. This was her time to shine and her time to be herself. This was her time to awaken.

The Joy of New Experiences

There is no question that we had been spending lots of time with Dante and Paulina since our first date with them. We had hung out with them three times over four weeks, and things were going so well that we had not really thought about Nate and Jennifer all that much. Vivian must have been missing Jennifers lips and touch because she asked me if I could get in touch with them to set up a date night soon. Nate was happy to hear from me when I reached out. He told me that he was just about to text me, too, because Jennifer was missing sexy Vivian. We agreed that it had been far too long since the girls had some playtime, so we compared our schedules and set a date for the following Tuesday night.

Tuesday night finally arrived, and Vivian was excited to see them. She came downstairs looking incredibly exquisite this evening. She was wearing a black leather skirt and a tight white shirt that was so low-cut that it exposed almost all of her cleavage. She asked me if it was too much and wanted to know if she should change. I asked her if she was kidding me as I slapped her ass somewhat hard and told her to go get her shoes on.

When we arrived at the restaurant, we walked in and saw them sitting in a booth, but I instantly noticed something different this time. For years, they have always been seated on the same side of the booth or table, but tonight, they were sitting in opposite booths and facing each other. Interesting. They both stood up and greeted Vivian with a hug that was preceded by a glance down at her boobs and followed up with comments about how sexy her shirt was. She smiled, laughed, and told them she thought they both might like it. Wait, both?

"Now I have to try and really focus during this dinner", Jennifer laughed as she came to give me a hug. "We thought we would switch things up tonight if you don't mind sitting next to me?" she smiled as the words rolled off her lips.

"Alright, if I must", I smiled back. I glanced at Vivian and Nate. Nate still had his arm around the small part of her back.

"Sounds great to me!" Vivian said with a laugh as she began scooching her butt in her leather skirt across the leather upholstery of the booth.

Dinner went about the same as usual except for the unusual amount of touching that was occurring and Nate not being able to take his eyes off my wife's boobs. Jennifer had touched my arm a few times, which led to Vivian touching Nate's in return. I noticed Nate had touched Vivian's leg, too, as he asked her if her skirt was genuine leather or not. It was not. I was unsure what was occurring, but I was not complaining either. After dinner, Jennifer asked if we should go to our house and get in the hot tub. Silly rhetorical questions.

It was an absolutely perfect night for the hot tub. A slight breeze blew on that early spring night, and the nearly full moon lit up our yard with a sexy ambiance that cast shadows in every corner. Vivian entered the water first while Jennifer changed into her bathing suit. Nate got in and sat on the higher bench next to Vivian. I followed and sat in the other deep seat directly across from Vivian. Jennifer came outside and saw us three already in the hot water.

"Where am I sitting, y'all?" she asked in her sexy Southern accent.

"Wherever you want, baby", Vivian replied to her.

"Wherever I want? Alright then", she said as she dropped her bathrobe to the ground.

Jennifer swung one leg over the hot tub wall, followed by the other, and slumped into the hot water square on my lap. This was an interesting choice and not her typical spot in our tiny hot tub. She leaned back against my chest with her legs across the tub on Vivian's lap. Vivian was smiling. I was freaking out. After a few minutes, Nate scooched a little closer to Vivian, and to my amazement, he put his left arm around her shoulders. Vivian cozied up to him with her hands underneath the water. My imagination ran wild with what her busy little hands might be doing under that water. We all talked briefly, but I knew Jennifer could feel my hardness under her ass as she sat on me. I was a little embarrassed and a lot excited. This was all very new territory for us. Vivian had a determined look in her eyes as she raised one leg out of the water and placed her foot on Jennifers stomach and boobs. Jennifers hand began rubbing the lower half of Vivian's leg. After a few minutes, Nate commented on how long my wife's legs were as he placed his hand on her upper thigh and began to rub slowly. Vivian just giggled. What would happen next was going to change our lives forever.

Jennifer rose out of the water very sensually and leaned toward Nate and Vivian. She crawled slowly onto Vivian's lap and started to kiss her wildly like I had seen her do so many times before, but this time, Nate was right there. He had his arm still around Vivian's shoulders and now had himself a firsthand view of them kissing. They kissed and embraced for a very long time with Nate there watching them. I must admit that I was a bit jealous because I couldn't see much with all of Jennifers hair in the way. I sat there sipping my drink until I noticed Jennifer's hand gliding down Vivian's rib cage and disappearing under the water.

Vivian opened her legs wide and pulled one foot out of the water to place it on my chest. It was apparent to me now that Jennifer's hand was rubbing between my wife's legs. Jennifer removed her tongue from Vivian's mouth and started gliding it down her neck while slowly inching her way down Vivian's collarbone. Her free hand came out of the water to grasp Vivian's breast, and in one wild motion, she ripped her bikini top down to expose her excited and erect nipple to the bright moonlight. Vivian moaned loudly while Jennifer's mouth and hand gripped her breast, and her other hand rubbed tirelessly on her vagina. It was the most incredible sight, and I could not believe what I was witnessing. Just when I thought it could not get more intense in this situation, I realized that I was dead wrong.

Jennifer released Vivian's nipple from her licking and sucking, and she began to lean into Nate. Nate grabbed Jennifer's head as he kissed her ferociously, all while she continued working her hand between Vivian's legs. Vivian was breathing heavier and becoming more vocally loud. Her eyes were glued to them as they kissed a mere eight inches from her face. Nate's right hand came up out of the water so that he could start rubbing Vivian's right breast while also pinching her erect nipple in between his finger and thumb. He stopped kissing Jennifer and looked at Vivian, who was staring at him and biting her lower lip. That was all he needed to see. He leaned his head toward Vivian, and she opened her lips wide. That was it. My wife was making out with another man for the first time in over eighteen years, all while I watched in amazement.

Nate and Vivian kissed with such passion. It was evident that this had built up over the past two years of sexual tension. Nate and Vivian continued to kiss while Jennifer continued to rub and kiss and suck on Vivian's boobs. It was the most incredible and intense thing I had ever seen my wife do, but I must admit that I started to feel a little left out, seated across from them and not involved whatsoever. It was almost as if Vivian could feel that from me as well, because, at that moment, she spread her legs wider, brought her foot back out of the water, and started to rub my chest with her toes. I grabbed her leg and squeezed it gently to let her know I appreciated her gesture and all that she was letting happen to her.

Nate broke off their kiss and looked at me. He gave me a thumbs up and a nod as if he were seeking my approval and permission to continue. I gave him a thumbs up in return and nodded slowly only once. His mouth was on her other boob in an instant. There was my sweet Vivian with her legs spread open, Jennifer's hand rubbing her pussy, and both their mouths licking and sucking her tits while she panted in ecstasy. I started running my hand up her leg, which she had placed on my chest, when Jennifer turned around in the water and began to make out with me! It took me by total surprise for some reason, and I was stunned that I was now making out with another woman in front of my wife. Vivian's moans and heavy breathing continued and increased out of nowhere. When I got a chance to look her way, it was Nate who was now rubbing in between her legs while they were kissing again.

"Do you mind if I go back to your wife for a minute?" Jennifer whispered while smiling at me. I kissed her again and told her, "Please do!"

Jennifer turned back in the water and returned to Vivian and Nate. Jennifer started to kiss Vivian again. I ran my hand up Vivian's leg and met their hands on her. She was being rubbed and grabbed everywhere. I felt a hand on her ass cheeks and another hand on her crotch again. I started to rub her ass, too, when my hand touched the bows of her bikini bottom. She was not wearing a typical bikini bottom that you would have to pull all the way off her feet if you wanted to remove them. Oh no, she was not. She had on a pair where the front and the back were tied together on each side of her hips. Divine timing yet again. The universe wanted me to make my next move. I started to pull at her single knot, and the bow came untied. She stopped kissing and laughed when she realized what I had tried to do.

"Hey, what are you doing to my bathing suit?" she asked coyly.

"I am untying them to take them off. You don't need these. Your top is already missing", I smiled as I answered her.

"I agree", Nate added as he started untying the other side. Vivian laughed a nervous and apprehensive laugh.

"Nate! Leave them be if she wants them on!" Jennifer scolded him in return.

"It's ok", Vivian said, staring him in the eyes.

He untied the other side, showed us the loose strings, and dropped them in the water. I removed Vivian's bikini bottom, leaving her completely naked and hidden by only the bubbling water. I hung it over the side of the hot tub next to me. She wrapped her hand around Nate's head and pulled him into her as they kissed wildly. She opened her legs wide and put her foot on me once more. Jennifer moved in close again, prompting Vivian to switch back to kissing Jennifer. Vivian started to moan louder than she had before, so I had to explore underwater to find out what they were doing to her. As my hand slowly traced the distance of her long sexy leg, I went for her pussy, and I found Jennifer's dainty fingers rubbing on Vivian's slippery clit, while Nate's thicker fingers were sliding inside of her lips. I was in total disbelief at what was happening to my wife.

Vivian had turned to her side to reposition herself so she could take turns kissing Nate and Jennifer. When she also felt my hand on her, she lifted one leg a little higher. Vivian was utterly stuffed with their fingers, so I decided to play with her ass at the same time. I was unsure what her reaction would be, but this was too hot not to go for it. I started to rub my finger on her opening, and I slid just a little tiny tip inside of her, which she seemed to enjoy. She began to rock her hips back and forth in rhythm with our hands and movements. I knew what this meant. The three of us continued working on her body, rubbing and fingering her two holes until she reached a point where she could not withstand it anymore. Her moans grew louder. Her body started to shake and tremble. She took a deep breath, held it, and began to have a massive orgasm. She panted and whimpered as she came all over their fingers. It was so fucking incredible!

After she gathered her composure, she laughed and asked what we just did to her. We all laughed at that. I then sat back and watched in wonder as Nate and Jennifer played with her body continuously, all while making her orgasm two more times! Her body was exhausted and satisfied. After her third orgasm, we realized the time had escaped us as it typically did, and it was almost 4 a.m! We all hurried out of the water and went to bed quickly. Nate, Jennifer, and I did not have to work in the morning, but poor Vivian did have to get up in only three hours. I felt a little bad for her, but at the same time, I did not because she had just lived through a breathtaking moment of her life that not many people have ever experienced.

A Moment of Epiphany for Vivian

I awoke that next morning in a startled state of panic that made me feel as if I had overslept and was late for an extremely important appointment or something. I darted my eyes toward the alarm clock. It was nearly 8 a.m. and I was not sure why I was awake. My mind raced rapidly. I must have missed an important appointment! What day was it?

Wednesday, I think? I was not sure, actually. Why does my head hurt so bad? Oh yes. I was drinking until 4 a.m. and I remember now. Hot tub. Vivian. Vivian!! I sat up quickly and suddenly felt this overwhelming feeling that I needed to see her. I needed to talk with her. I needed to hug her. I needed to ensure she was alright after what she endured the night before.

I raced out of bed fast and threw on a pair of shorts that were on the floor near my dresser. I darted out of my bedroom door and made my way to the window that overlooks the driveway. Her car was still there! I had not missed her. Nate and Jenniffer's car was gone, too, so I knew they had already gotten up early and left. I went down the staircase and called her name, but there was no reply. I ran to the front door and unlocked the deadbolt as fast as I possibly could. There she was, backing her car out of the driveway. I waved my hands frantically to get her attention. She put the car in drive and cut the wheel to head down the street when I must have caught her eye with my flailing arms because she turned her head in my direction and stopped the car. She pulled over to the side of the road and got out. She had a slightly troubled look on her face as she approached me.

"Is everything ok?" she said with a hint of concern.

"Yes, baby. I just really wanted to see you and talk to you before you left. Are you ok after last night?" I said, wrapping my arms around her shoulders and cupping her head in the palm of my hand as I pulled her in close to me.

"I am ok. I am exhausted and a little sick, but I am ok", she whispered as she pulled away from my embrace to lean back and look me in the eyes.

"Is it my imagination, or did I have six hands in my vagina last night?" she asked with a smile on her face.

"Um…that happened!" I said as we both started laughing.

"Fuck!!! I was not sure if that actually happened or not. Damn it, I am a whore now. It was pretty cool, but you should go back to sleep. We can talk more when I get home tonight", she told me and followed it up with a kiss before returning to her car. I watched her drive away feeling so proud and so much in love with her that I could barely stand it.

After the kids were in bed that evening, we finally had a moment to speak about the experience she had just lived through in the hot tub less than seventeen hours before.

"Ok baby, I am dying to know how you felt last night with all that happened", I questioned her.

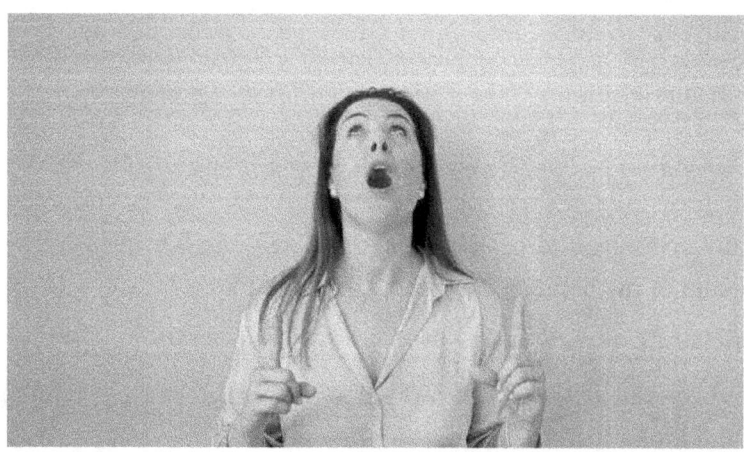

"Honestly? I loved it! It felt amazing to me to be the center of attention and to have all those hands on me, touching me all at once. It felt almost powerful", she said very confidently.

"It was awesome! I couldn't believe it when it was all happening. I couldn't believe that you and Nate started kissing. I couldn't believe it when Jennifer started kissing me. Are you ok with all that and what I did, too?" I asked her.

"Am I ok that you were kissing Jennifer? I mean, I was kissing Nate, so not much I can say about it, but honestly, it didn't seem to bother me. I guess I am just that comfortable with her", she answered.

"To be honest, I have not been able to stop thinking about it all day. It was so fucking hot! I know I used to be afraid of things like this, but I think I am looking forward to doing that again", she added.

"I can't stop thinking about it either. I remember how hot it was when I moved my hand in between your legs, and I felt both their hands there. One rubbing you, and one fingering inside of you. It was unbelievable. I have been hard all damn day thinking about it", I admitted to her.

"Then let's take care of that hard dick for you, baby, since I had so many orgasms last night from multiple people", she whispered as she slid her tongue into my mouth.

NAVIGATING NEW WATERS

To borrow a famous yet tiring metaphor, Vivian and I had unquestionably set sail into uncharted waters on that breezy moonlit evening. However, the issue was that neither of us knew how to sail, and the map to return home sank to the bottom of the ocean a while ago. I knew deep down there was no going back, so who needed a map anyway? It was time to sink or swim, and we were swimming just fine for the moment. Better than fine, to be frank. Vivian had found this new level of sensuality and rekindled passion in her that was driving me absolutely insane. All I had to do was remind her about all three of us fingering her to orgasm, and the beast inside of her was unleashed. We were enjoying some of the wildest and most passionate sex that we had experienced in our marriage, possibly ever. We were not just treading water but riding the waves of pure joy and pleasure that this new experience had given us. There is one major problem with swimming in the middle of the ocean, however, that no matter how careful you are, eventually you will find yourself surrounded by sharks.

Blood in the Water

Dante was the next person I thought about after Vivian got back into her car and drove to work the morning after Nate and Jennifer had changed our lives forever. She told me that I should go back to bed, and I tried to take her advice, but I gave up after one hour of lying there listening to the oscillating fan circulate air around my bedroom. I was far too excited to sleep at that point. I could not stop replaying the images in my head of her kissing both of them, of her moaning, and of her cumming from both of them. I also could not wait to text Dante and fill him in on what my innocent angel wife had done the night before. I grabbed my phone and started dishing on all the details.

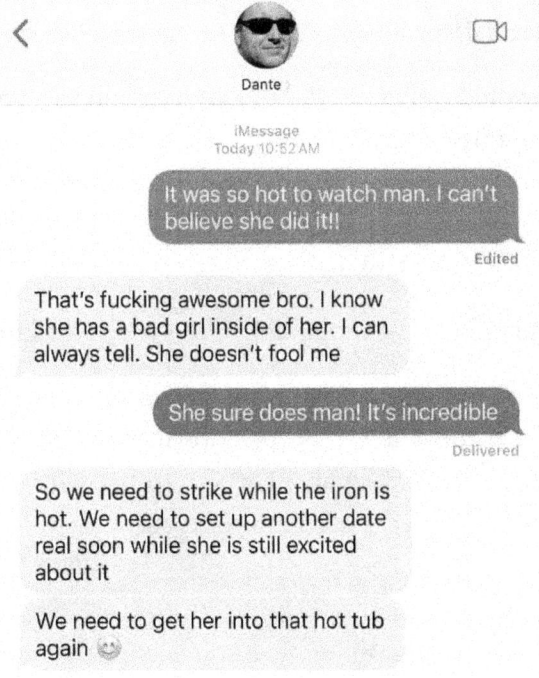

I waited a few days to raise the topic with Vivian. I wanted to give her time to let it all sink in before moving on to the next couple.

"Hey, babe. Dante was asking if we were free Saturday night and wanted to hang out with them. We have no plans per my calendar", I mentioned casually.

"Oh yeah? Alright. I like that it is Saturday. I don't think I can do work nights anymore after last week", she laughed.

"Yeah, a Saturday is a nice change. We don't have to worry about getting up early. We need to figure out what to do with them. We can go check out that new beer and wine cellar, or maybe I can do grilling here?" I said, gauging her reaction.

"Yeah, I would rather check out that beer and wine place, and then everyone can go home. I am not sure I am ready to have them here yet. Last time they were here was fine, but now they will be here later, and I am still scared they will try and attack me", she said jokingly.

"Hey, you are a professional now if they try attacking you!" I replied playfully.

"Well, they are still very professional, and not sure I am ready for all that. How about we go to the wine cellar and just see how it goes?" she counteroffered.

"Sure, baby. Wine cellar it is!"

That following day, I woke up and texted Dante to tell him the plan for Saturday night.

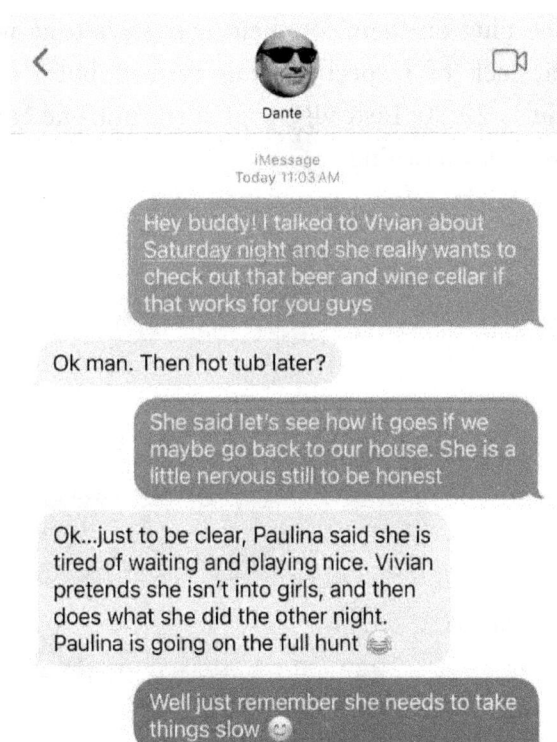

I did not really appreciate his words or his tone about my wife. I did not respond to him the rest of the day. I felt like their impatience with the pace at which things were progressing was going to force her into uncomfortable circumstances that would ruin our relationship with them. Maybe that would be ok if it did ruin it. Maybe I should have pulled the plug on them for their aggressive tone with me and their lack of respect for our wishes, but I did not. Hindsight is 20/20. Instead, I kept silent until he contacted me on Saturday morning.

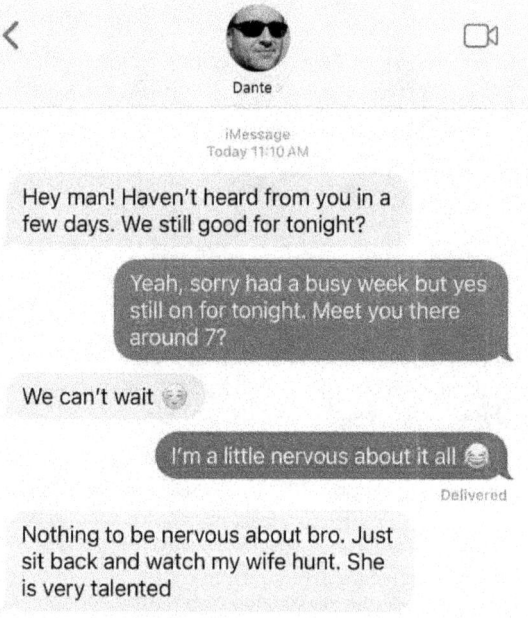

See! Nothing to be nervous about at all. Fuck.

Déjà Vu

Vivian entered the kitchen looking stunning as hell and ready to go. What else was new? I, on the other hand, was not prepared to go. I had been caught in the act of pouring us shots, in fact. Despite Dante's inspiring words of encouragement bestowed upon me, I was nervous! I was not just nervous but also apprehensive, guilty, and yet excited, all simultaneously. I felt like I needed a shot of peach whiskey to calm my nerves. It seemed like a good idea to give her one as well if she was to endure the shark attack that was likely going to occur in just a few short hours. Without a word, I held up a shot glass for her to take, and she did so without hesitation.

"To Sebastian and Vivian!" I said with a false sense of excitement as we clinked our glasses together.

"To us, baby!" she toasted with an enormous smile that led to us sharing a peachy whiskey kiss.

She genuinely seemed happy and perhaps even excited, making all my inner turmoil all the worse.

We strolled through the parking lot, walking hand in hand. My fingers spun her wedding ring around out of habit, adjusting it so the diamond was facing straight and not scratching my finger. I reached for the door handle and pulled it open so she could enter first. As she passed through the doorway, I looked her up and down and whispered how sexy she was into her ear, which prompted her to turn her head and give me a sweet kiss on the lips. That was the moment I realized that Vivian was wearing the same exact sexy outfit that she wore the week before, when we had dinner with Nate and Jennifer. Déjà vu.

The establishment we were at was very cool. All the walls were made with authentic bricks, combined with the unfinished cement floor beneath your feet, dimly lit by rustic-looking light bulbs hanging from the ceiling. This place definitely made you feel as if you were in a cellar. Then came the real selling point. The brick walls were lined with beer taps on both the left and right side of the room, and straight to the back was a small section of wine taps as well. In the center of the room were long tables with stools where you could sit and enjoy your beverage of choice. It was an impressive venue, to say the least.

I scanned the tables for our dates and saw Dante standing up and waving to us from the back corner near the wine taps. Vivian and I made our way through the sea of people until we approached their table and found them sitting across from each other rather than side by side. Another similarity to last week. Dante and Paulina stood to greet us with customary hugs and handshakes.

"Vivian, come sit next to me, girl", Paulina said as she led Vivian by the hand to their stools.

"Alrighhhhhht", Vivian said playfully, followed by her infectious laugh.

We sat down momentarily until we needed to get up and get some drinks in our hands, and then it was back to our seats. We talked about our kids and how work for all of us had been the past few weeks. Dante was getting a promotion that called for a celebration. We emptied our glasses in our bellies and got up to fill them again before returning to the table. Paulina commented that Vivian was too far away from her and then slid her stool closer. Vivian giggled. I could feel my heart rate accelerating. Paulina began complimenting Vivian on how beautiful she looked and how sexy her leather skirt was. Vivian giggled. My heart rate increased. Paulina touched Vivian on her arm at first, which progressed to her shoulder and complimented her even more. She asked Dante to take a picture of her with such a sexy woman. She slid her stool closer to Vivian. Vivian giggled. My heart rate increased a little more. We got up to fill our glasses a third time and returned to our stools. Paulina told Vivian that she had heard about her being a bad girl in the hot tub the week before with our "other couple" and wanted to hear all the details. Vivian did not giggle. My heart rate stopped.

I took a deep breath and held it in for a moment before exhaling slowly. I could not even look up from my wine glass to make eye contact with my wife. I was in utter disbelief that Paulina just went there with this information and betrayed my trust like that. I thought Paulina was a "professional" at hunting, so Dante said. How was pissing off your "prey" part of a successful hunt?

"Wow. I had no clue that my husband told you about that. I thought that was private between only me and him?" Vivian chose her words quite deliberately yet in a nonthreatening tone.

"Hey, there is nothing to be ashamed about here, girl. We are friends, and isn't that the point of all of this? It is great to have fun and explore, but how amazing is it to have someone you can talk to about it at the same time? Sebastian is very excited about it, and he told Dante that you were very excited about it, so don't be embarrassed! Own it, and let's talk about it! Hell, I want to be excited about it!" Paulina spoke loudly while leaning against Vivian's shoulder with her shoulder.

"Well, I guess you got a point", Vivian replied hesitantly. "But first, I have to go pee", she said while making a silly face that insinuated her bladder was about to burst. "Sebastian! Go refill your wife's wine!" she said quite loudly as she removed herself from the table.

"You look scared, Sebastian", Paulina said to me smugly.

"She is probably pissed at me now. I am not sure that was the best thing to say to her. She is extremely private, and I will be in trouble now for telling you about that", I snapped back.

"Bro, relax. Paulina knows exactly what she is doing. Why do you think I am sitting back and not saying much? She's got this. Trust us. Vivian is glad you told us, and she certainly wants to talk about it with someone other than just you. I told you. She is not as innocent as she makes you think", Dante reassured me. I glanced at Paulina.

"I will have her naked within an hour", she said and winked one eye at me. I was not sure that was what I wanted anymore as I grabbed her glass and got up to refill it. Vivian was sitting down just as I returned with her freshened drink.

"Thank you, my darling husband", she muttered to me in a neutral tone.

"Alright, gorgeous! Spill the beans. I am dying to hear what this other couple did to you!" Paulina said with exuberance.

"Oh, that?" Vivian laughed. "That was no big deal. Basically, we went into our hot tub with our friends, and we had lots of fun. I may have kissed both of them, and they may have both had their fingers inside of me!" she laughed hysterically.

"You bad girl!" Paulina pretended to be shocked.

"Yeahhhhh, I guess I was a little", Vivian responded shyly and playfully. Paulina smiled at me.

"What I am hearing is that we need to pay the bill, go back to your house now, and get in that hot tub!" Paulina added.

"I mean, yaaaaa, we can, I suppose. But you guys don't have bathing suits, do you?" Vivian countered.

"No, but we can just go in our underwear", Paulina quipped.

"I will drive home naked later if I have to!" Dante finally spoke. Vivian laughed.

"Well, I guess let's finish these drinks and go", Vivian answered.

I was shocked that Paulina's plan was working thus far, and I was shocked that I was somewhere in between excited and worried at the same time. Had I taken this too far?

I removed the hot tub cover and placed it on the ground to the side of the hot tub. Vivian was more than a little tipsy after her shot of peach whiskey and three glasses of wine.

She came outside and ordered me to get us all drinks, which I graciously did. Upon my return, I found Paulina and Vivian sitting beside each other and Dante sitting across from them. He really was letting Paulina take the wheel. The only open spot for me was on the high bench next to Vivian, where Nate had sat just a week prior. I was not sure how the girls were sharing this one seat next to me, but I did not ask questions. I got into the hot water. The three of us were so tight and so close to each other. It seemed as if Vivian was almost sitting on Paulina's lap but not all the way on it. The entire left side of my body was glued to the right side of Vivian's body. Vivian was shark bait, and it did not take long for Paulina to attack.

Paulina put her right arm around Vivian's shoulders and gripped Vivian's right breast in the process. Vivian just sipped her drink. Dante sat across from us and was almost eerily quiet. He was not his usual self at all. I looked at him and took another sip of my drink. He was staring at the women intensely. Vivian and Paulina were talking and giggling for a few moments. I remember their conversation died down, and there were a few seconds of awkward silence until it finally happened. Paulina shifted in her seat so that she could get her head on the same level as Vivian's, and then she kissed her. Vivian did not hesitate to return the kiss. Oh, how they kissed. They kissed for so long with so much passion and excitement. Paulina seemed as if she had been starving for this for so long. I was fortunate to have a firsthand view of them making out and feeling each other with their hands. That is when Dante tapped me on the arm.

"Hey, man. Switch seats with me", he demanded.

I did not bat an eyelash. This was the Paulina and Dante show. This was not my show. The raucous of him and I clumsily trying to stand and change positions in this small tub caused splashing waves of water, disrupting the girls' attention to each other.

Vivian laughed and asked, "What are you two guys doing?"

"Just changing seats, don't mind us", Dante told her. "It's my turn to get an amazing view."

"A view of what?" Paulina asked him coyly. "This?" as she pulled Vivian's bikini top up to her collarbone, presenting Dante with Vivian's hard nipples on her glistening skin.

Paulina started licking and sucking on Vivian's boobs while Dante and I looked on intently. She kissed each nipple as gently as she could before slowly making her way back to Vivian's wanting lips. Dante started to shift in the long bench, and I could tell from his awkward movements that he was pulling his boxers off. He confirmed it when he took them out of the water in his hand and placed them on the side of the hot tub. He then placed his right hand back under the water and began to stroke his cock. I could see the tip of his dick poking up out of the water as he stroked, and it was easy to diagnose that he was much bigger and thicker than me. I envisioned Vivian sucking on him in front of me and suddenly wanted it more than anything in the world. He continued to make himself harder and bigger while watching our wives enjoy each other until he apparently had enough of it.

Dante raised himself out of the water and sat on the edge of the hot tub with his engorged manhood in his hand. He said but one command, "Paulina." She stopped kissing Vivian and turned her head to look at him, and without hesitation, she pivoted her body around and slid his stiff meat down her throat. She sucked him and slurped on him as if she was famished for him. She gripped his balls in her left hand and got a hold of his cock in her right hand while she sucked. He immediately removed her hand and said sternly, "No hands. You know the rules."

"Damnnnn!" Vivian said and chuckled with her gaze glued to their sexual act. Dante was looking Vivian dead in the eyes.

Paulina stopped sucking, looked at Vivian, and whispered, "Come here and help me suck this girl."

I thought she would obey for a split second, but she hesitantly said, "I can't."

"I know you want this in your mouth, sexy. Just come over here and give it one lick", Paulina tried to coerce her. Dante remained silent and only stared at her.

Vivian did not make eye contact with me, which I thought was a bit unusual. I was waiting for her to glance at me for a glimmering moment so that I could reassure her with a look of approval, but she only watched them as if I were not there.

"I'm sorry, guys, but this is a bit too much for me. I am not comfortable with this at all, so maybe I should go inside now." She now appeared flustered.

"No, no, no, sweetie! It's quite alright. Dante is stupid for even doing this, really", Paulina said, glaring at him. "Let's just relax and finish our drinks for a bit. Dante will put that thing away."

"I am sorry, Vivian. I shouldn't have done that", Dante said, sounding sincere as he sank back down into the water.

We all took sips of our drinks while we listened to the sounds of the crickets. I remember thinking to myself that this was the end of our evening and perhaps the end of our relationship with them. They went too far, and they scared Vivian. It was game over, in my opinion, but the funny thing is, I have been wrong before, and I will be wrong again. Paulina was too fucking good. Dante was not mistaken. She apologized for going too far as she ran her fingers through Vivian's wet hair. The girls were lying on their sides facing each other in the water, which did not appear to be too physically comfortable, to be honest. Vivian did not say a word. She just stared at Paulina. Paulina stared at her in return until she closed her eyes and softly slid her tongue into Vivian's mouth once again. I was in awe. They had her on the brink of tears, I felt, yet there she was, back in an enthusiastic kiss. I was starting to see the powers that these two possessed, and I realized that I may have severely underestimated them.

They kissed for a few moments when Paulina said her arm was hurting in that position and suggested that they switch seats to face the other way. Vivian agreed and stated that her arm was hurting also. Paulina instructed Vivian to climb over her. Vivian put one leg over her and straddled her for a second when Paulina grabbed her, and they made out again with Vivian sitting on her lap. I could see Paulina's hands rubbing up and down on Vivian's back as she untied her bikini top and removed it. I expected my wife to freak out and end the evening with that, but conversely, she used her left hand to push the hair away from her face and place it back behind her ear as she leaned back down for more passionate kissing.

It was time for Dante to make another move as he started rubbing Vivian's ass with his left hand. After a few minutes in this position, Vivian finally made her way back into the water and was now snuggly nestled in between the two of them, with her tits floating on the water. She made eye contact with me for the first time in what felt like forever and smiled at me. I smiled back at her as she placed her legs on my lap and rubbed my stiff cock with her foot. I realized at that moment that she was checking on me. Checking to see if I was hard or soft because the moment she felt my hard shaft with her toes, she turned her head towards Paulina and started kissing her madly.

Dante reached across Vivian and removed Paulina's bra, which interrupted their kiss but prompted Paulina to put her erect nipples directly into Vivian's mouth while she kissed her husband. Vivian sucked and licked at her nipples while her feet rubbed my cock under my bathing suit. I quickly removed my bathing suit and threw it on the ground, and began stroking my throbbing dick against Vivian's foot. I wanted her to know how fucking hard I was. I wanted her to know how excited I was. I wanted her to know that I was absolutely okay with whatever was about to happen to her next.

She started to moan, and it took me a second to realize that Dante and Paulina were both rubbing her pussy frantically under the water. I extended my arms toward my gorgeous wife, grabbed her bikini bottom, and pulled them down her legs and off her. She did not hesitate to lift her ass off the seat to allow this maneuver to take place. It was an all too familiar scene given that this same eerily similar situation took place a little over a week ago. Apparently, this was our life now. In a flash, both of them had their fingers in her slippery pussy, while they both sucked on her nipples. I was rubbing her legs just as I was last time, so I figured what the hell, and I slid my hand up to her ass again. I could feel their hands all over her clit, and all inside of her as I rubbed and inserted a finger in her tight opening again. Her body trembled and shook; she took a deep breath and held it; she let out a releasing cry as the orgasmic waves overtook her body. She was most definitely getting spoiled, and I believe that she was starting to like three people making her cum hard.

A Moment of Epiphany for Sebastian

Sunday morning arrived, and it was unforgiving, as I suspected it might be. I woke up in a panic because it felt as if I was sleeping alone in bed, but there was Vivian's naked body hidden in the bundle of blankets. I slid out of bed quietly so as not to disturb my sleeping beauty and made my way to the kitchen to start cooking my girl her favorite foods for breakfast. I made myself an epic Bloody Mary loaded with celery, a hardboiled egg, pickles, and olives stuffed with bleu cheese before turning on the gas stove. I took a sip and there was not enough spice so I added some worchester sauce and red pepper flakes to give it some kick. It was delicious, and I knew it would cure this hangover very soon. The aroma of freshly cooked bacon spread throughout the house and must have woken up Vivian because it was not long before she stood before me in her extremely tiny silk shorts and her tank top that exhibited her erect nipples.

"Good morning, my darling!" I said as I embraced her in a warm hug and a kiss on the cheek. "How are you feeling, baby?" I asked because I was concerned that she might be as dehydrated and dizzy as I was.

"I feel like a fucking whore!" she said, trying not to smile.

I grinned at her while I placed my hands on her cheeks and embraced her tiny head. "Oh, that's official! You are a fucking whore!" I confirmed and chuckled as I kissed her soft lips.

We sipped mimosas while eating our breakfast on the back patio and discussed the events of the previous night. Vivian was surprisingly in good spirits after what had taken place just a few hours before. Now, don't get me wrong, physically, she enjoyed every moment of her earth-shattering three-on-one orgasm, with a second married couple in as many weeks. That was not the issue here. The issue was that she was still very apprehensive about going that far with Dante and Paulina due to not knowing them all that well or for that long. She compounded that apprehension and doubled down on it with anxious feelings that there was now the expectation they would place on her to repeat the same actions if not more.

She viewed them as "professionals" who were definitely going to want more from her. I tried my best to relieve her anxiety about the self-created expectations that she portrayed on them, but deep down inside, I knew she was absolutely correct. They were going to want more, and I knew they were going to take more. She also was not happy with me because I told them what she had done with Nate and Jennifer. She felt I betrayed her trust. I tried to explain that I was just so excited, and I had no one else to talk to but Dante. She understood that but made it clear that, to them, that story meant she was fair game for them to make their moves on her. I understood that but then reminded her that I think she enjoyed it also, which she did not deny.

After we cleaned up the breakfast mess, we decided to change into our bathing suits, pack a cooler, and head to the pool for the afternoon. There is nothing better than a lazy Sunday afternoon just floating in the water with some great music and a sexy little wife who is starting to develop into her sexuality. It was about 4 p.m. when we began to pack up our things to head home so I could grill some dinner. Vivian was excited about the T-Bone steaks I had on the menu for the evening. I was packing up our belongings when I heard the "ding" sound on my phone that alerted me that I had received a text message. It was Dante.

"Hey, baby. Dante just texted asking how we are feeling today", I announced.

"Oh yeah? Tell him we are good, just chilling at the pool", she said, smiling while folding the towels. I typed and hit send.

Ding

"He asked if we didn't get enough water last night", I read to her and chuckled.

"Haha, he is so funny", she said sarcastically.

Ding

"He said, but seriously, they had an amazing time with us last night, and we will have to do it again soon."

"Yaaaaaa, I had fun too, splashing in the water", she laughed while we walked to the car. I typed and hit send.

Ding

"He said he wants me to take a pic of you in your bikini and send it to him!" I laughed as we were getting in the car.

"What, he wants to see more of me already, does he?" she joked. I typed and hit send.

Ding

"He said fuck yes, he misses that sexy ass already. Now be a good girl and take a pic for him right now!" I relayed the message to her.

"Ok, I guess he misses me then. Let's send him this", Vivian said as she pushed her shoulders together, squeezing her boobs and showing lots of cleavage. I took the hot picture, and I hit send.

Ding

"He said mmmmm that's such a good girl right there. Enjoy your evening, and I will see you both soon."

"He is such an a-hole", she laughed.

I had an epiphany at that very moment. I may have had a few actually. It was a stark realization that I had not seen previously and had not crossed my mind. Dante was way more dominant and controlling than I initially thought he was through all our interactions, but it was Vivian who astonished me more. She had the ability to state her feelings in one moment and then change the perception of her feelings just a few hours later. It amazed me that she could go from "Ms. Terrified" of their expectations of her to laughing and following his picture demands just a few hours later. It is feasible that it was me just being a bit naïve. Perhaps what I should have been really paying attention to was the hint of a smile that appeared from the corners of her mouth when he called her a "good girl", while alluring her into taking a picture for him and rewarding her after with another "good girl", for doing as he said.

INTERLUDE: DANTE, PAULINA & THE HOT TUB

Do I believe in sex angels? Fuck yes, I do! There have been a few people who entered our lives during this scary and liberating time. Some became friends of ours for many years, like Nate and Jennifer, while others showed up exactly when we needed them most to push us to the next level of our journey and then disappeared like Christian. I have to admit that I was disappointed that I did not get to see my bartender, Christian, ever again. I am not sure if anything would have ever happened with me and him, but it sure was hot to think about.

Even though we did go out a few times and joke that we hoped he was working, I did make it very clear to Sebastian that I was not interested in meeting any men, women, or couples from online websites that wanted to just use me. I was all set with that. Sebastian always seemed to understand me, but then would somehow find a way to still push me and help me grow. I still remember the one night that he asked me about meeting Dante and Paulina. I had asked him before to delete the account he met them on, which he agreed to do, but maybe it was fate that he did not already.

I agreed to meet with them even if I was not sure about it, but I made it clear that I was not doing anything with them at all. It was just wanting to meet as friends. I liked them both instantly. They were just attractive enough to keep my interest, but they were both really funny and very personable, which I love. Sebastian and I connected with them right away, so that was awesome. I did notice that I was slightly attracted to Dante on the first meeting. I was more attracted to him than I was to Paulina. He was my type, and we certainly had chemistry. He was a smooth talker. Our first meeting with them was very nice, and I did want to see them again for sure.

I was surprised that they had invited us to their house for a party with their family and friends just a week later, but it showed me that perhaps they were serious about having us for friends and didn't just want sex from me. I had such a good time laughing with Paulina, and of course, Dante made sure that we had our next hangout on his calendar before we left. On our third get-together, Paulina was flirting with me here and there, but after my first glass of Merlot, I didn't mind so much. I kind of liked it. I typically would have been anxious by them both getting very close to me on the couch in the bar, but I had finished my second glass by that point, so I was feeling really good. I actually felt very free, sexy, and powerful. There was a little bit of body contact, for sure. They made me the center of their attention, which is what I was starting to realize I really liked. We decided to all go back to our house, and I was happy when our guests showed respect and didn't try anything with me that night. It was an awesome night, and the slow steps I needed.

INTERLUDE: DANTE, PAULINA & THE HOT TUB | 213

We were starting to hang out with Dante and Paulina a lot over a few weeks, and I was beginning to miss Nate and Jennifer. We found some free time to meet them for dinner, and I was hoping for some fooling around with Jennifer in the hot tub. I was really starting to enjoy that with her. I never would have suspected how that night was going to turn out and impact our lives forever. If it was just the dinner alone, it still would have been a thrilling night with the amount of flirting and touching that was happening by both of them on us. Nate had never looked at my body that much before or touched me like he was during dinner. It was very new, but I liked it a lot. It was very exciting each time I noticed him staring at my boobs, or when he touched my shoulder, or even my leg as he wanted to feel the material of my skirt. There was something exciting about him doing this in front of his wife and my husband with no worries at all.

When we all went into our hot tub, I thought it was going to be just the usual between Jennifer and me, but I was very wrong and pleasantly surprised with everything that happened. I couldn't believe it for so long; I was afraid to do the things that we did with them that night. Nate started to move closer to me, and I began to figure out what their plan was for this evening. I told myself in that moment to just enjoy myself and not be scared of whatever was about to happen. Honestly, everything seemed to happen so fast, and it was like a blur of excitement for me. Jennifer kissed me, Nate kissed me, Jennifer kissed Sebastian, and then Jennifer took it to another level when she rubbed me between my legs. It was so hot that I had to let go of my inhibitions and opened my legs for her.

I was so incredibly turned on by everything occurring to me that I did not even think about my husband across from me watching when I started to kiss Nate, too. It felt so strange to be kissing another man, but with my husband watching, made it even more strange. Then suddenly, it was Nate that was rubbing me, which felt so amazing. I was very wet, which was tough for me in the water, but I could tell how wet I was under my bathing suit.

I feel like I blinked my eyes, and I was completely naked with mouths and hands all over me. I never felt more incredible in my entire life. I cannot explain what it felt like to be switching from kissing a woman to kissing her husband while all three of them were sliding their fingers inside of me at the same time. My body erupted with such intensity. They all made me orgasm multiple times that night and made me lose track of time. I was exhausted and thoroughly satisfied. I quickly went to bed, but I remember having two thoughts before I passed out for the night, how incredible and life-changing that all was for me and how I was sure I was going to be embarrassed talking to Sebastian about this the next day.

I was so happy when I didn't seem to be too embarrassed to talk to Sebastian about it all the next morning. It was starting to feel completely normal to have these fucked up conversations with him. All day at work, I was distracted by the thoughts and memories of the night before. Fuck, it was so fun. The more I thought about it, the more I came to a realization about myself. I loved it. I loved all of it. I loved being the center of attention of the three of them, which sounds bad to say, but it was the truth. I loved having them all taking care of me. I loved how strong my orgasms were. I knew that I wanted more of it for sure. I knew my life had changed forever.

I was still riding high a few days later when we decided to go out with Dante and Paulina. I noticed that Paulina was much more talkative and attentive with me than she usually was. She was also touching me more than she usually did. She was definitely making

INTERLUDE: DANTE, PAULINA & THE HOT TUB | 215

me feel wanted, and I liked it. She took me by total surprise when she told me that Sebastian informed them that I was a bad girl in the hot tub with our friends the week before.

At first, I was very upset that he would tell them that, but then she explained it to me, and it all made perfect sense. I decided that I wanted to tell her and Dante about it. I am still a very shy person who doesn't like to talk about so much detail, so I told them very generally that I kissed both of our friends and that they both had fingers inside of me. I left it at that because I knew they could fill in the rest of the story on their own.

I don't have any clue what came over me next. Perhaps it was the wine. Perhaps it was reliving the story in my head. Perhaps it was the fact that it thrilled me to talk about it to others. Or perhaps it was that she was getting closer to me and making me have that desired feeling again, but when she called me a bad girl, and Dante suggested we leave to go to our hot tub, I agreed immediately. I glanced at Sebastian, expecting to see a very excited look on his face, but instead, it was a look of concern. I assumed it was because I was so dead set against them coming back to our house and telling him I did not want to go into the hot tub with them, but a girl can change her mind, can't she? Was I becoming a bad girl?

I could not believe I was in the hot tub again just a few nights later with a different couple and almost having all the same things happen to me. Things were going great until Dante decided to take his boxers off and make Paulina suck his dick. I actually really liked watching her suck that thing. He had a very nice-looking one, but I got very uncomfortable when they wanted me to help her with it. Truth is that a piece of me wanted to suck it, but not with her there helping me, and not with Sebastian watching. This was much too fast for me, and it made me very uncomfortable. This is exactly what worried me about them and not being able to respect my boundaries.

It made me very happy that Sebastian was not trying to convince me to help her even though I was sure he really wanted me to do it. I felt a sense of freedom and empowerment at that moment because I knew this choice was all mine and I wasn't going to be talked into it by anyone. I stood my ground, and things got a little weird, but eventually, it returned to normal. Before I knew what happened, all four of us were entirely naked, and I was orgasming from three people's fingers again. Yes, this was our life now.

The next morning, I definitely felt like a whore. I could not believe that I had two couples make me cum in a week and a half. For so long, I was worried how Sebastian would actually react if I ever did things that he wanted me to do. Saying you want your wife to perform sexual acts with other people is very different than seeing her do it, in my opinion. He also did nothing with Paulina last night, so it was all about me.

We went to the pool that day and just enjoyed each other, but in the back of my mind, I could not stop thinking about the fun I had with Dante and Paulina. I found myself thinking about Dante's hard dick and watching Paulina take it in her mouth. If I am being honest, I was very intrigued by the dominating way he spoke to her. I found it very hot how he commanded her to suck him and the way she listened to him when he took her hand away. This was a dynamic that Sebastian and I did not have, and I never felt it ever in my limited sexual experience. I was so intrigued by it. I could not stop thinking about the way he was looking at me as he filled his wife's throat with his large meat. He was staring at me as if he was calling to me.

I was lost in these dominating thoughts when Dante texted Sebastian. When he texted that he wanted me to pose for a picture in my bikini, I acted like I didn't want to and made a joke, asking if he needed to see more of me. Sebastian smiled as he texted, so I could tell he enjoyed it. I was turned on when his reply was that he missed my sexy ass and called me a good girl. He followed that up by telling me to take a pic for him right then. Was that an actual command? I got a little wet in that instant. Sebastian was still smiling, so I played along. I squeezed my boobs together and told him to send him that picture. I was tingling in anticipation of how Dante was going to respond. What sentence was my husband going to read to me next? When Dante responded and called me such a good girl for doing that, my pussy was soaking wet.

THE GOOD, THE BAD, AND THE UGLY

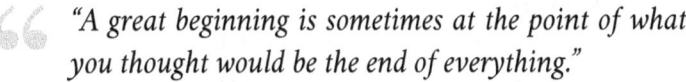
"A great beginning is sometimes at the point of what you thought would be the end of everything."

— DODINSKY, AUTHOR

Let me start off by going on the record stating that I did not want to write this chapter. I will take that one step further and let you in on a big secret: Vivian refuses to read this chapter altogether. I am praying that I can get her to even record the Interlude for this chapter when the audiobook is produced. Now, to be clear, it is not the entire chapter that bothers me. It is just one section of the story that brings up some bad memories for me. Vivian, on the other hand, despises this entire part of our story and, therefore, doesn't like any of it. It all just brings up some awful recollections for both of us that we try not to even bring it up anymore because it doesn't serve us to do so. You are likely asking yourself, so why bother telling this part of the story in the first place, Sebastian?

Some who studied English Literature might call this the climax of our entire story. I call it the defining moment in our marriage. I call it the critical juncture in the story and in our family. I would be doing a disservice to all of you if I left essential details out and made the story more vanilla just to protect our egos. Also, what good book can become a bestseller without a twist in the plot or a tragedy to pull at your heartstrings? The title of this chapter alone tells you why I had to include it as part of our "feel-good" story. This chapter encompasses all three aspects of human nature: good, bad, and ugly.

Let's start with the bad and the ugly first and cover why Vivian refuses to read what just might be my finest piece of writing in the entire book. In this part of the story, Vivian and I both make incredibly bad choices in the pursuit of pleasure. We made choices that we thought were being made for the ultimate greater good and the happiness of each other. We both used horrible judgment when trying to decide how to keep pushing our own boundaries, as well as each other's. We are both ashamed of some of the despicable actions that we decided to make that caused each other nothing but grieving heartache and nearly destroyed us as husband and wife. We chose not to communicate with each other openly and honestly, and it was nearly our demise. We fell into a web of manipulation, dishonesty, and deception. We were both willing to go to extreme measures to make each other happy, even if that meant risking it all in the name of progress.

Enough of that nonsense for now; let me tell you the good in this now and why I knew I had to write this chapter as it truly occurred. I wrote this chapter with pure honesty, not for us, but for you. I wrote it for all the husbands and wives out there who have made significant mistakes along the way and jeopardized their marriages. I wrote it to serve as an inspiration to the spouses whose hearts are broken and trust is shattered, to show you that there is a path of hope and happiness that can be found in the darkness. I wrote it to help serve as a lesson to you all and to help you not repeat the same mistakes we have made, which you still might, but that's alright. You can see your way through if you genuinely love each other.

In a lot of ways, this chapter tells a story that was our darkest moment thus far in our twenty-two years of marriage, but we refused to let that define us. Conversely, we chose to let it define us with our love and resiliency. We want to be that inspiration so that your marriage can rise out of the ashes and survive. Fuck that, it doesn't have to just survive, we are living proof that it can thrive again! We are living proof that you can build back trust again and be even stronger than before. We are living proof that you can increase your communication and continue to grow from tragedy. We are living proof that no matter how dark things look in your marriage after a series of devastating mistakes, you can always find your way back with love. Love conquers all.

After making the decision to move forward with this chapter, I still struggled with how to actually write it. I wrote one entire section, re-read it, changed my mind, and scrapped the entire thing to start over. Initially, I intended to write this chapter as I had written the rest of the book with tons of detail, as well as with my photographic memory of past conversations and text messages. I recognized that I could not follow that same structure out of love and respect for my dear wife. I came to the realization that I can still tell this story in total honesty and purity without laying out her personal conversations that embarrassed her and hurt her so much. The chapter ended up being shorter than it might have been otherwise, but I am still proud of it, nonetheless. Finally, we both highly recommend not to try this next part at home.

THE DOWNWARD SPIRAL

My alarm clock told me it was time to roll out of bed that following Monday afternoon and get an energized start to the work week. I was getting dressed to head out to the gym when I started thinking about the interaction between Vivian and Dante the day before. It was so hot when I texted him pictures of her in her bikini. I kept thinking about her smile and reactions when he got a little dominant with her, then praised her. Vivian had always been such a powerful presence since the day I met her. Strong personality, defiant, and obstinate are terms I could use to describe her. In sixteen years of marriage, I had never known her to want to be told what to do or take orders, like she did yesterday with Dante. I was a little taken aback by it, but then maybe I was overthinking the situation, as I sometimes have a tendency to do. She had changed so much and so fast; I guess it would be naïve of me to think that she was not capable of growing in the realm of sexual domination. I just could not imagine her being submissive to me, so there was no way she could be submissive to anyone else. She was a tough woman, and that is what I love about her.

I was just about to leave for the gym when I received a text from Dante.

I had to take a few minutes to think this one over. Dante was correct in what he said about her needing to be more comfortable with him, but I was not sure I liked the idea of him texting her on his own. If anything, I should tell her he asked me first to ensure she was on board with this.

However, there was a part of me that wanted to see what choice she would make on her own.

If I was being honest with myself, I knew this was not a great idea, but the wheels were in motion now.

When Desire Takes Control

Fifteen minutes had passed, and my brain was already wondering if she had answered him yet. I did not leave for the gym yet because I decided to unload the dishwasher first and hang around in case he texted me back. I had this feeling of anxiousness that I had not felt in a very long time. It was not a good anxiousness to be clear, like waiting for presents on Christmas morning. It was more like the pit forming in your stomach kind of anxiousness. Do you know when your intuition tells you something bad is going to happen, and you are watching it unfold in slow motion? I could not stand it anymore, so I went to the messenger app and clicked both their profiles so that their icon was now on my recent view menu. They both had green circles, so I knew they were on the app simultaneously. Were they talking to each other? I decided to text him.

My heart was racing. What did Dante mean she was bad? They were chatting for like fifteen minutes! How could she be bad that fast? She is not even bad! Maybe he was exaggerating to get me going. That's what it must have been. My heart started beating faster with every minute that passed.

I was waiting for some screenshot pictures but then another text came.

The truth is, I was putting "LOL" so that he would think I was excited and all was good, but inside, I was crumbling. How could my Vivian go from saying hi, to seeing a picture of his dick in twenty-five minutes? I was getting agitated now, and my adrenaline was increasing so much that my body was slightly trembling. That's when I got a text with six screenshots of their conversation. I knew this was wrong and an invasion of her privacy, but I thought, fuck it. I was getting angry. I needed to see how this conversation went down.

The conversation started out innocent enough with him sending her a scuba GIF of a man blowing bubbles underwater and him telling her how much fun he had the other night. From there, I could see he started saying little dirty things, trying to gauge her responses, and unfortunately, she had fed into him just as he was hoping. What bothered me the most about that first screenshot was that he told her she did not have him fooled and that he knew she was a bad girl. That exchange led to him telling her that she was a bad girl trying really hard to be good, but it was getting harder to do, to which she replied that he should stop seeing through her.

What the actual fuck?! Did I just read that right? In five minutes, she just told him that she was a bad girl trying really hard to be good? My wife? I knew she was pushing her boundaries, but this was admitting to him that she is someone she does not even let me see. I was so sad and irritated by these screenshots, but I had to keep reading. I felt heartbroken and could not even process the information. However, there was a piece of me that was excited by this at the same time.

The rest of the screenshots were ten times worse. Vivian doubled down on his "failing to be a good girl statement" when she admitted to him that she wanted to suck him that night in the hot tub, but she could not bring herself to do it with me and Paulina there. All of this led to him sending the picture of it to her, which she seemed to like very much. That was all I needed to see for the afternoon. I was in shock, to say the least. I was not sure what just happened. I was confused about who my innocent little wife was behind my back. I felt blindsided and betrayed, only from words without action. Then I got a text from Dante.

THE GOOD, THE BAD, AND THE UGLY | 229

Dante

iMessage
Today 1:54 PM

> Are you ok? That was a lot to take in. I know

>> I am not sure how I am. I didn't expect her to say those things to you. I didn't expect her to want your cock in her mouth. I thought it would just be a normal conversation of getting to know each other more.

> Just be cool. You promised. This is what you want for her right?

>> Yes I do. I am fine. Promise. Just in shock I think

> This is going to benefit you soon. You watch. She will come home super horny tonight. You're welcome 😊

>> And I can't tell her that I know she was messaging you today?

Delivered

> Nooooooooo

> If she wants to come home and tell you then let her. She may not be comfortable yet. If you tell her that you know you will ruin it for her. And she will not want to message me again

Vivian arrived home from work at her usual time. When I heard the garage door opening, I got nervous suddenly. I was unsure how she would react when she came through the door, and I tried my best to keep cool, as Dante recommended. Would she be cool? The answer I learned was no. She walked in as I was finishing up some dishes.

"Oh heyyyyyy! There is my gorgeous wife!" I laid it on her pretty thick.

"Heyyy." She replied very quietly.

I turned around from drying my hands and went to her for our customary kiss and a quick hug. Oh my, oh my, she had guilt written all over her face. Vivian did not even make eye contact when she gave me a swift and tight-lipped peck on the lips. Her eyes looked to the side of my head as she kissed me and broke it off to turn to her lunch bag for dirty dish removal time.

"What's going on, babe? You seem down or off. Is everything alright?" I asked lovingly.

"Yeah, nothing's wrong. I just had a long day at work. Shit kept happening all day", she replied distantly.

Ding

She received a Facebook message. She grabbed her phone off the counter, turned away from me to exit the kitchen, walked into the bathroom, and closed the door without uttering another word. Interesting behavior I thought. I immediately picked up my phone and went to the messenger app. Dante and her were both online. My heart rate sped up. I put my phone down and started to prepare dinner. Five minutes had gone by, and she was still in the bathroom. I checked my phone, and they were both still online. I continued with dinner. It was almost done, and I was excited about the aroma of sage that engulfed our kitchen. Ten minutes had gone by, and there was no sign of Vivian leaving the bathroom yet. I checked my phone, and they were both still online.

I served our dinner on our plates and started to get the table set for us and the kids. I was hungry, but my mind was consumed with wondering if they were, in fact, messaging each other right now or not. Fifteen minutes had gone by when I heard Vivian laughing in the bathroom. I walked toward the bathroom door to tell her that dinner was ready, and I could hear her watching a video on her phone. I checked my phone, and the app said Dante and her were both offline and had been away for four minutes. I refreshed my phone, and they both changed to five minutes away. They had both gone offline on the app at the same exact time? Perhaps it was just a coincidence.

During dinner, she seemed to relax and return to her usual self. I noticed, because I was really paying attention, that it took her nearly twenty-five minutes to even look at me. After dinner, it was still a little awkward between us as we cleaned up the dishes and the kitchen. Vivian was quieter than usual, and so was I, due to the entire vibe being off. I started to get upset because I had hoped that she would tell me about her conversation with Dante today, and she had plenty of opportunities to do so. I kept asking myself if she was really going to keep this from me.

As we were finishing up, she told me that she was going to take a bubble bath and would see me upstairs. Left alone with my thoughts, they wondered profusely. I could not stop thinking about the picture of Dante's throbbing cock that he sent to my wife or her replies back to him. I looked at the screenshots again of her telling him that she wanted to suck it the other night. I returned to the thought of them potentially messaging each other for over ten minutes tonight with me in the next room. Were they messaging now? I checked my phone, and they were both offline for Eighteen minutes. Both of them were offline for the same exact amount of time yet again. This was a bit too much now, and I could feel myself getting angry with this level of discussion behind my back.

I headed upstairs to shower, and on the way up, I kept thinking that I should ignore Dante's advice and tell her that I knew he reached out to her earlier that day. What was so wrong with that, anyhow? I would not ask what they talked about; that was between them, but I was not too fond of her thinking that this was a big secret right now and that she was succeeding in keeping me in the dark. I had it all planned out in my mind how I would say this. She was still in the bathtub when I entered the bathroom and turned on the shower for myself. The shower was separate from the bathtub, and there was a piece of glass between them so we could see each other while we washed. I brushed my teeth and stepped into the hot water. There she was, soaking in her bubble bath with wet nipples, just peeking out beyond the suds while she listened to soothing and relaxing music on her phone.

I had my speech ready to end this charade that we were playing. This is not what we did as husband and wife. We did not keep secrets of this magnitude from each other. I was simply going to say that Dante texted me earlier that morning, and we talked about the fun we had the other night. He mentioned that he thought it would be good for the two of them to get more comfortable and get to know each other, so he asked me if I minded that he reaches out to her. I thought it was fine, so I said yes. I hoped she was okay with that, and I apologize for not checking with her first. It was perfect because then she would be aware that I knew he was texting her and that he was decent enough to ask me first.

As I was about to speak, I had one issue with this idea that crossed my mind. Vivian's reaction. I assumed she would respond with, "Yeah, he reached out and said hi and that he had fun the other night", and that would be it. However, that might not be it. What if she really stopped messaging him because I knew? What if that stripped her of the thrill of talking with another man secretly, or even worse, what if she got defensive with me like she sometimes did? It did look a bit scandalous that it was now almost 9 p.m., and she had not mentioned his reaching out yet. Could I put her in a position where it makes her look deceitful for hiding this from me all evening? I remembered Dante's words telling me not to tell her yet and to be cool. I felt that the longer this went on without me speaking up, the messier it was going to get. I decided to put my faith in her and him and wait this out a few days to see how it was going to transpire.

Vivian started to drain the tub and got out to towel off. We still had not spoken since I got in the shower, and I did not like the awkward tension that was between us. She went into the bedroom and closed the bathroom door behind her. The tension in the air was a familiar one that usually exists because I am in trouble for something, but this time, I could tell it was her guilt and worry that was keeping her quiet. I decided not to let it phase me the rest of the night. This would not last long, for sure. I anticipated that she would tell me very soon about their messaging or tell him that she could not message him anymore. I turned the shower off and grabbed my towel. After I was dry, I opened the bathroom door and noticed it was pitch black in our bedroom. Had she turned out the lights and gone to sleep without even saying goodnight to me? Am I in trouble for something? As I shut the bathroom light off, my eyes adjusted, and I realized she had lit two candles on the end tables at the sides of our bed.

"Come join your naked wife in bed, my sexy husband!" Vivian spoke seductively.

Majorly confused about the woman who seemed to be avoiding me all evening, I slid under the blanket beside her, and she pounced on me immediately. She pushed me flat on my back, got on top of me, and started kissing me very aggressively with her mouth wide open and tongue moving frantically. This was the way she kissed me when her level of horniness was in the stratosphere. This was not her everyday passion and kissing. Something, or someone, excited her to this intense level, and I knew for sure that it was not me. She grabbed my dick and whispered, "I want this fucking hard cock in my mouth now", and she started kissing down my chest and stomach until she reached her prize. Her wet mouth surrounded my cock as she slid the entire thing down her throat. I let out a quiet moan followed by a "Fuck Vivian!".

She ravaged my manhood. She sucked and slurped on it like she needed it to survive. She used her hand to grip and twist it while she sucked fast. She was moaning and making sounds of pleasure while she sucked. She honestly was sucking me like she had never sucked me before. I could feel that I was not going to last much longer, so I told her that she needed to stop because I was going to cum. It was customary that I would stop her there so that we could have sex at that point, but on this night, she was on a mission. She kept sucking.

"Baby, you need to stop. I'm going to cum." Her pace quickened. There was no stopping the flow of hot semen that was about to erupt out of me like molten lava.

"Alright, baby, now!!!!" I managed to blurt as she removed her mouth. I held back loud moans of pleasure as my orgasm gushed out of me, spewing up into the air and oozing all down her fingers that squeezed me so tightly.

"Damn baby, that was incredible!" I gasped, trying to catch my breath.

"I just wanted to suck the fuck out of you tonight", she whispered while stroking my cum covered cock. She cleaned me up with a towel and then lay on her back, waiting for my mouth. I opened her legs and got my tongue into position. I asked her if she was ready for what was about to happen to her.

"Lick my fucking pussy!" she demanded. What the fuck? She never talked like that in bed, ever! I started doing as I was told. She was soaking wet before I even touched her with my lips. I licked her and savored every drip of her juices. She grabbed my hair and pulled my face into her while wrapping her right leg over my shoulder and down my back. I was not eating her long before she started lifting her ass off the bed while grinding herself against my lips. I felt the wet warmth inside of her, and I instantly felt her muscles gripping and contracting on my soaked fingers. She came loudly and for a very long time. It was a very intense orgasm for her, too. Dante was correct; their dirty messaging today definitely paid off for me.

Stuck

I woke up the next afternoon and grabbed my hard cock like always do. I squeezed the fuck out of it while remembering how insane Vivian was last night for it. Then I quickly thought of Dante and checked my phone with an anxious feeling in my gut. There was a text from him that only said, *"Hey bro".* I answered him back with a *"Hey what's going on?"*. There was no response for a few minutes, so I went to the messenger app and there they were both online. I sent her a text that said, *"Damn baby! Woke up hard thinking about you last night",* to see if she would go offline to answer me. Ten minutes passed, and they were both still online. His icon said away for one minute all of a sudden. He texted me.

Then he was gone. I tried my best to get my day going, but knowing that she was talking to him right then turned me on and ate at me equally. It was a real dilemma I found myself in. I felt stuck. On the one hand, I was very happy for her that her desire had taken control and that she started to feel empowered and was exploring her newfound independence.

On the other hand, was it really independence if she was hiding it from me? I checked my phone, and she had not seen my text yet. She purposely ignored me and continued talking with him. I found that to be a different level of fucked up when you know your spouse is trying to reach you, and you don't even open it to read it because you are fucking around with another person via text. I checked the app, and they were both online. I was getting more agitated. Just then, he texted me.

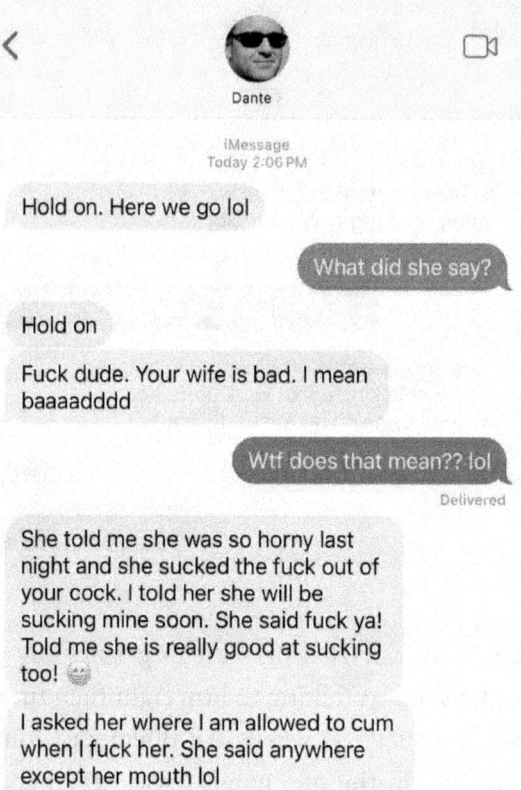

Well, there it was. Vivian was already talking about fucking him. Something I wanted her to do so badly for eight years now, and she was talking about doing it without me knowing.

The truth is I was hard. I was so conflicted with betrayal and lust inside of me at the same time. I was royally fucked. Dante sent me a screenshot that I was not ready for, and it fucked me up for the rest of the day. Vivian essentially told him that she liked the way he dominated his wife, and she liked the way Paulina listened to him. Vivian then let it be known that she wants to listen to him and do what she is told. She wanted to follow his orders. I was beyond disgusted. The love of my life was submitting herself to a dominant man after playing in a hot tub one time and texting with him for a total of two hours if that. I was furious.

Furious at who exactly? I had created this situation myself. I kept telling myself that repeatedly. Could I be furious at Dante? He was sending me screenshots because he thought I liked it. Furious at Vivian? Absolutely. But I also felt this love for her and had this overwhelming feeling that I did not want to ruin this for her. I wanted Vivian to experience this so severely that I was willing to put my feelings aside so that she could explore the situation. That was supposed to be the point; it just was not supposed to be behind my back. I was strong, though, and I knew I could endure this for her. They continued messaging for almost an hour and a half before they went offline. Just then, I finally got a text from Vivian.

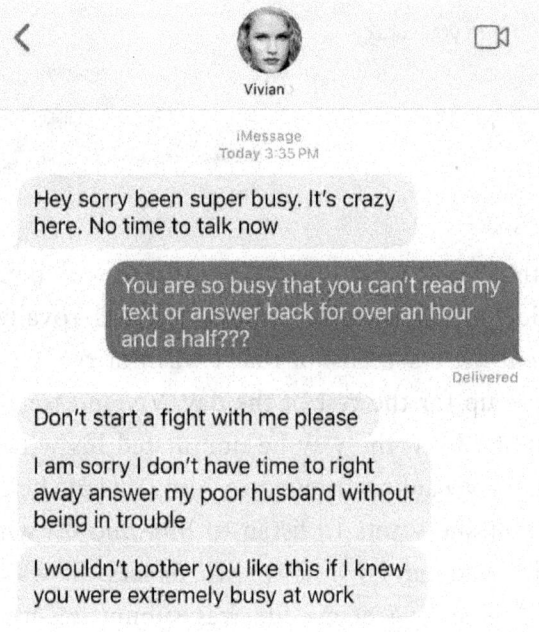

I stopped responding to Vivian after that zinger. I was in utter disbelief that she was blatantly lying right to me and making up false stories. I was livid!

Strained Trust

This toxic behavior continued for the rest of the week. Vivian would spend almost two hours messaging Dante daily and then come home and complain that she was busy at work all day and could get nothing done. She was coming home and acting so suspicious and would barely look at me, but then on my nights off, she would fuck the living hell out of me. I played it cool, and Dante kept feeding me with screenshots of my shocking wife. I was not doing well with any of this by the end of the week, so I started to let Dante know it. I made it clear to him that this had been going on far too long, and I was not happy with her deception. This is not how it was supposed to be. He reluctantly agreed to talk with her. He assured me that he would fix this. He was going to suggest that she include me and remind her that this was my idea and this is what I wanted. He then was going to recommend a way for her to let me know that they were talking and make it seem like it was just starting that day if I could ignore that it had actually been a week already. I agreed. I could forgive the past discretions if we could move forward together. Unity is all I desired.

I received my customary text from Dante the next day, but it was not the news I had hoped for. He backed up everything with screenshots of their conversation so I would know he was not lying to me. It was very important to him that he had my trust and would not do something I did not want him to do. He said none of this was fun and pointless if not everyone involved was having a good time. In their message, Dante did an excellent job telling her that maybe she should tell me they are talking or at least want to start talking. He reminded her that this was all my idea and that I would be very excited if she were being a bad girl and pursuing another man. Her response to him broke my heart.

Vivian told him that she really wanted to tell me and that the guilt was killing her. She told him she did not know how to have that conversation with me yet because she was scared. She told him that she did not know how I would react and did not quite trust that I would be excited. She thought I would freak out. She then told him that she thought it would be better to do this on her own first to see if she could even go through with it without pressure from me. She told him that once she gains confidence, she can tell me maybe, but I could never know how long it had been going on. Devastated is not the best word I can use to describe how I felt reading that.

THE LINE CROSSED

I did a shit ton of soul-searching for the rest of that afternoon; let me tell you. I was a decimated prisoner trapped in my own head. "What have I done?" was all I could ask myself, but the problem was that "myself" was not giving me back the answer I wanted to hear. How have I pushed her this far that my wife was ready to have sex with another man without my knowledge? Where was the trust? Where was the loyalty? Did she even love me anymore? Did she ever love me? These were the self-deprecating thoughts that tore at my insides. This was all my fault. When I messaged him back that afternoon and let him know that this was not the way this was supposed to go down, the following conversation ensued:

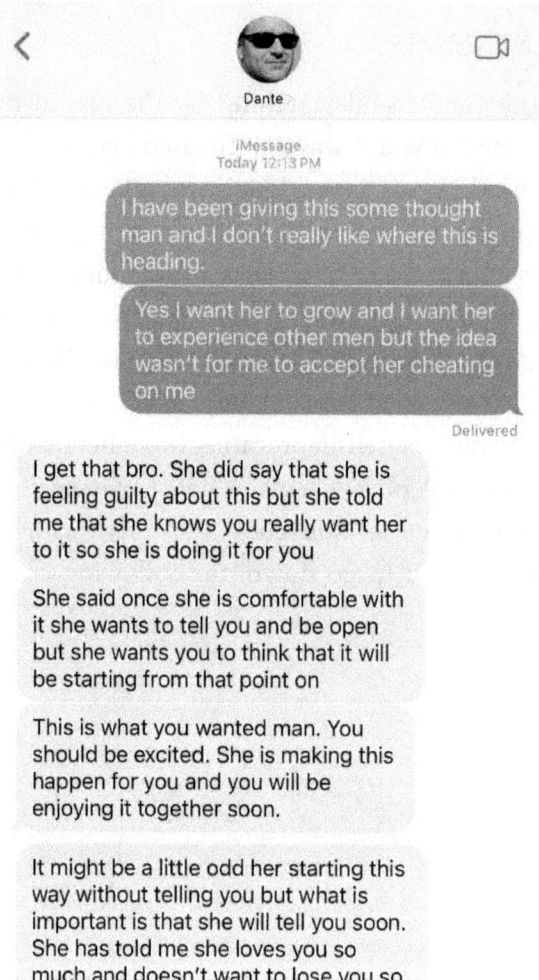

Well, it was reassuring that she wanted to be careful so she wouldn't get caught!

Dante did have a point to a certain extent. I had worked so hard to get us to this point of our journey, hence why I was beating myself up over it. Vivian's growth and happiness were both significant to me. I liked that he was right about me planting the seed in her. We just needed a sex angel to sprinkle some water on her to make her grow. Was this any different than her interest in Christian? Christian helped her grow; why should I be upset that Dante was helping her grow? This was just such a monumental step that I didn't anticipate, but if Vivian wanted to have sex with another man, then I should not stand in her way. Her comfort in telling me about it would come with time, much like all of this had come with time. I just needed to let her grow and be patient with her. I answered him back.

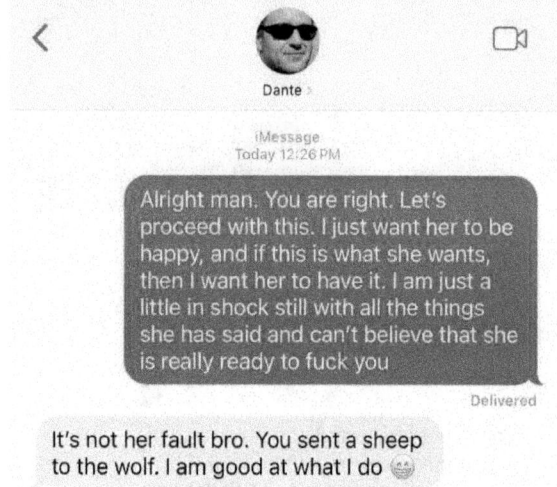

Well, I guess I fucked up again because there I was, comparing him to a shark previously when I should have seen he was really a wolf.

The Secret Encounter

It was a Tuesday night, and the stage was set for the main event that would change Vivian for the rest of her life. Dante ensured I was aware of what was happening and that I was good with it all up to that point. The plan was that I would go to work; Vivian would feed the kids dinner, shower, drop our youngest child at soccer practice, and meet him at a local hotel for fifty minutes only before having to leave to pick up our child. I started work earlier that night, so I would not see her at home. I texted her that I had to go in earlier for a meeting. I was guessing that she was relieved by this news because I was sure she could not handle seeing me before this act of indiscretion that she was about to commit. The truth was that I could not handle seeing her.

Dante texted me at 6:22 p.m. that he was at the hotel and that she was on her way, and he asked me if I was doing okay. I told him I was not. Thankfully, no one was in the office around me because I could not sit still. I was pacing in circles. I was nauseous. My armpits were sweating through my shirt. I was a mess, to say the least. He responded back to me.

And like that, he was gone. It was 6:30 p.m, and I knew that I needed to hold it together for the next fifty minutes. I tried to focus on work, but when your wife is at a hotel and she is fucking another man for the first time, work does not exist. Holding it together was my main focus, and I failed miserably. With each minute that ticked away, my anxiety grew with the images in my head of what they were doing to each other. She was tasting another man, no doubt, or she was being tasted after fifteen minutes had passed. The feeling in my body is something that I cannot forget to this day.

My adrenaline took me over. My heart was pounding the entire time, and I was visibly shaking. My body temperature dropped, and I was suddenly cold despite sweating through my shirt. It was my hands that were the most freezing. My palms were sweaty, but all my fingers were ice cold. Blowing on them could not bring me warmth. There was still that nauseous feeling in my stomach that would not subside, but it was the relentless tightening in my chest that really drew my attention. All the deep breaths in the world could not calm me. My body felt like it was shutting down. I was scared that my marriage was shutting down. It was 7:10 p.m when I heard the text on my phone. It was Dante.

He let me know that she just left his hotel room and asked if I was good. I was honest with him that I was freaking out, but overall doing okay. I asked him how it went. He asked me if I really wanted to know. I was catching on that this was his game. I told him that I needed to know after everything I had gone through in the last forty minutes. But was I ready? He proceeded to tell me that they essentially did all of the things in those forty minutes. I do not think I need to go into details on this with you all. Use your imagination as to what he made her do; she was happy to follow directions. All I can say about it is that Vivian had sex with another man.

The Aftermath of Adultery

It took me a few hours to calm myself back down to the level of a normal human being. It was about 9:30 p.m. when Vivian texted me, saying good night and that she loved me and was going to sleep early because she was exhausted. I bet she was exhausted after everything I read. I was so furious with her that I did not even respond to her that night. Maybe she will think I was busy dealing with an issue? After all, I do not always have the time to answer my "poor wife" when I am busy at work. Sound familiar? Yeah, I was bitter as fuck. I was just cheated on. Give me a break.

Dante texted me the next morning, asking if I was still okay. I was not, but I played it off as if I was. He thought it was an excellent idea to let me know that Vivian texted him as she was driving home and sent him a blowing kiss emoji. Awesome! He then told me that Paulina wanted to go out with us Friday night, but I was disgusted by this entire scenario and did not really want to. I told him I would check with Vivian, to which he replied that he just asked her, and she said, "Fuck yeah!". He told me to ask her anyhow for appearance's sake.

When Vivian came home from work that evening, I could not even look at her, and she was not really looking at me. I got the same peck on the lips and the same awkward treatment after the first day they messaged each other. I learned she was terribly awful at unfaithfulness. I decided it was time to break the ice and talk to her to ask her about Friday.

"Oh, by the way, Dante was asking about us going out Friday night", I said to her without looking up from washing the dishes.

"Oh yeah? Ok, sure. We haven't seen them in so long. That sounds fun."

I could feel the anger building in me, knowing she was with him just last night.

"Cool. I will let him know", I replied coldly.

That night, Vivian came out of the shower and climbed into bed naked with me. She reached her hand over to me and felt my boxers, and her hand stopped in surprise.

"Oh. What is this?" she asked playfully.

"My boxers."

"I can see that. I expected you to be naked. Is nothing happening tonight?" she asked, confused.

"I didn't know if anything was happening."

"Well, it's your first night off. We always do something on your first night off", she said, more perplexed.

"Ok. I wasn't sure", I answered, taking off my boxers.

We started kissing, and all I could do was imagine her kissing him. She tried going down on me to wake up my flaccid cock, but all I could do was imagine her on her knees, looking up at him with his large cock in her mouth. I was hurting, and my brain was telling my dick to take the night off because she did not deserve it. She gave up trying to harden me and actually got upset at me for not working for her. I was so angry with her that I do not remember the words I yelled at her, but I know it ended with her crying and me leaving the room and slamming the bedroom door.

It was déjà vu the next night minus the slamming of the door part. That night, she just rolled over, and we said no words to each other. I could hear her crying after she asked me why I was being so mean to her. There was no saying "good night". There was no telling each other "I love you". I could feel all my anger and hatred growing. I was happy that I had to work the next two nights. During the days, we barely texted, sharing only necessary texts about the kids and whatnot. She knew I was pissed at her, but I assumed she did not know why.

Friday night date night came, and boy, was I excited! I hope you could sense the sarcasm as I was laying it on pretty thick. Bonus points if you know the movie reference! Dante and I decided the four of us should meet up to play pool and have some drinks. I anticipated Vivian would be nervous on the way there, but she seemed fine, which surprised me. When we arrived, she gave them both a big hug and commented on how long it had been since she had seen them. She was prepared for this, and I was not. I was not sure I knew who she was anymore. We had a few drinks, and Vivian was flirting and having fun with Paulina, and I felt sick to my stomach. The girls went to the bathroom and left me and Dante alone to chat.

"I will tell you what. It is pretty hot all four of us hanging out tonight when your wife and I just fucked a few days ago", Dante said with a smile.

"Yeah, it is a little weird. I actually can't stop thinking about it," which is all I could answer.

Just then, Vivian exited the bathroom with no sign of Paulina. I could tell by the way she was walking that she was getting very tipsy. Her following action left Dante and me with no doubt she should switch to water. He and I were sitting on high stools with our feet on the pegs and our legs in an open position. She approached our table, walked right up to Dante, and got so close to him that she was in between his legs. He looked at her with a "What the fuck are you doing" look, and she made a shocked face that someone makes when they realize they just fucked up immensely. She quickly turned away from him and stood between my legs, dancing indifferently to the music on the jukebox. I could not even put my hands on her. I was beyond embarrassed and disgusted as he looked at me with wide eyes just as Paulina approached the table. It was the final straw for me; it was a long and silent drive home for the two of us, and it was another night of going to bed without me speaking to her.

The next morning, we had to get up and go to another drinking event with a group of friends that we had not seen in a while. Things were fairly normal until they weren't. When it was time for us to leave, Vivian made a statement in front of all our friends that I was too drunk to drive home and that she should drive. She was right, and on any other day, I would have gladly given her the keys, but on this day, her embarrassing attack on me in front of all of them set me off. I reached my boiling point with her. I was a volcano that laid dormant for far too long, and this was my time to erupt. I went off on her in front of our friends which was not warranted, this I know. I gave her my keys, and when she started driving down the road, I exploded. Again, I do not remember all that was said in that state, but I know we both screamed at each other; she cried and yelled, "Why do you hate me" and I hollered, "Fuck you," and "Fuck off" many times. Upon arriving home, we both slammed doors and ignored each other for the rest of the afternoon.

Later in the evening, I sat on the couch and watched her cook dinner for the kids. I had been drinking water for a few hours, so I had begun to sober up a good amount. I looked at her and remembered what I loved about her. I felt sad in my soul about where we were and what I had created. As I chugged my water, I glared at her and decided that this was the night to fix us or ruin us. This was the night to come clean and tell her everything. Fuck Dante, I could not live like this anymore. I could not live with a cheater. It was causing me nothing but misery. There was no fun in letting my wife sleep with another man and carry out an affair if I had to pretend that I did not know anything about it and could not enjoy any of the benefits of it at all. Call me selfish, I guess, but it was time to bring the house down. After dinner, we began cleaning up the dishes, and I finally decided to speak to her.

"Hey, after the dishes are done, I was thinking we could sit out by the fire and talk. I have some things I have to say."

"Sure, I can put them to bed and join you at the fire", she said with a worried tone in her voice.

"Ok. Sounds good. I will get it started." I replied emotionlessly.

Picking Up the Pieces

I sat mesmerized by the dancing flames and the smell of smoke that filled my backyard. There is something so quiet and peaceful about a fire as you try to gather your thoughts and contemplate the end of your marriage and your family. Vivian came out wrapped in a blanket and sat down next to me. She said not a word. We both stared at the fire, not speaking for what felt like an eternity when, in reality, it was probably only five minutes. Vivian broke the ice.

"So, what did you want to talk to me about, baby?" she asked with a hint of nervousness in her voice.

I could not answer. I just glanced at her and returned to staring at the fire to give me strength.

After a few minutes, she spoke again, "What is it, honey? It's obvious you are not happy with me lately, so please tell me what it is so that I can work on fixing it".

I again looked at her and took a deep breath, "I do not know how to say it or how to start. I feel like I am going to puke."

My anxiety kicked in, and I started to take deep breaths. Vivian looked concerned. I took a deep breath, said, 'I...'" and stopped because I could not let the rest of the words flow freely. I feared the rest of the words would lead us to a divorce. I started to shake from adrenaline, which was very visible to her. She put her hand on my arm.

"Hey, calm down. Do not get so worked up. Please just say what you need to say because you are starting to scare me."

We locked our eyes for a few seconds. Vivian's facial expression comforted me and made me feel that everything was going to be alright. Perhaps that was just wishful thinking on her part. I finally got the courage to speak.

"I have made a big mistake. I fucked up really bad, and I am scared."

"What did you do?" she whispered nervously.

"It's not what I did, really", I answered back in a shaky voice.

"Ok, what did I do then?" she whispered again, more nervous than previously.

"I….I know about your affair with Dante", my eyes filled with tears of heartache.

Her gaze left me and shifted to the orange embers as tears began to build up in her eyes. I was ready for her to fight me. I was ready for her to deny it. I was ready for her to scream at me.

"Ok", she said very calmly. "Are you going to divorce me?" she asked quietly.

"So, you are not denying it?" I asked, a bit confused.

"No. I fucked up. I am so mad at myself for fucking up so badly", as the tears slowly streamed down her cheeks.

We sat in silence with only the sounds of the crickets and what was left of the crackling flames. I added three more logs to the firepit. It was going to be a long night. Vivian wiped the tears from her eyes and finally broke the awful silence.

"I am actually very relieved that you told me you know about this. It was pretty obvious that you knew already based on how you have been treating me lately. You have had so many comments and have been so angry with me a lot. It was giving me anxiety, and I have been wanting to tell you, but I was so scared, and I did not know how to. I am so happy that you finally said something to me. It is a very big relief; you have no idea. So now you can just yell at me or divorce me if you want because I am the worst person ever."

I had not formulated a response to that; in fact, I had not formulated any response after letting her know that I was aware of her cheating. I was letting this conversation flow on its own.

"Why Vivian? What made you do it? What made you have sex with him and not want to tell me when you knew I have wanted this for you for so long?"

"I don't know. I was stupid. I think part of it was that I knew you wanted it for me so much, so I told myself that even though I couldn't bring myself to tell you, that somehow, it's what you wanted, and you would be okay with it", she tried to rationalize.

"Do you even love anymore?" I asked her.

"What? Yes, of course, I love you. Why would you ask me that? I hope you don't think I have any feelings for this guy. I am so happy you know about it now, so I am not trapped anymore, and I can end it with this guy immediately."

"Well, I didn't say that you necessarily needed to end it with him", I told her.

"I hope you are joking me right now. I am disgusted with myself. I am repulsed with this entire situation, and it is done starting now. I want nothing to do with this guy ever again, and I will tell him that tomorrow", she snapped back at me.

"Now, just hold on. Before you text Dante saying all that, please let me talk to him so I am not in trouble with him", I replied.

"Why do you give a fuck if you are in trouble with him? You are the husband, and he fucked me behind your back! You should be sickened with him and be done with both of them, too!" she scolded me. A perplexed Vivian continued, "Like I said, it was obvious that you knew about this, so I would like to know how you found out in the first place?"

"I was aware the entire time", I spoke softly with shame.

"What do you mean you were aware the entire time? What does that mean?" she asked while glaring at me.

"It means I knew everything from the start. I knew about the first day that he wrote to you because he asked my permission first. I knew about the dirty things that you said to him right away, which shocked me. I knew about you telling him that you wanted to suck him and him sending you a picture of his cock. I knew that you wanted him to tell you what to do so you could follow his directions. I knew about you telling him that you wanted to follow his directions and do what you are told. I knew the night you broke my heart and went to that hotel and sucked and fucked him. So no, he didn't fuck you behind my back. He was being respectful to me and making sure that I was ok with everything each step of the way. It is YOU that fucked him behind MY back!"

"Ok, wow!" is all she could say as she stared at me in shock. "I knew you guys were talking, but I didn't want to believe it. I can't believe you would actually allow him to do all this to me. I am your wife! When he asked you if he could message me, you should have said no immediately! You don't let some guy text your wife!" she screamed angrily.

"I told you that I fucked up and made a big mistake, didn't I? I actually did not see an issue with him sending you a message. He thought it was a good idea for you two to get comfortable with each other, and I agreed with him", I defended myself.

"Well then, you should have told me that right away instead of keeping it a secret", she said.

"Trust me, I wanted to tell you right away. But when you started saying dirty things to him after ten minutes, he thought it was best not to tell you. He said you would not continue to get comfortable and open up if you knew that I was aware that you guys were texting. And don't talk to me about keeping it a fucking secret, either! You and him message for twenty minutes, and you're telling him you want to suck his dick. That's disgusting, and I didn't expect that from my fucking wife. What I expected from my loving wife was that you would have come home from work and at least told me that he texted you that day and made sure I was cool with that. So why didn't you Vivian? Instead, my sneaky wife comes home from work, guilty as fuck, and won't even look at me or make eye contact with me for two hours! I didn't expect that my wife would lie to me and say she can't respond to my text because she is so busy at work after texting with him for two hours and telling him that he can cum anywhere he wants as long as it's not in your mouth! Now those are some fucking secrets!"

"What are you talking about? You're watching me to see if I am making eye contact with you? What am I a prisoner here? And I barely talked to that guy. I always would tell him I am too busy to answer and would just write to him that I hope he has a nice day and stuff like that. I am not sure what he was telling you, but he was always asking me personal questions and trying to get me to talk dirty with him, and I never said any of those things that you are saying now", she yelled. I was growing angrier and starting to lose my temper with her.

"You're a fucking liar! Trust me, I could not believe that you would say any of those things either, and I told him that. So, he sent me screenshots as proof of what you were saying and showed me that you wanted this. Am I really supposed to believe that you just texted nice things like a have a great day at work, and then somehow that led to you on your knees looking up at him with his cock in your fucking mouth!"

"He was sending you screenshots of our private conversations and telling you private details of what he did to me? And you wanted to hear that?" she asked eerily quiet now.

"Yes, and trust me, I did not want to hear or read that. But it showed me what you wanted, so I kept letting you be happy and do what you needed", I answered more calmly.

She stood up from her chair, crying more now, "Fuck you both! You both disgust me and make me want to puke. I am done with all of this. Just please divorce me now so that I can move on with my life after we both just destroyed our family.

You should have never pushed me to this, and you should have never told me all of this!" she screamed at me and headed for the house.

"You probably shouldn't have showed up at his hotel room and fucked him either, but sure go ahead and blame me!" I screamed back. She slammed the door behind her.

I sat outside alone for about an hour while waiting for the raging fire in the firepit to die down, along with the raging anger in my heart and in my head. As I made my way up to bed, I hoped Vivian's raging anger had died down too. I entered the dark bedroom, where I found her in bed sobbing in pain. I got undressed and lay down next to her. She was on her side facing away from me and was hyperventilating and struggling to catch her breath. I could tell that her nose was stuffy from crying by the clogged sounds of her trying to inhale. I placed my hand on her side and gently rubbed her. After a few minutes of not speaking, I asked her if she could roll over and face me, which she did after a long pause of indecisiveness. On our sides facing each other, I placed my right arm under her head and rubbed her back with my hand while my left arm went over her back. My hand caressed her head and stroked her hair.

Her crying had subsided, and she now focused on slowing and controlling her breathing. There is no doubt that she just suffered through a panic attack for the last hour and was just coming down. My heart ached for her. I apologized to her for my role in this entire event, and she told me how sorry she was for lying and cheating on me. We talked for the next three hours and told each other why we both made the choices that we made in this entire disaster. I explained to her that I only truly wanted them to text so that she would be more comfortable with Dante if we were to play in the hot tub again. I told her how it shocked me when she opened up to him so quickly, but it must have meant that she really liked him, and it made me happy. I let her know that there were many things that she told him that bothered me. I reminded her that her keeping the conversations a secret from me was killing me, but I again let it continue because I did not want to ruin it for her. I was honest also in letting her know that there were parts of it that I did like, and it did turn me on. What destroyed me was her willingness to have sex with him and purposely keep it from me, even after he told her that she should include me. I told her how sick I felt and the anxiety it caused me to give him the green light and have sex with her. It was the hardest thing I had ever endured, but I went through it for her.

She shared with me her feelings from the first day. She did not think it was a big deal when he first messaged, but she felt it was inappropriate when he started saying dirtier things to her. It also excited her at the same time. I asked her about his comment about her being a bad girl who was trying really hard to be good and her telling him to stop seeing through her. She admitted there was some truth to that, but she mainly said it to keep the conversation flowing. She realized she did get excited when he sent her the picture of his dick, and a small piece of her did want to suck it in the hot tub that night. Her biggest roadblock was that she was still unsure she could do anything like that in front of me.

She wanted to tell me they were messaging each other, but she was conflicted about how I would react. She said she did not see it going further than a few times, so it was not worth mentioning. Then something happened.

She was unsure what it was but said it felt like she was under a spell. She told me that she was not sure if Dante had manipulated her or not, but she could not stop how fast it had progressed. She said she felt stuck and trapped, and I sympathized with her because I felt the same exact way. Vivian started to cry again and said that something inside told her I knew all about their conversations. She said she knew how badly I wanted this for her, so she decided to go through with it and have sex with him. She knew it was wrong to keep it from me, but she felt I knew all the while, so she went through with it mainly for me. She did not think she could go through with it if we were open with each other about it, so she kept it silent. She regretted it all so badly and could not stand the thought of losing me and prayed that I could forgive her someday. She was not aware that I had already forgiven her. We held each other tightly. We both cried. We grew so much closer that night. Closer than we had ever been. That was the night that defined us because that was the night that we became invincible and indestructible.

EXPLORING BOUNDARIES TOGETHER

Despite all the pain and turmoil that we endured that evening, we both grew so much closer at the same time. I would argue that we both learned how to forgive at the highest level of forgiveness that a married couple could attain. We were both grateful that we survived the potential disaster and became stronger for it. I knew at that moment that there was literally nothing she could ever do that would make me divorce her. We held each other that night with a new sense of purpose and a newfangled level of intimacy. I will never forget the way she clung to me, as if I was the most essential thing in the world to her. It is what I had been missing during all of this adversity. Notwithstanding our renewed love and appreciation for each other, there was still one important aspect that we needed to decide on that night: Dante's fate. I knew he would be texting us both in the morning, and Vivian and I needed to be united in how we would respond to him.

I took the position that she should continue to see him but with everything out in the open. No more secrets. No more lies. I felt that we went through all this hardship, but for what purpose? Was it all for nothing? She had a great relationship with him, she was very comfortable with him, she had already had sex with him, and I still was turned on by the thought of her sucking and fucking him. That had not changed. I did not want us to go and throw it all away, or that meant all I went through, and the torture I put myself through for her, would be in vain.

Vivian took the position that she wanted to end it all with him immediately. She despised the fact that he told me about their conversations without her knowledge. She despised that he manipulated us both to his advantage. She despised that I allowed it all to happen and that I put our marriage at risk when I should have put a stop to it all. She loathed the fact that he and I had talked about her and shared secrets behind her back. It was getting late, and she was falling asleep, so she agreed that she would take a couple of days to think about it. She wanted me to tell him that we had this immense discussion and everything was out in the open between us now. She wanted me to tell him that she would be deciding if she wanted to continue this sexual relationship with him or not, and she wanted me to make it very clear to him that she did not want him to message her until she made her choice.

The Decision

Vivian and I woke up the next morning, and we were immediately in each other's arms, holding one another tightly. We were both very much aware of how dangerously close we put ourselves to the flames. I kissed her deeply and cherished every part of her as I peeled her clothes off slowly and made sweet and passionate love to her. We both orgasmed and just held each other longer than we usually would. There certainly was a new sense of appreciation for one another that was on a higher level than we had experienced in all our years of marriage. Sometimes, you need to stare death in the eyes to appreciate life to the fullest. Vivian made us an exquisite breakfast that morning that consisted of eggs, sausage, bacon, tomatoes, cucumbers, avocados, and toast with jam. The kitchen smelled amazing, thanks to her breakfast, which was fit for a king. I made mimosas, which is what I am good at. We talked more about Dante while we enjoyed our feast, but there was still no indication of how she was leaning.

Monday afternoon, I woke up feeling very nervous to tell Dante everything that had happened that weekend. I knew he would be furious with me, yet I should have been the one furious with him. I picked up my phone and sent Dante a text with my shaking hand.

I proceeded to tell Dante the entire story, what pushed me to absolute anger, what drove me to tell her the truth, how our screaming match exploded, and how our makeup discussion saved us. I told him about how she felt betrayed by both me and him. I explained to him how her initial reaction was to end it all with him, but how I tried my best to convince her that maybe that was not the only option. I told him that she agreed to take a few days to think about everything and that she would consider her next path forward. I told him not to message her during this process as she needed her unclouded judgment to guide her on if she should continue this journey with herself in the middle of him and me. He agreed that he would not message her and stated that there was no way she was going to continue this path as she was not ready to be a true hotwife yet.

The following weekend had arrived, and it had been a week without us even mentioning Dante's name. He and I texted sparingly, but I could see that he was separating himself from me, likely due to the impending ending of our arrangement. I woke up that Saturday afternoon after working the night before and was preparing to go back for another night of fun at my job when Vivian asked me to sit outside to talk briefly. I knew she had decided at that moment, and I was ready to support whichever conclusion she reached.

To say I was blown away when she told me that we could try continuing with Dante would be a drastic understatement. She said she was a little damaged by everything that had gone down already but was willing to give it one more try because it might be different now that she can be open with me with no secrets between us. She wanted to make a few things clear, however. If she changed her mind for any reason, she was out, and he and I needed to accept that. She said she did not want him texting me with details about her actions. It was alarming to her that we were sharing so much, and if she were to find out that we were doing that again, even once, she was out. She also said she did not want me to ask her for any details of what she does. She was just not ready for that, but she said perhaps one day she might be. She was adamant that she would decide how much to tell me, and if I did not like that, she was out. She reminded me that she was only doing all of this for me because she did not need any of it, but I got the sense that she was not being completely honest with herself. I, of course, agreed to all her terms, as did he after he got over his initial shockwave that she even wanted to fuck him again.

Vivian Becomes a Hotwife

Vivian and Dante picked up their text conversations the day after she decided she wanted to give hotwifing a legitimate try. Dante and I both understood our roles and understood that information sharing had to cease and desist. We still chatted a few times that next week, but it was brief and extremely vague. I found myself wanting to know how their conversations were at least going since the only information I was getting from her was in line with her past statements; "Yeah, we text here and there, but I am always too busy at work". I knew that was not accurate, and she was still holding back due to her shyness about the subject matter. Vivian had established clear-cut boundaries, and it was crucial that we adhered to them. I am not saying that I did not try to push Dante for something juicy now and then, but he did a fantastic job deflecting me. After four days, he could see that I really needed something to tide me over, so the most he admitted to me was that she was back. He said it took her a few days, but she was back to talking sexy with him, which he felt was a fantastic sign. That's all I needed to know. I was so happy she was back to texting comfortably with him and that I had not ruined that for her. On Friday afternoon, I received a text from Dante that absolutely made my day.

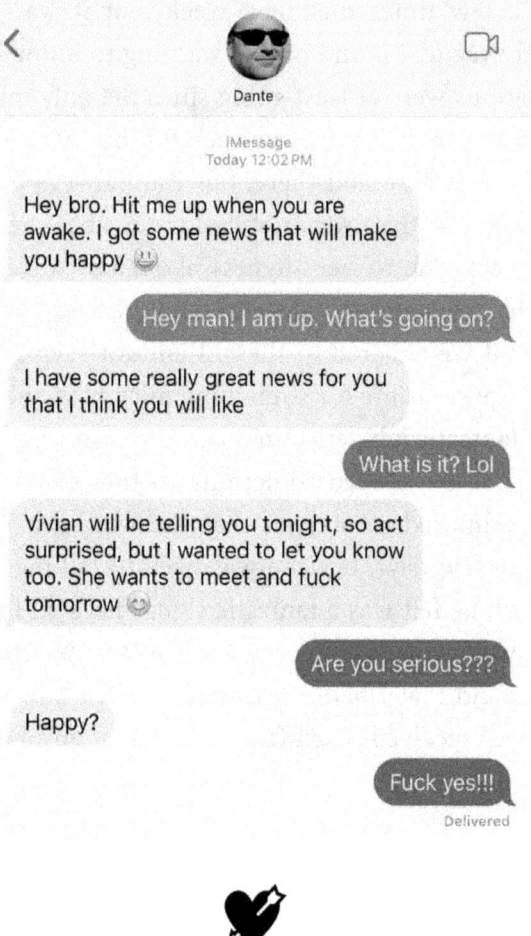

Vivian was absolutely, 1000% terrified to look at me or even talk to me when she got home from work that evening. I was so glad Dante told me what was happening so I would not be too worried about her behavior. If I am being completely honest, it was almost fun to watch her squirm a little bit. After dinner, she poured us two glasses of wine, and we went to sit on the couch to watch television. As I searched for the remote, Vivian saw her chance and knew she had to step up and find the courage to broach this subject with me.

"Hey, I have been meaning to tell you; Dante was writing me today for a little bit", she started nervously.

"Oh yeah? I have been meaning to ask you how that is going with him, but I didn't want to press you."

"It's going alright, I guess. Like I said, this guy always wants to text me when I am at work, and I don't have time for that bullshit", she laughed.

"Yeah, I know it sucks. You are always so busy."

"Yeah, so anyway, he was asking me what I am doing tomorrow morning and if I wanted to hang out with him, but I told him that I would talk to you", she admitted while looking down at the wine glass in her lap.

"Yeah? That's great, baby! What time? Hang out like go get lunch or something?" I asked, knowing full well what the answer was going to be.

"Noooo. He wants to hook up with me. He is only free in the morning, so he wants me to meet him very early in a hotel, which is perfect for me because I have shit to do tomorrow. If that's alright with you, of course. This is so fucking weird! This conversation is so fucking weird. I can't believe I am telling my husband this right now!" she joked with embarrassment.

"Of course, I am ok with it, baby! That's awesome! So, you are going to just go meet him and have sex?" I asked happily.

"Yeahhhhhh", she replied shyly.

"Fuck, baby! You are really going to do it? I love it!" I responded while giving her a big kiss on the mouth. "My dick just hard from you telling me this!"

"Well, that is good, I guess. So, fucking weird. Anyhow, I have to get up early and leave around 7:15 which is good. I want to leave the house before you wake up", she added.

I was a little taken aback by that, so I asked, "Why before I wake up?"

"I don't know, I just don't think I can see you before I leave. If I see you, I might change my mind and not go at all. I am not sure I can handle all this."

"Can I see you after when you come home?" I asked her a little confused by her statement.

"Yes, of course. That is different. It is already done at that point, and I have to come and see you at some point", she said, laughing.

"Well ok, I guess that is fine. I really wanted to see you before you go and give you a big hug and a kiss, but that is fine, love. What are you going to wear? Something really sexy?" I questioned.

"I don't know, dude. I haven't thought about that at all, but can we stop talking about it now? I don't like talking about this with you. It makes me uncomfortable", she requested, growing impatient.

"Sure, baby", I told her while turning on the television and feeling quite content.

Saturday morning came, and I can assure you that I was up at the ass-crack of dawn. It was 6:30 a.m. as my arm extended and reached for Vivian on her side of the bed, but she was no longer there. My heart started pounding. She was getting ready to leave soon, and there was no way I could go back to sleep in this mental state. I also knew she really did not want to see me before she left for her date of morning sex with Dante, but I could not help myself. I could not just lie there in bed for another forty-five minutes when I wanted to hug and kiss her before I sent her off to another man's throbbing penis penetrating her wet vagina.

Vivian was cooking herself breakfast, and as I made my way down the stairs to enter the kitchen, she turned and looked up at me with a slight guise of irritation on her beautiful face.

"I was hoping you would stay sleeping, baby", she recapped as she went back to scrambling her eggs.

"I know, darling. I am sorry. I woke up and immediately thought about what you are going to do today, and there was no way I could sleep again. But we will not talk about that anymore. This is just a regular workday. I am going to do the dishes, and you will go get ready, and you will leave for work", I suggested with a smirk on my face.

"Ok, so you want breakfast before I have to leave for work?" she asked, accepting my role-playing suggestion.

"Yes, please!"

After we ate, Vivian went upstairs to shower and get dressed quickly, and I attended to the breakfast cleanup as promised. I had just finished drying and putting away the last pan when I heard her coming down the staircase. I immediately felt my adrenaline turn on. I felt nervous and had the same pit in my stomach that I had felt when she met him previously, but at least this time, it was all legit and out in the open. Even still, it is a strange feeling you have when you let your woman go off to have sex with someone else. I turned to look at her as she was putting her shoes on and grabbing her coat; she was intensely nervous. She could not look at me, and her behavior was making me more nervous at that point. I felt afraid to look at her as well. As she zipped up her coat, she spoke with a shaky voice while looking down at the floor.

"Just so you know, I am not coming home right away after. I don't think I can come right home. I need to go out and do some shopping and not see you right away."

"Sure, baby. Whatever you need to do", I responded. "Get going. You are going to be late for work. Have fun at work!" I added with a warm smile.

"Ok, bye", she responded while walking over to me. She gave me a kiss while we both looked in each other's eyes. Hers were glossy from tears that were beginning to swell. We both said I love you to the other before she looked at me one more time.

"This is so fucking weird", she said as she turned and walked out the front door.

I got dressed and decided to work out in my home gym. I needed to be distracted from my racing brain and increased heart rate. All the images of Vivian and Dante danced around in my head. I pictured her moaning as he went down on her, I pictured her on her knees looking up at him as he fed her his stiff meat, and I pictured her legs around his waist as he drove it in and out of her repeatedly until he pulled it out and released all over her body. I got through my workout the best I could before giving up. My thoughts were still racing. I decided to take a shower, and before I knew it, I had a raging hard-on of my own. I could not resist my urge to pleasure myself under the hot water while I imagined myself and Dante both releasing at the same time.

Approximately two hours had passed since Vivian left the house when I received a text from Dante.

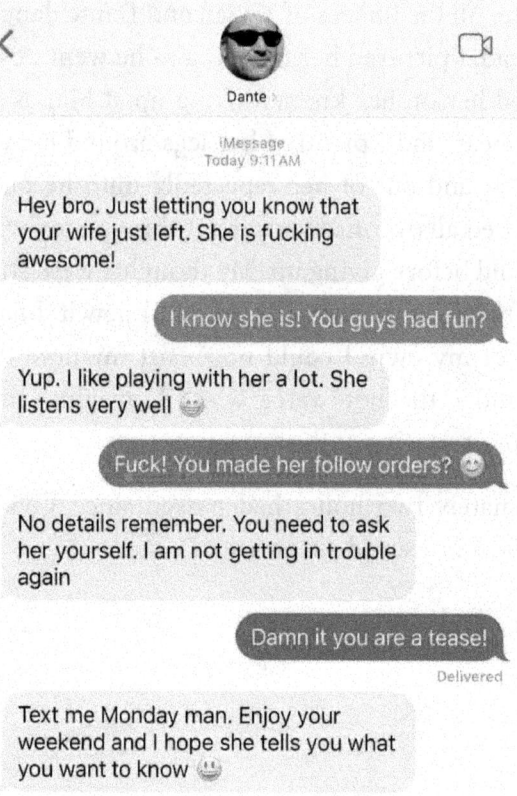

And just like that, he was gone. I kept myself busy for the rest of the late morning with minor tasks such as changing our bedding, washing the laundry, and vacuuming the house. Two more hours had passed, and Vivian was still not home. I did not love her strategy of not coming home to avoid seeing me, but I respected her wishes to handle it that way. At least I knew that she had already finished with him hours ago and was just making herself happy with some shopping now.

It became lunchtime, and my kids wanted me to make them some grilled cheese sandwiches, which just so happened to be my masterpiece specialty, so I got on it right away. I called the kids down when the perfectly grilled deliciousness was ready, and they ran to the table and started wolfing them down immediately. They sure loved them. I began to wash the frying pan when I heard the sound of the garage door opening, which caused my heart to almost leap out of my chest in anticipation of seeing my wife. Vivian walked into the kitchen and said, "What's up, what's up?" as she typically did when she was feeling good.

"Mama's home!" our youngest shouted while running to Vivian and wrapping her hug around her waist.

"Mama is home!" I yelled with a big smile on my face while running to Vivian and wrapping my hug around her shoulders.

"I missed you!" I stated as I began placing a hundred kisses on her lips, cheeks, neck, and forehead.

Vivian laughed and said, "I missed you too."

"I hope you had fun at work and with your shopping", I asked while looking into her eyes.

"Yaaaaa I did", she said and laughed a nervous little laugh as she shook her head from side to side in disbelief.

"Awesome", I said and smacked her ass before walking away to continue washing that frying pan. I decided to give her the space and time that she needed to process what she had done that morning before trying to find out anything more.

Later that night, we were both relatively quiet as we brushed our teeth and showered. I was lying in bed stark-naked when Vivian turned out the light and crawled her unclothed body in next to mine. We both wasted no time as we wrapped our arms around each other in such a tight embrace. I held her close and stroked her hair. I wanted to ask her details, but I did not know what to say or how to say it. All I knew was that she made me so happy, and I felt this incredible burst of love in my heart for her. I discovered at that moment what compersion felt like. That is when she whispered shyly and playfully.

"Your wife was a bad wife today."

"She was?" I asked, copying her tone exactly. She nodded her head.

"You were a bad girl?" I followed up.

"Yaaaa", she answered while nodding her head again.

"Is it because you had sex with another man that was not your husband?" I questioned her while rubbing her back with a little more intensity than I was before.

"Mhmm."

"Did he put his hard cock in your mouth?" I started to squeeze her skin in my fingertips.

"Yaaaa. I had no choice. He opened my mouth with his fingers and slid it down my throat."

"Fuck, you really were a bad girl. Did you let him lick your vagina until you came on his face?" I started aggressively squeezing and rubbing her breasts.

She nodded her head, "He spread my legs open and started to lick me. He made me to cum. It was not my fault."

I slapped her ass hard and started to swirl my hands around both cheeks. I felt her fingers slowly wrap around and grip my throbbing and dripping cock.

"Well, my bad wife, did he then slide his dick inside of you and fuck you hard?"

"It was an accident. I tripped, and I fell, and I just landed on his dick", she joked innocently.

"Oh, you just landed on his dick by accident? So, you just decided at that point you might as well just keep riding?" my fingers explored her soaking wet pussy.

"Mhmm."

"Let me guess. You accidentally made him cum too?"

"Yaaaa. On my boobs by accident!" she started to breathe heavily from my fingers exploring her clitoris.

"So that's it then. You are officially my sexy little hotwife now?" I asked, barely able to keep my leaking cock from exploding in her hand.

She once again nodded, "Mhmm."

"You are not officially a hotwife until you fuck another man and your husband on the same day", I whispered in her ear as her body began to shake and break out in intense convulsions of orgasmic waves.

When her trembling subsided, I pushed her onto her back, spread her legs wide open, and inserted myself deep inside of her. I was so hard that she made a whimpering sound as I glided up in her. I laid on her chest, and we wrapped our arms around each other again. We slowly grinded our hips in unison as our mouths kissed each other overpoweringly. I could no longer hold it as I pictured her and Dante in this similar embrace just hours before. The thought of Dante's cock feeling the inside of my wife as I was now and imagining the tightening in his balls that served as a precursor to him of what was about to erupt out of him. I arched my back. My body bucked. I gripped every inch of her that I could possibly get my hands on as I let burst after burst of hot cum flow out of me and fill up the inside of her uterus. I collapsed on her in exhaustion as we lay there in satisfied silence. Vivian was now officially a hotwife!

Three's a Crowd

The next morning, Vivian and I woke up, and we engaged in mind-blowing sex yet again. I joked with her that every man should let their wife have sex with someone else if this was the intense outcome. While she agreed with me that both sessions were ridiculously intense, she cautioned me that she was not really sure if hotwifing was for her. I was a little astonished by this declaration, to say the least. I was running purely on the assumption that she loved every minute of what happened to her the morning before with Dante, the night before with me, and then five minutes before with me again. She said that she wanted to be honest with me, and while she had fun with Dante at that moment, she was not a fan of how it made her feel beforehand or afterward, for that matter. She told me that my intensity the night before was incredible and that she loved making me so happy, but she was not sure if what she did made her happy. We both agreed that maybe she just needed more experience to gain that confidence, and we both agreed that it is weird telling your husband about your sexual exploration with another man, but there is some fun in it, too. We were both glazing over our recent past with Dante, which was a problem.

Vivian and Dante continued texting for another two weeks or so when it finally appeared that they could meet up again. As fate would have it, that night landed on her menstrual cycle, so they both decided not to waste money on a hotel room. She agreed to meet him in a parking lot in his car just to talk and get to know each other better and increase their comfort level. She came home that night with all smiles, which prompted me to ask her if she was a bad wife again. She told me that she was a bad wife, but she did not want me to get upset about something. I assured her that whatever it was, it was ok with me. She told me they talked for maybe thirty minutes before they started kissing. They kissed for a long time when he started rubbing her and making her very excited. She told me that he unzipped his pants and took his hard dick out for her to wrap her tiny little mouth around. She again reiterated that she hoped I was not upset, but when he said he was going to cum, she kept sucking and took it all in her mouth.

Up to that point in our marriage, she had never let me do that with her, so I was a bit shaken and hurt, but I tried my best not to show her that. What was significant at that moment was that she trusted me to tell me this pertinent piece of information. I asked her what made her do that when she had never let me do it in her mouth in our over seventeen years of marriage. She said it was not really her fault. Dante left her no choice. She told me he made her take her hands off and only use her mouth. He said hands were cheating. Like he told Paulina in the hot tub, I remembered. So, she held herself up with her hands and was only moving her head up and down to suck his thick cock. She asked me that when he said he was going to cum, what choice did she have? To stop sucking? She had to take it in her mouth.

I was angry with him as he knew this was the one place she told him that he could not cum with her, and he knew that she had never let me do that. He knew that I felt that, as the husband, that should be my role to be the first to do that with her, not his. I knew I needed to calm down as I promised her that she could tell me anything. I quickly told myself that this was all for her growth, and Dante's words quickly rang in my head, saying that this would eventually benefit me. I remembered his message that I planted the seed; he was the water to make her grow.

I again reassured her that it was all part of the growth process for us both and asked her if she liked it. She said that she choked on it and spit it all back out on his cock, which made me laugh. I was relieved that she had not swallowed it for some reason. I asked her if she had fun overall, and she said that she did because she was able to talk and get to know him more. She said that she was much more comfortable and relaxed with him this time, and she thought maybe that was what prompted her to let him release in her mouth. She also felt more comfortable coming home to tell me about it all. I kissed her and told her how much I loved her, and then we went up to shower and go to bed. In bed, she attacked me instantaneously and sucked me so fucking amazingly that I could barely stand it. I imagined her sucking

Dante and him blasting his hot load all in her mouth when I felt my own load about to erupt. My little hotwife stunned the fuck out of me when I told her I was about to cum, and she mumbled to me, "mm-hmm", but did not pull her mouth off.

A week had passed since Dante pushed my wife to expand her boundaries and engage in a new activity that she previously opposed wholeheartedly, but could he pull off another magic trick from his book of spells? He texted me to let me know that he was talking to her a lot about MFM, and he told her that she would be doing it soon since she wanted to follow his directions and do what she was told. She admitted to him that she did not know what MFM meant, so he explained it to her. Now, I know you all remember from Chapter 2 that MFM means a Male-Female-Male threesome, but I had yet to fill her in on the acronyms of the lifestyle. What was important from their discussion was that she told him that it sounded hot, but she was not sure she could do that yet. She was not sure she could stand for me to see her have sex with another man, let alone participate with her. I was not sure she could either, if I was being honest, but it thrilled me to the core, nevertheless.

He told me that since he and I were not allowed to be texting about these sorts of subjects, he wanted her to talk to me. He wanted her to tell me that she wanted to be with two men. I knew this was not for her, and I almost felt bad for her if he was going to force her to do something that she did not want to do, but at the same token, I did not feel bad. She was the one who wanted to listen to his direction. She had asked for this. Had she asked for this, or did I force it all upon her I thought to myself? Regardless, I was supposed to say nothing to her and wait for her to approach me.

Another week had passed, and I heard nothing from Vivian on the subject of her taking two dicks. Dante had told me they talked about it a lot. She was asking questions as to what she would do or how it worked because we were not really watching porn together, so her knowledge was limited. He told me he gave her some scenarios that the three of us could play out, and he said she seemed intrigued. I was also intrigued. Vivian came home that night and finally broached the subject with me.

"Hey, so Dante was texting me today, and he was telling me that he really wants to do MFM, I think he called it, but he wants to have a threesome with me and you both", she said to me with not much excitement in her voice.

In my best-surprised voice, I exclaimed, "Oh damn! He wants to do a threesome? That sounds awesome to me. I am guessing that is too soon for you, though, right?"

"It's very soon. I mean, what the fuck? I had sex with him once and sucked his dick once and told you about it, and he thinks I can have sex with him and you together that fast?" She was irritated.

Vivian was correct that it was too soon, but I could not see that with my own eyes. I was blinded by the excitement of all we had accomplished and all that might possibly be. I reminded her that I had been in the hot tub with her and had seen her kiss and get fingered by Nate and Jennifer many times. I also saw Dante fingering her in the hot tub with Paulina. I told her I loved seeing her do it all, so if that was the sticking point for her, she need not worry. Vivian was quick to point out that kissing and fingering was not the same as sucking and fucking. She had a minor point.

I know Dante had kept working on her because he felt that once we did this threesome together, it would open up our entire world of sexual gratification. Another week or so had passed when he texted me that we needed to set it up because she had finally agreed that if the situation were perfect, she would do it. I told him that as luck would have it, we had just found out that both our kids had sleepovers that following Friday, if he could come over that night. He said he would make it happen. He said he would suggest that night and instruct her to tell me that it was happening, to which I agreed. Deep down, I did not see Vivian going for this, so I did not take it too seriously. She came home from work that night, gave me a kiss, and said, "So, it looks like you, me, and Dante are having a threesome Friday!"

Friday afternoon finally arrived, and I was nervous as fuck! I woke up and started cleaning the house for our guest's visit that evening. Dante and I had been texting all week about this event in terms of him asking me what I would like to see her do and what I wanted to try in my very first threesome ever. I know he was also talking with her about this all week, but he kept their conversations very close to the vest. It felt exciting and yet awkward at the same time because Vivian and I were about to live through this amazing experience together, but we were the two who were not talking about it. Anytime I mentioned the upcoming naked free-for-all, she got tense with me, so I decided just to let it be.

Vivian came home from work to find dinner ready for her and the kids. She walked in the door and gave me a look of apprehension that told me she was not doing well. She asked me to pour her a shot quickly because she needed alcohol to calm her nerves, to which I obliged. After dinner, Vivian went upstairs to shower while I cleaned up the kitchen and dropped the kids off at their friends' houses for their sleepovers. Upon my return, I found the house was darkly lit with the aroma of apple-spiced candles filling the air with delectableness. Vivian came down the staircase, looking simply breathtaking. She was wearing a new red dress that I had not seen on her yet, that was so short that it put her gorgeous long legs on full display. This dress was unique in the fact that the zipper was on the front and not on the back. It had a big silver loop that drew attention to her chest and trailed all the way down to the grand prize.

"You look simply stunning, darling", I proclaimed as I gazed at her in awe.

"Thank you, baby. I can't believe this is happening tonight. Can you make me a strong drink, please?"

"Of course, my sexy vixen", I said to her as she laughed.

Dante would be arriving soon, and my nervousness was starting to sink in. I grabbed a beer and downed it rather quickly as Vivian sat watching me while sipping on her vodka faster than she was accustomed to. She looked so beautiful, and there was a radiant innocence about her that I knew would be stripped away after that evening. She was the mother of my children, whom I had loved for so many years, and I was about to watch her do unspeakable things with another man before my very eyes. Perhaps it was my innocence that was about to be stripped away as well and I had not even realized it. My deep contemplation was interrupted by a text on my phone, and I knew in an instant who it was and what it was going to say.

"He will be here in ten minutes", I softly spoke to her.

She chugged the rest of her vodka and extended her glass out to me, signaling that she required another. After inserting a full drink back into her hand, I noticed her sexy bare feet.

"Which sexy shoes are you going to wear, darling?" I asked her curiously.

"I am not going to wear any shoes", she answered quickly. "What is the point of wearing shoes if everything is about to come off me soon anyhow?"

"Well then, you should just take that dress off now and open the door naked", I replied with a smile.

"You should open the door naked", she quipped back as she was interrupted by a loud knock on the door. We both stared at each other in silence for a few seconds with a look of knowing that our marriage was about to become even more altered than it already had been. This was yet another immense point of no return for us. I went to the front door and opened it to invite our guest in.

There in the kitchen, the three of us stood as we surrounded the island, each with a drink in our hand. Dante could tell as soon as he walked in that we were both edgy as hell. He asked us both if we were nervous, which we confirmed. He suggested we just go talk in the kitchen and lighten up the mood a bit. He also reassured us that nothing had to happen whatsoever if we did not want it to. I think that made us both more relaxed. He joked with Vivian that she was not even this nervous when she met him in the hotel alone. That made her laugh, which made me smile. We all began to relax as we made another drink. Dante somehow even convinced Vivian to pose silly for me while I took pictures of her bent over the island. The man knew what he was doing with an inexperienced and anxious couple without a doubt. She was smiling and laughing when he reached over and unzipped her dress down a little to expose her cleavage to us.

"That is better", he said, staring at her with a thirst in his eyes. "Let's all go sit on the couch."

I turned on the television and the three of us snuggled on the couch with Vivian squeezed in the middle. Wasn't this a familiar feeling that reminded me of our days with Martin? How far we had come. Dante and Vivian sat staring at the television, much like she and Martin used to, with nothing happening whatsoever. I remember thinking that I felt a bit awkward sitting there next to my wife and the man that she had already had sex with twice, but they looked afraid to touch each other. The answer came to me then, and I knew immediately what must be done. I needed to remove myself from the scenario.

"I am getting another beer in the garage. Do you need one, Dante?" I asked as I stood up from the couch.

"No, I am good, man, thanks."

"Cool", I said as I turned and walked away from them.

I took my time out there, opened a beer, and slowly indulged in a few sips. I checked my social media accounts on my phone and took a few more sips. It was not much, but I felt like they got a full thirty seconds of alone time, at least. Thirty seconds is all a wolf needs to slaughter a lamb. I opened the garage door slowly and quietly and entered the mud room, where I purposely left that door open. I opened the door just a bit and peered around the corner. I could hear Vivian exhaling profound breaths that were interrupted every now and then by the nervous laughter that she typically released in situations like this. Around the corner, I could see Vivian leaning to one side, with her left leg spread wide as Dante faced her. He was playing with her pussy on my couch.

She moaned some more, giggled some more, and eventually asked where I was. Dante told her I was getting a beer in the garage and asked her if she could give him a tour of the upstairs since he had never been up there. She nodded, and they got up off the couch and vanished up the staircase. I had already been gone for approximately a minute at that point, and I was not sure how long I should leave them alone without upsetting her. I slowly crept up the stairs and made my way to our bedroom to find our door closed, which bothered me a bit. Why the hell did they close the door on me? As stupid as this sounds, being that it was my bedroom in my house, I was not sure if I was supposed to walk in or not. I heard my wife giggle, so I took my opportunity, knocked, and turned the doorknob.

"Why are you knocking, baby?" Vivian questioned me as I closed the door behind me.

I hurried past the closet door and turned right to enter our room, where I found them sitting on the bed beside each other. The scarlet shade of her face matched the dress on her body. No doubt I interrupted something that was happening in here.

"I don't know. I didn't want to interrupt whatever you were doing in here", I muttered nervously. I could feel my hands shaking from my nerves.

"Your wife was giving me a tour of the bedroom, is all, and we were just talking", Dante said. I looked at him and noticed his khaki shorts were unbuttoned and unzipped.

"Do you mind turning these lights off, and do you have any other low lights you can put on bro?" he added.

"And put on some music, Sebastian", Vivian interjected.

I played some music on my phone and set it on the end table. I had some candles set up around the room that I started lighting as they watched me with great intent. When I was done lighting them, I turned off the overhead light. The mood was set. Dante stood up off the bed and gazed at Vivian. She giggled again with nervous anticipation as I watched on.

"Why are you laughing?" he asked her in a very serious tone.

"Because I am nervous, and I don't know what to do", she replied.

"Lay down on the bed", he said in a more direct and dominant tone. Vivian complied.

Dante took off his shirt and threw it on the floor. He slowly lowered himself down on top of my wife and started to kiss her slowly as I still stood there soundlessly, watching in wonder. As they kissed, I watched as Vivian raised her right leg and slowly rubbed it up his leg until she reached his lower back. Dante raised his left hand to Vivian's face and gently squeezed her chin as their tongues twirled together. He shifted his body off of her so that I could see what he was doing to her. His hand slowly started to make its journey down her entire body, fondling her breasts over her dress before making its way down her stomach. He barely brushed over her vagina before moving his hand to the baby-soft skin of her inner thigh. She spread her legs open for him.

Dante began to rub his hand under Vivian's dress slowly, and I could hear just how soaking wet she was becoming as she began to moan. After playing with her pussy and getting her hot, he stopped, and his hand came back up to his mouth. He began to lick her juices off of his fingertips as she and I both watched him with great intent. He stared at her with each lick and suck he took while she stared right back at him. My cock was rock solid and dripping. After Dante enjoyed tasting Vivian off himself, he grabbed the giant silver zipper that dangled just above her tits, and he began to unzip it ever so slowly. Inch by inch, I watched as Vivian's dress began to reveal her body to us. He made his way down until the zipper became undone. He pushed the left side of the red fabric off of her, followed by the right side, until there my wife was with her naked body exposed to this man on our bed. She had no bra or panties underneath. Her erect nipples told me that she was just fine with her current situation.

Dante inched his way down Vivian's body and spread her legs wide open with no resistance. He knelt on the floor before her and began tasting the folds of her pussy while exploring her labia with his fingers. She began to take deep breaths, which told me that she did not hate what was happening to her. I still stood there silently while I watched him eating my wife out in front of me. All my dreams and fantasies had come true with each slow stroke he made with his tongue. That is when Dante stopped and looked up at me.

"Sebastian, come over here and kiss your wife", he directed me.

Without saying a word, I took off my shirt and my shorts and slowly made my way onto the bed, inching closer and closer to her naked body. She had her arms above her head as I reached her face. We made eye contact and stared at each other upside down before we started to make out passionately. After we broke off our kiss, my mouth and tongue glided down to her nipples, kissing and sucking on them. Two feet away, Dante enjoyed the deliciousness of her sweet pussy. Vivian could not withstand this intense pleasure for too long before succumbing to a powerful orgasm.

Dante stood up and examined her naked body, with her legs spread wide for him as she panted and tried to catch her breath. He removed his shorts, revealing the hard cock that he stroked in his hand. Dante took a condom out of his shorts pocket, opened the small package, and slowly unrolled the snug condom down his throbbing shaft. He grabbed her by her ankles and violently pulled her to him. He spread her legs wide and slowly rubbed the tip of his cock on her soaked clitoris. This was the moment I had waited so long to see. So many years of yearning for this was about to come true in this magical moment. He pushed the head of his swollen dick slowly inside of my wife as she let out a magnificent sound that was a cross between a sigh and a whimper. It was simply incredible to watch her enjoying this man filling her up inside like I had never been able to.

"You're such a good girl", he said to her as he put her legs on his shoulders. "Suck your husband's cock", he ordered her. She laughed her nervous laugh once again.

"Suck your husbands' cock!" he demanded her in a stern tone.

She wrapped her fingers around the shaft of my dick, and she began swirling her tongue around the head of it at first until he started pounding her hard. That is when she began sucking and stroking with aggression. I looked down at my dear wife as she now was working two hard cocks; one she stroked and sucked down her throat, while the other thrust inside of her pussy mercilessly. He pulled his shaft out of her and turned her legs to the side to slap her ass extremely hard. I could not tell if she liked that or not, but I know that I never hit her that hard during sex.

"Sebastian, lay down on your back. I am going to make this bad wife of yours suck your cock while I fuck her from behind." I did as I was told.

"Flip over and get on your knees", he instructed her. Vivian did as she was told.

Vivian lowered her mouth slowly down every inch of me like she had done a million times before, but this time, I watched Dante mount up behind her, slide himself into her again, and begin to thrust her violently. He was fucking my wife so hard that she could not even keep my cock in her mouth without it falling out. She put her head down on my inner thigh and only stroked me with her hand as her pussy was pounded into submission. He pulled out, and I could tell by his face that he was about to cum. He calmed himself down and gave her ass another hard slap, to which she winced in pain. He stayed on his knees and gave his next order to her.

"Vivian, lay on your back. I want to watch your husband fuck you while you suck my cock".

She was out of breath at this point, but she slowly rolled onto her back. I stood on the floor at the side of the bed, and now it was my turn to grab her ankles and pull her to me. I touched her with my fingers before I slid inside of her, but she was a little dry, so I got on my knees in front of her tasty kitty. She closed her legs and told me no because she just had a dick inside of her. I told her I did not care and opened her legs once again. He held her arms down on the bed and told me to lick that mouthwatering pussy. She was soaked in no time, as I knew she could not resist my mouth, and within a matter of moments, she was cumming hard again on my face while Dante kissed her.

When the aftershock of her second orgasm had vanished, I buried my manhood as deep inside of her as I could go. I still remember to this day that she was looking up at me with open eyes, which was unusual at that time because her eyes were almost always guaranteed to be closed during sex. Our eye contact did not remain long as Dante crept up on the side of her, turned her head towards him, stuck his fingers in her mouth, pried open her lips, and glided his throbbing dick down her throat. That was about as much as I could handle. I started to thrust into her faster and faster while her tongue and hand swirled on his shaft. He and I both began to moan right around the same time. That is when I saw the most beautiful and intense scene that I had ever witnessed up to that point in my life. Dante pulled his cock out of her mouth and let out a very audible moan while he sprayed his hot load all over her tits and neck. He bent over to kiss her, and that was it for me. I was tapping out. I pulled out of her and shot five or six streams all over her stomach and some that even shot up high to almost her neck. Dante had to get out of the way of my massive orgasm quickly.

"Holy shit, dude, you almost shot it at my face! Holy fuck man, I have never seen that much in my life!" he said to me as I continued to drain myself on my sexy hotwife.

INTERLUDE: WOLVES AND SHEEP

It is not easy for me to relive these memories. I have blocked this section of my life, and I hate to even give it any thought; forget about talking about it. This moment of my life almost cost me my marriage and my family, and it makes me feel sick to my stomach. The overall theme of this chapter of my life is betrayal. I felt betrayed by my husband for his part in setting this all up for me and for sharing details about me behind my back, and Dante betrayed me for not only hunting me but also for breaking my trust and sharing my personal conversations with Sebastian. The other reason I blocked this section of my life was because I was weak. I was weak because I also betrayed my husband, and I hate to be weak.

All my actions with Dante were embarrassing, desperate, and degrading, and I will never lower myself to that level ever again. At that time in my life, I was insecure and trying to please everyone. I wanted to be the "good girl" that everyone liked, and I would do anything, whether I liked it or not, just to be that person. It wasn't an enjoyable time, as I was guilty of being someone I did not want to be, but I kept everything inside because of my insecurities and closed-mindedness.

During that time, I had never really talked to my husband about any desires that I had or my thoughts of sexual exploration because perhaps I was blocked or ashamed. My thinking back then was that I was supposed to be a mom and a wife, and talking about my desires put me in the shameful category. So, I pretended to be fun and sexual, and I turned to Dante to maybe help me be that person, but I felt horrible guilt that made me feel terrible, even to this day.

Being pressured by wolves has been a weakness of mine my entire life, but I have grown since this disaster, and I will never let anyone run my life the way they want me to, especially betraying those I love. My affair with Dante was a learning lesson that perhaps was meant to happen, to learn and move on. I have learned since this nightmare to communicate, be more open-minded, and trust my husband rather than being afraid and ashamed. We all make mistakes in this life. What is important is that we learn the lesson being taught to us, and we move forward and grow.

Technically, I became a hotwife during this part of my life. What this taught me was how to communicate and experience all the things I wanted to experience sexually by being open, discussing, and trusting.

8

VIVIAN'S EMPOWERMENT

> *"Just don't give up trying to do what you really want to do. Where there is love and inspiration, I don't think you can go wrong."*
>
> — ELLA FITZGERALD, SINGER

Vivian lay on the bed, utterly exhausted, covered in the seed of two men, and she looked astonishingly glorious to me. I took a towel from the bathroom and cleaned her off, which I followed with a kiss on her lips. The three of us put on our clothes and awkwardly made our way downstairs. We sat on the couch and continued to watch television in an uneasy silence that was as uncomfortable as suffering through a root canal with no Novocain. After ten minutes, Dante had finally worked up the nerve to declare that he would head home. After we bid him adieu, I flopped back down on the couch next to my dear wife and rubbed my hand up and down her silky-smooth bare leg.

"So, baby. How are you feeling? Did you enjoy yourself and have a great night?" I asked her excitedly.

"I am still a little in shock. I am not actually sure how I feel, to be honest. What about you?" She asked me as she stared at the television screen.

"I thought it was incredible! It was so amazing to see you have sex with him. I loved going down on you and looking up and seeing you sucking on him, and I loved when you were sucking me, and he was pounding you from behind. It was mind-blowing!" I proclaimed as my second hand began rubbing her leg as well.

"Well, I am happy that you enjoyed it, baby. I really am. That is all I wanted. I am glad that I did it and experienced it, and I am glad that we experienced that together, but I do not think I want to do that again, so please don't ask me."

"Wait, you didn't like that? You seemed to have so much fun. You had two orgasms, so I thought that you loved it", I said to her, very confused.

"Yes, I came twice, which was awesome, but there were a lot of other things that I was not very comfortable with", she responded.

"Like what, baby?" I asked.

"I mean, to start, I am not comfortable with the fact that you were there and that you were watching me sucking his dick or him fucking me. You are my husband, and I was not comfortable with you seeing me like that", Vivian replied timidly.

"Ok", I replied, disappointed.

"And that was all just a bit too much for me. You can't push me that fast. I felt very dirty sucking and getting fucked at the same time. It made me feel like a porno movie, and I did not like that. It made me feel awful. I felt like a whore. So, again, I am very happy we experienced that together, and I am very happy that you got to see it and it made you happy, but please don't ask me to do that again."

THE NEW VIVIAN - RECLAIMING SEXUALITY

Vivian had extended herself and pushed her personal boundaries to make me happy, but then she proclaimed to me how it did not make her feel good about herself. It destroyed me that I made her feel terrible about herself. While the threesome with Dante was a monumental event for us, it did not make me feel good that she thought the way she did. I knew she was not ready for that. I knew it was too soon for her. To be clear, I did my fair share of beating myself up over it. I let Dante push her too far too soon. What was important was that she openly communicated her feelings to me on our taboo act of ménage à trois, that I heard her fully, that I respected her feelings, and that I did not ask her to do that with Dante ever again.

Empowerment of Saying 'No'

Dante was looking forward to hearing Vivian's reaction to her first threesome and expected her to tell him how much she loved having sex with two men at the same time. You can imagine his level of disappointment, which admittedly matched my own when she delivered the identical message to him that she had passed on to me the night before. He started working overtime on us separately, trying his best to convince her to give it one more try before deciding to scrap it forever. I knew it was best for me to stay out of it. Dante was working on her almost daily, filling me in on what he was proposing to her. She was coming home at night and not saying a word to me as usual, but this time, I felt sympathetic to her because I knew the tremendous pressure he was putting on her shoulders, but I was not supposed to know per her rules.

Dante supported Vivian in her objection to "sucking and fucking" two guys at once. He comforted her and convinced her that it was all too much and "we" should not have asked her to jump in head first into a rendezvous like that. I stress the "we" in that sentence because, as I remember it, it was entirely his idea, but I digress. He informed me that he was talking to her about his new brilliant idea to get the three of us together, and he felt that it was going well. He expressed to her that he wanted her to perform with him in front of me. He wanted me to sit in a chair this time and not be physically involved. His vision was the two of them getting naked in front of me. His desire was to own her and direct her to satisfy his every need while I looked on. I would not be allowed to touch her at all. I would have no interaction with her until he had his fill of using her, and she was finished doing all that he commanded. To my surprise, he said that the thought intrigued her, or so he thought. This entire idea worried me a bit because this did not sound like something Vivian would agree to. She had made it clear to me that she did not like me watching her. I was concerned that he would convince her of this, and I was apprehensive because of the effect this could potentially have on her mentally. He said she was on board and would talk to me that evening.

Vivian arrived home that evening and mentioned not a word of Dante's sexual plan for her. Our nightly routine of dinner, dishes, and bedtime stories came and went when Vivian approached me with a warm hug and asked if we could relax in the hot tub with a drink, which prompted me to retrieve two cocktail glasses from the cabinet and the bottle of vodka.

We sat in the hot water gazing up at Orion's Belt when Vivian finally mentioned her lover.

"So, Dante has been writing me this week", she began.

"Oh yeah? Are you going to try and meet him soon for that dick?" I asked her playfully.

"Well, I was trying to, but he doesn't seem like he wants to meet for that", she replied disappointingly.

"What do you mean, baby?"

"Well, I was trying to ask about a night this week that we could meet, but he doesn't seem interested in just me. He keeps only talking about the three of us again. I told him I don't fucking want that, like I told you, but he keeps forcing it", she replied angrily.

"What? I thought we were clear with him that you did not want to have a threesome ever again?" I chimed in.

"He does not want a threesome. He wants to fuck me while you sit and watch, and you are not allowed to do anything to me at all", Vivian reacted.

"Well, that sounds really hot, actually!" I laughed.

"Well, not to me. I told you I am not comfortable with any of this, and I am certainly not comfortable with you just watching me get fucked, either. I know you want these things, but I don't know if I can make you happy like this. It gives me anxiety to think about it."

I could see she was distraught by this. Dante had misread her. She was not intrigued whatsoever.

"Baby, it's ok", I told her while stroking her wet hair. "You know where I stand on all of this now. I absolutely do not want you to do anything you do not want to do ever again", I whispered.

"I don't know. I am terrified to speak. I have to be so scared to say any of this to you or him. I don't want to be in trouble", she said with her voice quivering.

This sentence broke my heart. What had I put her through? I felt nothing but anguish for her.

"Vivian. I do not ever want you to feel that way ever again. I wanted this for you so you could have freedom and be happy with new experiences. If that is not what is happening, then what is the point?" I asked her.

"I feel so much under pressure that I can't breathe sometimes. I don't want to disappoint you, but I have had enough. I can't do this anymore. Dante is very demanding of me and my time at work. He is demanding of me all the time. I am not saying that I am not open to doing this another time with someone else, but for right now, I think I need a break. It's all been too much for me right now, and I just need time to think about what works for me and what I want."

"Absolutely love. I never want you to feel like this ever again. All I care about is your happiness and what you want", I concluded.

"Ok. I will tell him tomorrow that I need a break for a while, and I will decide if I want to continue this more with him", she concluded sounding very relieved.

Vivian did just that. The next morning, Vivian took back her empowerment. She took back her power from Dante when she told him that she was done for the foreseeable future with him, which left his mind boggled. He did not see that coming, I fear. She took her power back from me when she told me the night before that she would no longer be doing things to make me or any man happy. She would now be living for herself and her experiences that made her happy, and I could not have been more proud of her for it.

Empowerment of Saying 'Yes'

When I woke up that next afternoon, I received a text from a thoroughly confused Dante. He was less than pleased with his conversation with my dear wife earlier that morning. Talk about shock and awe! There he was, believing he was about to fuck her good in front of me, to being slapped with the harsh reality that she may never let him touch her ever again. Apparently, he still pleaded his case for the two of them to play together after she told him she was uncomfortable with his proposed plan for the three of us. It was too late for him. Vivian found her empowerment and stood up for herself and stood up against the both of us. I was happy, and he was disappointed. He felt confident that she would be back around because he was the wolf after all, and in his eyes, she was just the powerless sheep. I told him that I hoped she might continue with him, but the truth was that I only wanted what was best for Vivian.

Later on that evening, she told me how the conversation with him had gone that morning and that she needed her space and needed to focus on work so she would not be answering him as much, if at all. He had left that part out when we talked earlier that day. I wrapped my arms around her and kissed her forehead.

"I am very proud of you, baby. I know this hasn't been an easy situation for you, and it wasn't an easy decision either", I told her lovingly.

"You're not mad at me?" she questioned.

"Mad at you? Not at all, my dear. We have had some amazing experiences lately that most people never get to live through. How could I be mad at you? I always only wanted the best for you", I reminded her.

"Ok, thank you for saying that. I was worried you were mad or disappointed. I know you want all this for me, but I just need a little break. I am not saying we can never try this again, but just not with Dante. Maybe we can find another guy sometime later when I am more comfortable. For now, I just want to focus on our relationship with Nate and Jennifer", she replied.

"Oh, you still want to continue with them?" I asked happily surprised.

"Yes! I really like them both, and I am getting more comfortable with the thought of you and Jennifer together. Maybe we can see if Nate will ever be able to hang out with me alone, too, so that will make you happy. I think we should continue to hang out with them and see what happens with all of that", she added.

"Well then, I didn't expect that. You just made me super hard, baby. Let's get you upstairs and get you naked!" I said grinning at her.

VIVIAN'S EMPOWERMENT

From housewife to hotwife, Vivian's evolution was a sight to behold. The woman I saw before me was not the housewife I had married but an empowered, confident goddess. Vivian was no longer the shy and timid housewife who was terrified of opening up her own sexual expression and opening up her marriage to the excitement of other people. She had put her trust in me and dipped her toes into the hot water of playing with two couples in a hot tub as I watched on. She had stepped out on the edge of monogamy by having multiple sexual encounters with another man, including one with her husband, and did not slip and fall. Vivian could have continued her sexual relationship with Dante at the behest of her own values and well-being just to please him and me, but it would have been detrimental to her mental health. Vivian chose her own path, however. She chose empowerment. She chose to make her own decisions. She chose to explore her sexual being as she saw fit. She chose to cut ties with Dante and Paulina entirely. She chose to continue to explore her sexual appetite with Nate and Jennifer. She chose to no longer be a helpless sheep. She chose to be a powerful lioness.

Defining Empowerment

What exactly is empowerment anyhow? I have heard the term numerous times in the workplace regarding management empowering employees as a career development tool. I might delegate some tasks to my subordinates, such as creating the work schedule, approving timecards, or even assisting in performance appraisals to empower an employee who may develop into a leadership role one day. But what about female empowerment, and how does it relate to Vivian in this scenario? According to the Cambridge Dictionary, empowerment is "the process of gaining freedom and power to do what you want or to control what happens to you" (https://dictionary.cambridge.org).

That definition is quite polarizing and almost comes off as two separate meanings in the case of Vivian's story. There is one keyword in there that defines the entire word "empowerment", in my opinion, and it may not be what you think.

The majority of you will believe that the meaning of empowerment is having freedom and power. This can be true to a certain extent until I raise this question. Was Vivian truly empowered when I gave her the freedom and power to have sex with whomever she wanted eight years prior? Sure, I empowered her, but did she accept it? Did she enjoy her freedom and power and have sexual relations with whomever she wanted? The answer is no. Did she enjoy her freedom and power when she lowered herself to having a sexual relationship with a man that she essentially felt pressured into? The answer is, yet again, no. The keyword in that definition of empowerment is not freedom or power; it is control. When Vivian took control of what happened to her, she truly gained her power and freedom. Vivian was finally empowered.

Embracing Body Positivity

The ripple effects of Vivian's new empowerment were astonishing. In my eyes, she was a new woman but was only starting to see herself differently in her own mind. No change in Vivian was grander or more impactful than the surge in her self-confidence. There were apparent changes in her self-confidence in terms of her feeling powerful and comfortable standing up for herself and not fearing the possible backlash of terminating a sexual relationship that was not serving her anymore. But then, there were other, not-so-obvious changes that were rising to the surface of her confidence levels. All the attention and adoration she received from Nate, Jennifer, Paulina, and even Dante fueled her body positivity.

What Vivian received from this improbable adventure was something that she could not have ever imagined in her wildest of dreams. As I am sure a majority of women who have been married for more than a decade with children can relate to, Vivian had grown complacent in her sexuality. In her own words, she felt "like a mom" who had lost her sexual confidence and prowess. Vivian felt that the level of attractiveness and sexual magnetism that she had enjoyed in her youth had dissipated and was traded in for a minivan, toddler toys, and unimaginative and non-explorative sex with her husband forever. Oh, the power of what compliments and validation from others can do to a woman's confidence, no matter how shallow that might seem on the surface.

Flirting and being hit on by a bartender in front of her husband made her feel desired again. Meeting a new dominant man for a taboo sexual encounter made her feel vibrant and alive again. She felt erotic again. She began to see her body in a more positive light than when she felt she was "just a mom". Something extraordinary occurs to you when you start to feel liberated enough to feel comfortable being seen naked by others who want to taste you, devour you, and make your body shudder with pleasure. Vivian's self-confidence in her body image started to shine through as she began updating her wardrobe to sexy short skirts and tight leather pants, coupled with jaw-dropping lingerie and thong panties. When Vivian looked in the mirror now, she saw a brand-new woman. She saw a sexually liberated woman.

Empowerment and Liberation

Liberation is a funny thing when it comes to opening up a marriage and empowering your wife to sleep with anyone that she desires. Most people I tell this story to fall into the misguided category of believing it was me who liberated Vivian and broke the chains to her sexual freedom, but they are all incorrect. It was Vivian who liberated herself. It was Vivian who finally found the way to unlock the chains of her own mind as she guided herself to the freedom that I only showed her existed. She had finally reached the level of safety in our marriage to use the key of empowerment that I slid into her hand; the only question was how far she would go before locking herself up again.

Vivian was displaying a new sense of pride in her freedom that left me feeling euphoric. She started to express herself more vocally when it came to her sexual attraction to others. She had begun to lose her inhibitions with me. Vivian no longer felt angst about discussing men that she wouldn't mind letting fuck her, and she was even starting to show more allure toward women. It brought us much closer indeed. Vivian was beginning to show signs of embracing her true self for the first time, probably ever, and that was more than evident the day she was talking to my brother Alexandre and his wife, Katie.

The four of us had a few drinks one night when the topic of Gerard Butler came up, and Vivian suddenly got courageous in front of them both.

"I loveeeeee Gerard Butler. He is so damn hot. I would not kick him out of my bed!" Vivian said with a laugh.

"Wow, you aren't worried about saying that in front of Sebastian?" Katie asked her while sending a glance my way.

"Fuck no. Sebastian doesn't care. He actually encourages me", she quipped back.

"Really?" Katie asked, stunned, and glanced at me again. I shook my head slowly and made a face that told Katie it was not a big deal to me.

Vivian responded, "Yes, and I love it! I am totally free to say what I want in front of him and not worry about it at all. I love my freedom! He supports me fully, and it's pretty awesome."

"Wow, that is pretty interesting. I can't imagine having that freedom from Alexandre", Katie said while Alexandre made a face that displayed his agreement with that assessment.

I stared at Vivian with so much admiration, pride, and love. I felt pure happiness inside that she truly loved the freedom that she now lived, and she was so proud to have something that she now understood other wives did not have. This was my precious gift to her that she had graciously accepted. I thought there was no way our lives could radically change more than they already had, but later that night, I received a text from Nate that proved me wrong. My job now was to ensure that Vivian would not reinstall the chains and padlock of self-confinement and throw away the key.

UNEXPECTED ENDEAVORS

Our life was as stable as it had been in a very long time. Vivian was no longer a practicing hotwife, but only because the right man had not come along and swept her off her feet since Dante was jettisoned out of her life. Her happiness and self-confidence were at an all-time high though, which was fantastic. We continued to have dates with Nate and Jennifer, and Vivian continued to be pleased by them both at the same time. We even progressed to Nate going down on Vivian and making her orgasm profusely while Jennifer and I watched and made out with each other. It was hot as fuck! We were all having a great time together every couple of weeks, and Vivian and I even carried out discussions on the topic of this potentially leading to full swap sex with them eventually. Vivian was not ready for that yet. She was not ready for me to have sex with another woman, but did admit that she felt we would eventually progress to that someday. I was not as sure about that, but it did not matter to me. I was having a blast with my wife, and I thoroughly enjoyed watching them pleasure her. I figured we would keep it at this level until our relationship with them would eventually fade, so you can imagine my surprise when Nate texted me asking me if Vivian and I would like to go to a swinger's sex club with them.

Dreams and Desires

Nate was more than excited to tell me about the swinger club he just discovered online, which was only an hour away from us. It was called Dreams and Desires and he asked if I had heard of it. I had not, but I was super intrigued. He sent me some pictures of the club he found online, which looked amazing. No people were in the pictures; they were just shots of the empty club, but it looked beautiful nonetheless. This place had it all, including a large dance floor. Vivian loved to dance. Nate had pleaded with Jennifer to go check out the club, but she was not comfortable with that idea at all. He then filled me in on a critical piece of information: Jennifer had finally agreed to go, but only if Vivian and I agreed to go with them. I laughed at the premise but promised Nate that I would do my best to make his "dreams and desires" come true.

I was rather nervous when I first brought this up with Vivian for fear of her reaction, but at this point, I was becoming a professional at presenting her with terrifying requests. Her response was on par with what I had expected; she reacted in shock and let her emotions take over her initially.

"A sex club? I hope you joking right now! You think I am going to go there and just fuck a bunch of people or something?" she asked incredulously.

"No, I do not think that", I said calmly. "Nate wants to go check it out and see what it is all about, and Jennifer would only feel comfortable if we went with them. I would not expect you to do anything, baby."

"Then what is the point of going? To watch other people have sex?" she questioned me.

"I don't know Vivian. Just to go and support them, I guess? It might be fun. Nate sent me a few pictures. I can show you at least. It looks cool, and there is a big dance floor, too", I replied.

"Oh, there is a dance floor?" Vivian's stance softened.

"Yeah, check these out!"

After we looked at the pictures together, Vivian nodded her head as if she was thinking and contemplating.

"Ok, if I can dance there, then I will go, but that is all I am doing. I am not doing anything else but dancing only!" she concluded.

"Oh, yeah, let's go dance and have fun. I know you always complain that I do not dance, so I promise I will dance with you." I smiled as I pulled her closer to me.

"And, maybe some hot guy or hot girl will want to dance with you too. Maybe they will try to make out with you, though", I added as I smiled.

"Well, yeah, I guess that will be fine too. But I am doing nothing more than that!" Vivian added.

Nate and Jennifer were both ecstatic that Vivian agreed to check out Dreams and Desires with them. Nate was convinced that this would change our lives and our relationship with them forever. We picked the date and booked rooms in the same hotel near the club since it was such a long drive for all of us. When the night finally arrived, the four of us met for dinner beforehand. Vivian and Jennifer were both visibly nervous already. I was also very nervous, but I hid it better than they did. After dinner, we went back to our rooms to shower and change. Vivian stepped out of the bathroom and looked delicious as hell. She still had nervousness written all over her face but kept saying that she was excited to dance, so I assured her that we would tear up the dance floor.

We decided to drive separately to the club and meet Nate and Jennifer there in case they found anyone they wanted to hook up with and needed to leave. We did not want them to be bound to us. It was a short five-minute drive from our hotel to Dreams and Desires, which was nice, so I was not too concerned about having a few drinks. I needed a beer or two just to muster up the courage to get out of the car and walk into the place. We arrived in the grim parking lot, but it felt as if we were not in the correct place. The warehouse-looking building that stood in front of us with no sign or windows did not look very inviting. Vivian's tenseness grew. We walked toward the only door on the side of the building and stopped as we were unsure if this was right. It was very inconspicuous, to say the least. That is when we saw the door open, and a sexy man and woman came outside and walked to their car. We were in the right spot, and a slight sense of relief came over me, but it dissipated fast as I realized it was time to walk in.

Vivian and I took deep breaths as I gripped the door handle and pulled the heavy metal door open towards me. We were immediately greeted by the rhythmic sound of thumping techno music. As we walked into the darkly lit first room, I saw people standing in line at a window and a muscular man guarding the door to the next entrance with "SECURITY" written across his black t-shirt. I took another deep breath. This was it. We walked up to the window hand in hand as the half-naked woman on the other side asked if it was our first time. We were asked to sign waivers and pay the fees to become members before the large security man patted us both down and escorted us to a little room to his left. All new members were required to watch a video of rules and etiquette before they were allowed to enter.

When the video concluded, our security man escorted us out of the room and opened the door to the actual club. We were hit with the increased sound of techno music and strobe lights. Vivian and I were now members of a swinger's club. I never in a million years saw that one coming. Vivian gripped my hand tight as we strolled into the larger room. The first thing we noticed was there were sexy people all around us, and most of them were half-naked, if not entirely naked. We were both mesmerized. Directly in front of us were tables with booths where people sat, drank, and talked. Beyond the tables sat an empty dance floor, but a dance floor like no other. This dance floor had a giant television screen hanging above it with pornography videos playing. I pointed that out to Vivian. She was less than impressed.

To the left, I saw the beaded-off VIP section that had a few black leather couches where some people were sitting and talking. To the left of them, there was a pool table with people actually shooting pool. I found this to be most interesting because I didn't think even the most avid pool player in the world would want to play nine ball with a room full of half-naked people and porno on the television. To our right were six cabana beds with curtains that aligned against the wall. There were people already sitting on them talking, so I figured you would have to get here much earlier to claim those. We both looked at each other, and I gave her a kiss as we decided we both needed a drink before sitting at a vacant table to wait for our friends. Vivian looked highly overwhelmed.

After about ten minutes of watching all the gorgeous people walk by us, Nate and Jennifer entered the door. I ran over to them and brought them back to where Vivian sat. We were both so relieved to see them but gave them a moment to adjust as they looked around the giant room in bewilderment. Jennifer looked fine as hell. She was wearing a very open and revealing shirt, with a bra that pushed her cleavage up and out into your face. She was stunning, as usual. After they gained their bearings, we all grabbed another drink and decided to explore the back side of the club.

There was so much eye candy to ogle at as we passed the cabana beds and made our way down a narrow-looking hallway. There were boobs, asses, cocks, and vaginas everywhere. It was like a surreal dream that I never thought I would find myself in. Along the left side of the hallway were rooms with beds where people would go to play. All the doorways were equipped with chains hanging from them, and all the rooms had windows. As they explained to us on our new swinger orientation, you could play in any room that was empty. You had the option of closing the door and the curtain on the window for maximum privacy. You could open the curtain to let the voyeurs get a peek if you were so inclined. If you felt friskier, you could open the door entirely but put the chain up so people could watch but not enter. An open door with the chain down meant you were inviting absolutely anyone to enter that room to join you. It was early, so all the rooms were still empty.

As we neared the end of the hallway, we could see the bathrooms were straight ahead of us, with an option to continue to the left and the right. To the left, the hallway and sex rooms continued in a big horseshoe shape that looped back to the dance floor. To the right, we found the giant dungeon room. Here, we saw more rooms along the wall, with some couches scattered about. The difference here was the giant cross shaped like an X set up to the left of the room, with other stations nearby, where people could be whipped with an audience looking on. The cross looked very imposing, and they were strapping someone to it as we walked in. They had their back turned to the audience, and they were naked, with their hands and feet shackled to the cross. Then the other person began to whip their back and ass with various tools while curious minds watched on. Vivian seemed intrigued with this room, but Nate and Jennifer wanted to move on.

As we walked back to the dance floor, Vivian told me she wanted to dance, but no one was out there yet, and I was not one to start a trend. Jennifer wanted to get more drinks and sit at a table between the dance floor and the cabana beds, so that is what we did. Vivian looked displeased, and an uncomfortable look on her face told me she was not enjoying this experience. After about ten minutes, Jennifer stated that she needed to go pee, so Nate got up and went with her, leaving us alone. Vivian stared at the one naked woman that was now dancing all alone on the dance floor with the backdrop of people fucking on the television screen.

"I'm not sure how comfortable I am here", Vivian yelled over the loud music. "I wanted to dance."

"I know, darling, but there is nobody out there yet. It's still early. Unless you want to dance with the naked woman", I joked. Vivian did not find my response amusing.

As I turned my head to the left, I saw a couple sitting on a cabana bed, and they were having themselves a great time. The man was leaning against some pillows with his pants down to his ankles. His partner was on her knees with her hand stroking his thick hard cock. They both stared out at all the people until she lowered her mouth down over his shaft. She sucked him slowly while his hand gripped her head, guiding her up and down on his cock. I tapped Vivian's arm and pointed in that direction, only for her to glance for a second and turn her head back the other way, almost in disgust. I could see this was turning into a big mistake. I went and got us both another drink to try and ease her discomfort, but I could tell it was all for not.

"Can we go find where the hell they went?" she asked me angrily.

I took her by the hand and led her toward the bathrooms again. The crowd was filling up, and walking freely was getting more complex. As we slowly made our way down the darkly lit corridor, we turned to the left to see another woman engaged in oral sex with a man with the door open for our viewing pleasure. The gorgeous woman was on her knees, staring up at her man with her lips wrapped around his thick meat. The top of her dress was pulled down, exposing her giant breasts, while her partner lightly pinched her nipples. Vivian wanted to keep moving. As we neared the women's bathroom, we saw Nate and Jennifer talking with a beautiful couple in the corner of the area. We came to a stop and stood there watching them, not really sure how we should proceed.

"Damn, that is a hot couple they are talking to", I said to Vivian.

She glared at them briefly before turning her head in the opposite direction. I recognized the expression on her face as she diverted her attention back down the empty corridor toward the club's entrance. Unfortunately, I knew what was coming next.

"I don't want to be here anymore. I want to go to the hotel", her quivering voice said to me the split second before she darted off in the direction of the exit, leaving me standing there alone and confused.

"Vivian! Vivian, stop!" I shouted to her before finally catching up to her.

I put my hand on her shoulder to slow her progress, "Vivian, what the hell are you doing?"

She turned, revealing her teary eyes.

"Can we just leave, please? I don't want to be here!"

"Vivian, why are you crying? I am so confused what is happening here. What exactly is the problem?" I asked, both agitated and confused.

"I just want to leave. Is that alright?" she asked as she began crying more.

"Well, yeah, I mean, we can leave, but I am so confused as to why. You were just fine. What the hell happened that you are this emotional out of nowhere?" I questioned.

"Do I have to have a reason to want to leave? You begged me to come here even though you know I didn't want to. I told you I wanted to dance, but this is all too much for me. I am not comfortable with all this sex stuff everywhere. And then we came here with them, and they just ditch us right away? Jennifer is all over that other girl and basically ignoring me like I am trash or something. I am not going to stand here and be ignored and watch that. I am better than that. I am not comfortable, and I want to leave! You can stay here and have fun. I can go to the hotel by myself. Just let me leave, please".

"Vivian, you are being ridiculous. I am not staying here without you, but we can't just leave them like this. We came here together!"

"Just text Nate and blame me that I need to go. I really don't care. They will be fine. I do not want to talk to them. I don't want them to see me emotional like this", she snapped at me.

"Well, I am sorry, but you have thirty seconds to get your shit together because Jennifer just spotted me, and she is waving to me for us to go over there and join them."

Exhibitionist Sex Angel

I waved back to Jennifer and held up my index finger, signaling that we would be there in a minute, as Vivian did her best to wipe away the tears as best as she could without totally obliterating her mascara. While she worked to wipe away her tears, there was no way to wipe away the look on her face. Jennifer had waited for us long enough and decided it was time to make her way to us.

"She is coming", I alerted Vivian.

"Fucking great", she responded.

"He guys, y'all need to come join us so I can introduce you to our new friends", Jennifer said excitedly until she saw our demeanor. "What's going here?" she asked, sobering her tone.

"Not much", Vivian answered, "I am not sure I am feeling this place. It's a bit too much for me."

"Yeah, I get that. Are you ok? What happened?" Jennifer asked while touching Vivian's hair.

"Nothing. I am just really overwhelmed and not sure I want to stay", Vivian admitted while avoiding eye contact with Jennifer.

"Ok, well shoot, here comes Nate with this couple that we just met that are super nice. I will pull him aside and let him know that we have to leave."

"No, it's fine, really. Just me and Sebastian will go back to the hotel. I don't want to make you leave. You should stay and have fun with them", Vivian added snarkily as Nate approached with the new couple behind him.

"What's up?" Nate asked me and nodded with a large grin on his face. Jennifer knew it was time for her to take over the situation and try to save the night. She grabbed Vivian by the hand.

"Guys, these are our friends that we came here with. This is Vivian, and this is her husband, Sebastian", Jennifer announced with her big smile. She turned and faced us, "This is Tom and Brittany, our new friends!"

Vivian and I exchanged handshakes and pleasantries with Jennifer's new catch. Tom was a good-looking man with a beard that I assumed Vivian would find attractive, but the prize of this catch was Brittany. She had sexy, flowing blonde hair and wore the tightest white dress imaginable. It put all her assets on full display. Jennifer did her best to catch Vivian up on all she had learned about her new friends. Jennifer was so good at that. She knew everything about them already. How long had they been married, what they did for work, how many kids they had, how old they were, and the fact that it was only the second time they had gone to the club. Their first night happened to be the night before. They had to drive over two hours to get there, so getting a room for two nights and going to the club on Friday and Saturday was worth it. They said they loved it so much the night before they just had to come back. While Brittany was finishing that sentence, the trajectory of the evening and our lives would be forever altered.

An adorable girl with blonde pigtails, wearing glasses, Daisy Duke shorts, and a little white tank top, walked up behind Brittany and tapped her shoulder. Brittany turned to her, yelled, "OMG", and hugged the girl.

"I can't believe you are here again tonight too!" Brittany said to her.

"Yeah, that was not my plan, but my husband had to work, so I said fuck it! I am going back tonight!" the adorable blonde girl exclaimed.

Brittany turned toward us all, "You guys, this is Lily. We met her and her husband here last night. It was their first time coming here too, so we instantly clicked! I can't believe you are here again tonight, too!" she said, turning back toward Lily.

"I was not going to come, and then I got here, but I was not going to stay. I was actually about to leave, and then I was like, wait, I think I know those two", Lily said.

"Well, I am glad you came over! These are our new friends", Brittany announced to her while gliding her hand toward us like a magician does during a big trick reveal.

Of course, Nate and Jennifer shook hands and talked to her first. Then adorable Lily smiled at me as we shook hands and said it's nice to meet you. I am a sucker for pigtails and glasses, so I was smitten. Lily approached Vivian last, the same Vivian who, at the moment, was looking very unapproachable and miserable. Lily smiled at Vivian as they shook hands.

The five of us stood in that little section of the corridor for what felt like twenty minutes, just talking and getting to know each other. Jennifer was all over Brittany and Tom, yapping away and still asking them a million questions. Nate would interject now and then, and then he would look at me and smile now and then, to which I returned a smile. He and I were in heaven. Amidst all that, and the chaos of the techno music and naked people passing by, there was Lily and Vivian. Vivian and Lily. I was a spectator. It was like a cat-and-mouse game. Lily was all about Vivian; that was obvious, but Vivian was still a bit guarded from all that had just gone down minutes ago. For each minute that passed, however, I could see Vivian would soften. Lily complimented her on her outfit. Vivian softened. Lily told her how much she loved her accent. Vivian softened. Lily reached up and lightly rubbed two fingers on the side of her shoulder. Vivian handed me her cup and asked me to get her a drink. I asked Lily if she would like a drink, to which she smiled and said, "Yes, please". I was gone.

I could not get those two fucking drinks fast enough. Through the crowds to the entrance, I scurried, making my way through the sea of boobs to the bar. With two ice-cold beverages in my hand, I glided my way back to our slice of heaven in the corridor, only to find Vivian and Lily had disappeared. Jennifer informed me that they had gone to the bathroom together. Patiently, I waited as I talked to Brittany. She was exquisite and super nice, but I did not feel a spark between her, Tom, and us. I could see, however, that there was a great connection between them and our play friends, which did not bother me in the slightest. As I talked to Brittany, I could see my wife and Lily returning from the bathroom, but much to my surprise, they held hands as they approached me.

"Hello, ladies!" I said as I handed them their drinks.

Vivian smiled as they continued holding hands and sipped their drinks. Jennifer noticed the hand-holding, as well, but did not get upset or jealous. Conversely, she gravitated to Brittany and stood very close to her. Jennifer knew very well what the next move was, and within a few minutes, she took the bull by the horns.

"Hey y'all, I am thinking we should go check out the dance floor!" Jennifer spoke wild-eyed.

"I've been wanting to dance all night", Vivian responded with a smile.

"Will you dance with me, Vivian?" asked Lily.

"Of course!" answered Vivian, still smiling.

"Come on!" yelled Jennifer, turning down the corridor hand in hand with Brittany.

Nate, Tom, and I smiled at each other as we followed our wives happily. Nate and I fist-bumped each other. When we reached the dance floor, we men found a spot against the wall that would allow us to enjoy the view of our women without being in the way of others. I watched Vivian's body move with Lily's under the strobe lights. They were so beautiful. They danced in rhythm while still holding hands and holding their drinks in the other. Within minutes, Jennifer and Brittany began making out as they grinded on each other's bodies, which caught the attention of adorable Lily. Within seconds, Lily and Vivian were kissing. They danced as their tongues swirled together in unison. The four women danced and kissed for a few minutes until they started talking and hugging each other. That's when they began walking back towards us, still holding hands with their dance partners.

"So, we were thinking we should get out of here and go back to the hotel!' Jennifer screamed over the music to me and Nate.

I looked at Vivian, who was having her hair played with by adorable Lily, "Yeah, you want to leave?"

"Yeah, let's go after we finish these drinks?" Vivian shouted.

"Do you have drinks in your room?" Brittany asked Jennifer.

"Yes, we have tons!" Jennifer responded.

"Awesome!" replied Brittany.

The girls finished their drinks, and we made our way to the parking lot. Outside, Lily asked if she could ride with us rather than drive herself. She was feeling a bit tipsy and felt that was not the right choice, to which Vivian and I both agreed. At the hotel, we all decided to go hang out in Nate and Jennifer's room as they had a master suite that had much more space than us. I did not have any time to talk to Vivian to ensure how comfortable she was with all of this, but the smile on her face as she and Lily walked through the hotel hallways told me she was feeling just fine.

In their room, things started to heat up immediately. We put on some music, all made a drink. The master suite was a great idea because of the couch, the chair, and the king bed that was around the corner out of view. Our room was tiny, with just two queen beds. After a few minutes of us all taking a shot, Jennifer again knew what to do.

"Hey, y'all. I have a great idea that I think you will all like!" she said, smiling. "Let's have all the men stand where they are, and let's have all the women kiss them and then rotate", she added.

"Ok, but there are more women here than men", Nate responded.

"I will sit out the first round, then mix in", Lily added.

"Perfect, let's start with our men", said Jennifer.

Vivian came to me. This was my chance to catch up with her.

"Are you alright with all of this?" I whispered to her as quietly as I could. She smiled and nodded.

"Ok, go!" yelled Jennifer.

Vivian and I kissed. We started laughing halfway through, which I assumed was caused by the ridiculousness of the middle school game that we were playing.

"Ok, switch!" yelled Jennifer after about thirty seconds.

"I love you", I whispered to Vivian.

"I love you, baby", she whispered back.

And with that, she was gone. Jennifer came to me. We were familiar enough that kissing her felt normal. I opened my eyes and saw Vivian sitting out this round, sipping her drink. She glanced at me and Jennifer, but then diverted her attention to Lily and Tom.

"Did you miss me?" Jennifer asked me.

"Of course I did", I answered, causing her to smile before yelling, "Switch!"

Brittany came up to me, and we kissed. It did not feel right, but I tried to turn the passion on for her. There was still a disconnect. I realized that night that sometimes people just do not click sexually. Vivian was now kissing Tom, and it felt like she was feeling the same vibe.

"I like kissing you", Brittany said to me.

"I like kissing you too", I said, smiling back.

"Switch!" Jennifer bellowed.

Lily approached me, "Hi", and she smiled.

"I have been waiting for this all night", I whispered.

"Me too", she whispered back.

Her tongue entered my mouth. I kissed her wildly with the intent of letting her know my full intentions for her that evening. She got the message. She paused our kiss to remove her glasses and place them on the desk behind me. I grabbed the back of her head, pulling her into me, as my hands began feeling her amazing breasts and the inside of her thighs. Her hand gravitated to the boner that was protruding from my pants.

"Ok, the end! Everyone kissed everyone, correct?" Jennifer questioned.

"I did not kiss everyone!" answered Lily as she turned to my wife.

Lily took charge, and things turned crazy from that moment forward. She did things to Vivian that I never anticipated. Ever! This sex angel swooped into our lives and changed us both forever. Lily placed both hands on Vivian's face and passionately kissed her while the five of us watched. Her left hand slowly moved to the back of Vivian's head, and she grabbed a fist full of her blonde hair within her fingertips while her right hand slowly made its way to her tits. Lily squeezed her breast briefly before moving her hand in between Vivian's legs. Vivian's kissing sped up, and her arms went up onto Lily's shoulders, wrapped around her neck, with her left hand on the back of Lily's head. The two women pulled each other's mouths deeper into their own.

Lily's hands started moving toward each other until they settled on the base of Vivian's shirt, where, after a slight pause, she began to lift her shirt up and off over her head. My eyes were glued to them, minus the brief glance I gave to our friends, who were all watching and smiling with eagerness to see how far this might go. Vivian giggled as Lily unclasped her bra, slid the straps down off her shoulders, and let the black lace fall to the hotel room carpet. Lily's hands squeezed Vivian's tits together as her mouth frantically licked and sucked on her erect nipples. Vivian decided to return the favor.

Vivian removed the little white tank top that we all wanted to see hit the floor, revealing Lily's huge and supple breasts. They were beautiful and perky, as Lily was over twenty years younger than Vivian. Vivian kissed and sucked on her nipples in a much slower and methodical manner, truly savoring each flick of her tongue. Lily threw her head back in ecstasy and moaned as she scratched her nails into Vivian's bare-skinned back. Vivian's mouth glided up Lily's chest as she dragged her tongue up her neck, finding its way back into Lily's mouth. The women hugged each other and rubbed their breasts together slowly. My eyes wandered over to the other side of the room to find Jennifer had Brittany pinned against the wall and they were making out passionately as well. Nate and Tom sat on the floor with their backs against the wall while they took in the shows around them.

My eyes shifted back to my love and her adorable Lily to find that Vivian's miniskirt was sliding down over her juicy ass and down her sexy long legs to join her shirt and bra on the floor. There Vivian stood in the center of the crowded hotel room in her thong and watched in amazement as Lily undid her own daisy dukes, slid them down to the floor, and revealed her beautiful, shaved pussy for all of us to see. They once again kissed like each was starving for the other. Lily stopped kissing Vivian and looked deep into her eyes.

"You are so fucking hot! I am so glad I met you tonight!" Lily said to her.

"I am glad too, and you are also so hot", Vivian said, giggling nervously.

Lily turned to the couch, removed two throw pillows, placed

them on the floor, knelt down on one of them, and stared up at Vivian.

She extended her hand to Vivian and said, "Join me, you sexy thing."

Vivian took Lily's hand and knelt on the pillow before her. Lily started kissing her again while both women ran their hands all over each other's bodies. Vivian's hand found its way to Lily's vagina while her fingers began to spread and explore the lips of her lovely flower. A large smile spread across Lily's face as she rose high on her knees, put her hands on Vivian's shoulders, and gently started pushing Vivian backward until she was lying on the carpet. Lily used both of her hands to grip the edges of Vivian's thong panties with her fingertips, and she began to pull them down slowly. Vivian again giggled her nervous laugh that I was accustomed to, but she then lifted her ass off of the floor so that Lily could remove those panties with ease. I decided to sit on the floor next to them with my drink in my hand and my hard cock in my pants.

Lily's mouth went to work. She slowly moved her tongue over the folds of Vivian's glistening vulva. She started at the bottom and worked her way up to Vivian's clitoris, which caused Vivian to moan loudly. Lily gently slid her fingers inside of my wife, which caused Vivian to grab Lily's hair and pull her face into her deeper. Vivian was trying to stay quiet, but that was nearly impossible when a sexy woman was going down on you in front of five other people. Lily was not tasting Vivian very long when Vivian began to raise her hips off the floor and grind her pussy into Lily's face. I knew what this meant and knew what was coming next.

Vivian took a deep breath and held it, causing her face to turn bright red, until she let it all out in a loud crescendo of moaning as her hips bucked in orgasmic rhythm.

"HOLY FUCK!!!!!" Vivian cried out in pure exhaustion, trying to catch her breath.

"Mmmm, you are so fucking delicious!" Lily exclaimed as her hands were rubbing up and down Vivian's legs.

"Y'all, that was fucking hot!" Jennifer called out.

Lying on the floor completely naked, Vivian covered her face in embarrassment, "Fuck, did that just happen?" She shook her head and laughed, "Oh hey, everyone, did you enjoy the show?"

The feedback she received was a unanimous and resounding "Fuck Yes!". I kissed her lips, and she laughed as I reassured her that it was hot as fuck.

"You came fucking hard, baby!" I told her. Lily smiled.

"Um, fuck yeah, I did. Holy fuck!" is all she could muster.

Out of nowhere, a topless Jennifer appeared next to Vivian on the floor, and the two of them started to kiss as their hands were all over each other's bodies. In a flash, Lily spread Vivian's legs wide up, which prompted Vivian to start to laugh as Jennifer's tongue swirled in her mouth. Lily worked on Vivian's pussy again, causing her to orgasm in record time. Poor Vivian was out of breath and thirsty, so I made her and Lily another drink. As we all had a drink, I noticed Brittany was now topless too, and she and Jennifer were lying on the floor kissing over against the wall. I looked at Nate and Tom and raised my glass to them.

"Holy fuck, boys!" I mouthed to them as they laughed and raised their glasses back to me.

I turned to Lily and asked her if it was ok that I go down on her to repay her for what she did to my wife. She politely declined and said maybe later, but there were no worries because she absolutely loves doing it, and Vivian was the most delicious she ever tasted. Lily and I toasted to that and took a sip of our drinks. Lily put her cup down and looked at Vivian, who was still sitting on the floor naked with her back against the wall.

"Vivian, I think you need to get on your hands and knees for me. I want to see that delicious ass", Lily directed her. It was almost as if she knew how much Vivian enjoyed doing what she was told.

"Oh, ok!" Vivian said as she laughed.

Vivian turned over to her hands and knees, and bent down to place her head on one of the pillows. Lily crawled up behind her slowly and began licking and fingering Vivian's pussy until she came yet again for the third time, which caused applause from the viewers in the room. Each orgasm got stronger and stronger, and Vivian got louder and louder. Lily seemed to be getting tired at that point as the time grew closer to 2 a.m. Lily got up off her knees and relaxed her naked body, lying on her back on the couch. I crept on the floor toward her and started to make out with her. She was a fantastic kisser. She was very skilled with her tongue. That was clear. I praised her for her incredible skills because Vivian had never cum so hard and so many times in one night.

Vivian joined me on her knees on the floor at the edge of the couch and started to kiss Lily, too. They smiled at each other just before Lily suggested that Vivian should sit on her face.

A fatigued Vivian climbed up onto the couch and positioned herself with her legs on each side of Lily's body. Her hands leaned up on the back of the couch as she lowered her pussy down on Lily's face one more time. This was the best view I had seen all night. I watched as Lily's tongue spread Vivian's lips and her fingers slid deep inside of her. In the bedroom around the corner, I could hear Brittany and Jennifer moaning loudly, with one of them climaxing, but I was not sure who it was. I looked at Nate and Tom, and they were still sitting on the floor, but this time, they had a perfect view of the work Lily was doing to my wife.

I decided it was time to involve myself just a little bit. I spread Vivian's ass cheeks wider for the men to gain the best view of my wife. I leaned over, and I started to lick Vivian's ass while Lily licked her pussy. Both of our tongues swirled in close proximity when I saw Lily looking at me. I glided my tongue to reach hers as we kissed and swirled them together before continuing to lick her ass and pussy. I slid my fingers inside of her at the same time that Lily had her fingers inside of her, and that was all Vivian could stand. Vivian's body shook and trembled with orgasm number four, causing her to collapse on top of Lily.

What a fantastic night that turned into. It was nearly 3 a.m. when we all decided to call it a night. Lily was putting her clothes back on when she turned to me and asked if she could stay in our room with us because she did not think she should drive. I reminded her that her car was at the club, and we agreed that I would drive her there in the morning to get it. Our room had two queen beds, so it worked out well. Vivian was too exhausted and drained to worry about putting on her clothes, so she decided to make her "walk of shame", as she calls it, and walked down the hallway of the hotel completely naked. I am sure she is still on their security footage somewhere. Vivian, Lily, and I had a great night's sleep in one bed together.

Choice That Changed Everything Forever

Later the next morning, the three of us awoke to a day of sunshine, headaches, and the thick tension of awkwardness with a naked woman that you just met the night before. Vivian had a tough time making eye contact with Lily, and they briefly said good morning to each other while she made her way to the bathroom. Ibuprofen and water helped with headaches, and sunglasses shielded our eyes from the sun. Lily and I did our best to cut through the awkwardness as I joked with her that she would have to forgive us for not knowing how to act the morning after our first threesome with a woman. She laughed when Vivian added that it was her first time having four orgasms in front of a group of people, but she was doing great so far. When we arrived at Lily's car, we hugged and exchanged our departing pleasantries when Lily asked us if we were on SLS and if we wanted to connect with her. I had no idea what SLS was, but she informed me that it was an app for swingers to connect with each other. I told her I would get that app and create an account for us immediately. She verbally told us her SLS ID name and told us to look her up and that she would love to hang out with us again. I was super excited about the prospect of us seeing her again, but I knew Vivian, and we had a lot of discussions to be had after that eventful evening. Luckily, we had an hour's drive ahead of us.

"So, that just happened!" Vivian joked with a smile.

"Yep, it sure did!" I retorted. "How are you feeling after cumming four or five times while being watched?" I added.

"Seven times max!" she laughed. I was relieved to see her in high spirits.

"I can't believe that fucking happened. You were so amazing last night, baby!" I said to her.

"You will have to fill me in on most of it because some of it was a blur, and I was like, what the fuck is happening to me?" Vivian admitted.

"Well, I can tell you that you came so fucking hard multiple times. I have never seen you cum that hard. It was incredible", I responded.

"I mean, she was fucking really good at what she does. She was amazing!" she said. "So, can you tell me everything that happened again? I had a great time with her, but I much more wish it was all private. I feel embarrassed that they were all watching or what were they doing the whole time?"

I spent the rest of that hour rehashing all the distinct memories of that night that I would carry with me forever. I was concerned that she would be mortified with reliving it all and might never want to go to the club ever again, but I was extremely relieved and excited when she took the opposite stance. Vivian admitted it was very exciting to be pursued by Lily. She said it was thrilling to be stripped naked and fucked by her in front of others. She said it was embarrassing, and she could not believe she did it, but it was awesome at the same time, and she was glad that she did. What truly amazed me the most was when she said that she liked Dreams and Desires and would like to go again, maybe just her and me alone however.

I was so damn excited when she mentioned that because before Lily swooped in and saved the night, I anticipated that she would never want to step foot into that place again. She admitted that Lily definitely saved the night for us and wanted to go home before Lily magically appeared, but to her credit, she was open to trying again. She confessed that she felt highly overwhelmed at first because it was such a tremendous shock to her, and perhaps she did not handle it as well as she thought she could have. Couple that with a bout of jealousy over feeling neglected by Jennifer and Nate, and she cascaded into overreaction. Hence, her current proposal that we go again by ourselves. Vivian said maybe we could attempt another visit sometime in the following month or two, and I was just fine with that idea.

When I returned home, I did not waste much time before I started trying to find the SLS app on my phone. I could not find it by searching in the app store on my iPhone, but a Google search led me to www.swinglifestyle.com, the self-proclaimed world's largest swinger community. On the homepage, I found the button to download the app, and within minutes, I was setting up yet another couple's account online. I never thought I would be doing that again after the debacle between me and Vivian on AFF. I must have learned my lessons from my previously highlighted mistakes around that profile because I went to Vivian immediately to gain her input on what we should write and what pictures of us we should post. I almost passed out from shock when she agreed that our profile could say that we were looking to meet other couples and encourage single men to say hello.

She was not very interested in trying to meet another single woman at that point, however. Yes, we slept naked with Lily just hours before, and yes, we both made out with her at the same time, but that was as far as it went. She was still not ready to see me with women, and I again was perfectly fine with that. Because of that, she did not want me to try and find Lily on the app, which made me feel bad. She again reiterated that she had a great time with Lily, and Lily was talented as fuck, but she was not sure she was ready to actively pursue that relationship. I got her to agree that if we ever ran into her at the club, we could see how it went, but only if we ran into her naturally. Time would only tell if Lily's talented mouth would ever taste Vivian's sweet juices again or if she was another sex angel that just magically appeared to help us transition to the next phase of our lives.

A week had gone by on the SLS app, and we had received messages from some nice-looking couples who were interested in Vivian, as well as messages from dozens of single men. There were some couples that piqued her interest, but almost all of them were looking for other couples. As far as the men were concerned, I did not bother showing her the messages from them as they were either not her type or looked like super egocentric douchebags that would write, "Hey, she is sexy!". That is until I got a message one night from a man named Richard.

Richard first caught my eye with the message he sent me because he actually wrote a small paragraph with some content that he actually put a little bit of thought into, which was refreshing.

"Hey guys! I am up late tonight and couldn't sleep, so I decided to check my phone for some reason, and I am really glad I did. I came across your profile and liked what I read. It sounds like we have a lot of things in common and I am thinking that I may actually be a great match for you guys if you would like to chat. The wife is absolutely beautiful, and you both seem really cool and look like a lot of fun. I think we may be looking for the same things based on what you wrote. Hopefully, we can chat a bit and see if I am correct. Have a great night! Richard."

It was not mind-blowing, but it was enough to entice me to look at his pictures and not immediately delete his message. Wow, I was very happy I did. Richard was very good-looking, but his pictures differed from others on these sites. His pictures were of him in natural settings. Him wearing a suite in his car. Him on a beach with his shirt on. No pictures of his dick. One picture with his shirt off, but he had a genuine-looking smile that I just knew Vivian would like. I decided to respond to him that night.

"Hey, Richard, Sebastian here. My wife is Vivian. Thank you for your message. Vivian is in bed sleeping, but I also could not sleep, so I was on my phone. I know the kind of men that my wife likes, and I think she will like you. I will show her your profile and

pictures and see if she likes you and would like to chat more. Is that fair? I will be honest, my wife is a bit picky, so I can't guarantee that she will be interested, but I think you are her style. I will let you know more tomorrow. Have a great night!".

I did not expect that Richard would write back to me within seconds, but I was excited that he did. We started chatting, and the conversation went on for a good thirty minutes. Throughout that duration, Richard showed me a great sense of humor and realness about him. He asked me why I thought he was her style. I told him she loved tattoos and she loved humor, which I now knew he possessed. *"Score two points! I have that going for me, at least!"* he wrote. Richard asked if we had been to Dreams and Desires because he was not sure if he had ever seen us there. I told him briefly about our Saturday night the week before, to which he replied, *"Fuck Yeah! Glad she had a great time!".* I told him that it was our first time, and he was amazed she had such a great experience on her first visit.

He told me that if she was interested in him and wanted to meet after I showed her his profile, maybe we could meet there the following Friday night. I did not know this then, but Friday nights were the only nights single men were allowed entry into the club. He was not allowed on Saturdays. I told him we had a deal on my end, but again, I also didn't want him to get his hopes up. I told him it might be too soon for us to go again since Vivian wanted to wait a month or two. He assured me whatever she wants is great. We agreed, and I told him that I was going to bed, and he said good night. I then received another message from Richard.

"Hey, Sebastian, I believe in full transparency, so I wanted to admit two things. One, my name is not Richard. It's a fake name I use until I get to know people and trust them. My name is Mateo, LOL".

Mateo actually made a lot more sense to me than Richard. His dark olive skin complexion in his pictures did not scream Richard.

"Two, again, this is for full transparency, so you know what I am working with", and he attached a picture.

Fuck's sake. This was going to be a gigantic issue.

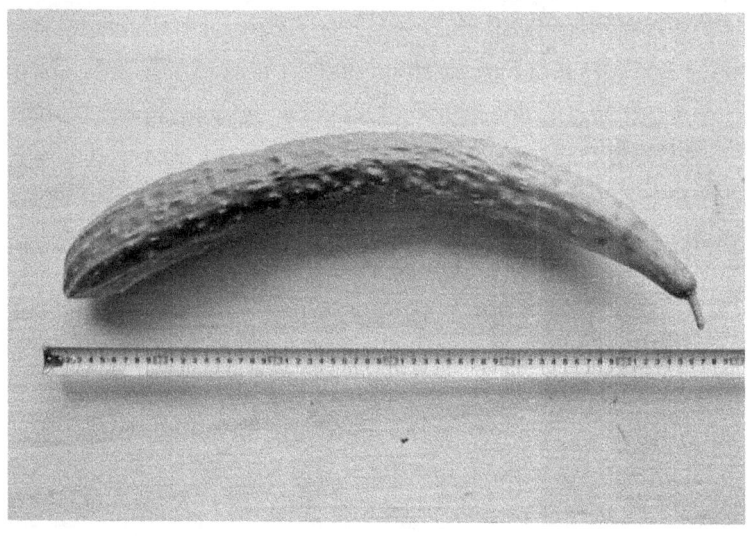

I was unsure when would be the best time to ask Vivian if she would like to meet Mateo at the club. Honestly, I was more worried about asking her to go to the club so soon after our first visit. I decided that it would be best for me to only show Mateo to her and to wait a few days before broaching the subject of meeting him at the club. When Vivian came home from work that evening, it was easy to see that she was flying high. She was in such a great mood that it made me want to talk to her about it all immediately, but then I was afraid of ruining her good mood. When we were finally alone, I decided to start the conversation, but Vivian had the same idea.

"Jennifer texted me today a little bit, which is strange because I never hear from her ever, but she wanted to talk about what happened last week after the club", Vivian began.

"Oh yeah? Nate and I have talked about it almost every night this week. It was so hot. What did she have to say about it?" I asked her.

"Well, we talked about how hot it was too, but she admitted that Lily and I actually made her very jealous. She said it was fun to watch, but it really made her want me more now."

"Wow, really? That is funny. She was the one making you jealous that night, but then you went and had amazing fun, and she got jealous. So funny", I said.

"Yep, exactly. She was more jealous, thinking I was going to see Lily again. She assumed I would be hooking up with her much more now after that night. I told her no, and she was very relieved", Vivian said before laughing.

"Damn, really? That is interesting!" I added.

"Yeah, very interesting. Anyhow, she was saying that we should go to the club again soon, but I don't want that."

I was not sure how to respond to that, then she clarified, "Well, I do not want to go with them, I mean. I want to go again soon for sure, but I want you and me to check it out on our own really."

"About that", I said and smiled at her. "We got a message from a single guy last night that I think you might like. I know your type."

"Oh yeah?" she said, smiling back.

We sat down on the couch, and I pulled up Mateo's profile. I showed her his pictures first, and she raised her eyebrows. She agreed that he was her type of guy. She said he was handsome, and she also liked the picture choices that he made. I read her the profile information he wrote and what he was looking for, and she really liked the things he wrote. Then I read her the messages he and I sent to each other, the compliments he made of her, and the super nice things that he wrote that made me like him and feel he was trustworthy. She laughed at what I wrote to him about her being picky, and maybe she would like him, but maybe not. I then decided to just go for it all, and I proceeded to tell her that if she wanted to meet him, he offered to meet us at the club Friday night. After contemplating a few seconds, she said she would go to the club and meet him, as long as there were no expectations that she would do anything. She reminded me that she was not a whore and was not going to make a habit of fucking people that she just met. I assured her there would be no pressure and I would tell him that as well.

Mateo was thrilled that we would meet him at the club on Friday night. He fully understood that did not guarantee him any action with her whatsoever, but in the event that he did come back to our hotel with us, he wanted to make sure what her boundaries were, as well as mine. He was so thoughtful and respectful to us both that I knew there was no chance that she would not like him. I just hoped he was the same in real life. There still was a huge issue to deal with, and that was the picture he sent me of his cucumber. I asked him how big it was, and he informed me that it was ten inches, and I could tell from the picture that it was thick, too. He asked me what she thought about that picture, to which I admitted that I had not shown her that one and had not talked about it with her. I told Mateo that I was not sure she would agree to meet him if I told her about that because of her past thoughts on the subject matter. I told him that she does not care about huge dicks like that, it is the opposite, so I wanted to let her meet him and decide if she likes him without that factoring into the equation. If she changed her mind after seeing it and was afraid of it, that was on her, and that is how it was meant to be. He agreed to proceed without her knowing. He said I knew her best.

We checked into our hotel room that Friday night and were both ready to go. There were no nerves as we were now quite aware of what we were walking into. And there was no pressure on Vivian at all with Mateo. I explained to her that single men were allowed entry into the club on Fridays, so if she was not feeling a spark with Mateo, we could part ways and find another man or couple if we chose. Vivian added that we do not have to connect with anyone. We could just walk around and explore the club on our own. We could watch people play or be whipped; it was all up to whatever we felt like doing. It was so freeing! We toasted to us with a shot of peach whiskey, showered, dressed, and made our way to Dreams and Desires.

Vivian looked absolutely amazing. It looked as if she was trying to drive Mateo mad with her outfit pairing. She had a tight white shirt on with no bra so you could see her nipples through the material, a tight black leather skirt, bare sexy legs, and black lacy heels that featured her painted red toes. She was fire, and she knew it. We strolled into the club, but this time with an air of calm and confidence. We agreed to meet Mateo a bit earlier so that there would not be such a large crowd to impede us from finding each other and chatting.

We got drinks, stood by the cabana beds, and watched the people slowly file in. There were definitely lots of couples already inside, but there were indeed lots of single men, too. Even though we were early, we still witnessed some single guys going up to couples and talking with them. This was so fascinating to me, yet intimidating, because we made eye contact with one guy, and he immediately approached us. He introduced himself to us, and we all shook hands, but I knew this was not the guy for Vivian. He asked if it was our first time attending because he had not seen us before. I told him we were very new and that we were there to meet a guy that we messaged with on SLS. This guy was relentless and asked if he could just hang out and talk with us in case our guy did not show up. I agreed, but Vivian was not even looking at him. She stood with her cup in her hand and held my hand with the other, but her head was turned toward the dance floor. She was not giving this clown the time of day, and he did not deserve it, to be honest.

Just then, I felt a tap on my arm. I turned to see Mateo standing there with a warm and inviting smile. He asked me if I was Sebastian, to which I confirmed, and I let go of Vivian's hand to shake his. He was dressed very dapper with a gray pin-striped suit, gray dress shoes, and a white buttoned-down shirt that was open enough to show the perfect amount of his chest and tattoo that peeked out from underneath. I told him it was nice to meet him and turned toward Vivian, whose nipples were rock-hard under her see-through shirt due to the low temperature of the club. I put my arm around her waist as she stepped up close to me and extended her hand toward Mateo. She smiled at him and told him it was nice to meet him, but Mateo displayed his smooth demeanor by leaning in to drop a gentle kiss on her cheek. He stepped back, put his hand on his chin, and looked her up and down with a Chesire Cat like grin.

"You are a bad photographer, Sebastian because your wife is way more beautiful than the pictures you take of her!" Mateo said to me, prompting Vivian to laugh loudly.

I already could tell she was very pleased with Mateo in person, as could the ignored, relentless pursuer who took a sip of his drink, turned, and vanished into the strobe lights. Mateo suggested we sit at a vacant table and get to know each other better. The three of us sat on the same side of the booth, with Vivian nestled in between the two of us. My left hand rested on her right inner thigh as her body turned toward Mateo while they talked. They covered several topics in a short time, such as their accents, where they were both from and what they did for a living, to name a few. We decided to get up and get drinks at the bar, but just as we got there, Mateo leaned towards me and spoke softly into my ear for only me to hear.

"Sebastian, I am going to take a walk, and I will come back in about five minutes. I want to give you both a chance to talk with each other about how she is feeling and what she thinks", he said to me.

"Sure, ok, man!" I responded.

He continued, "If she is not feeling it, just go somewhere else for a few minutes. When I come back, if you are not here, I will just go home. No issues from me, and I will not message you again."

"Oh! Ok, man. I mean, I can tell she likes you, so it's all good, I think", I said, surprised.

"I just like to make sure is all, with no pressure. If you guys are still here when I get back, I will take her by the hand and give you guys a tour of the club, as long as you are ok with that", Mateo added.

"Absolutely, man! I am good with all of it, as long as she is, and we will know if she is not good with it. Trust me!"

He patted me on the chest twice and turned to her. He told her he was going to the bathroom and would be right back, and she smiled and nodded. As he walked away, I put my arm around her neck, prompting her to turn and look at me, and I kissed her lips. I asked her what she thought so far, and she told me that he seemed very nice. I asked her if she liked him and wanted to continue hanging out with him or not, to which she assured me she was very comfortable with him. So, the bar is where we stood and waited.

After about ten minutes of Mateo being in the bathroom, Vivian started to question me where he had gone. I was wondering the same thing, but I assumed he was really giving us all the time we needed. I had started to wonder if perhaps he was not feeling it and had left us when I saw him returning with a giant smile on his face as he approached us.

"Do you guys want to go walk around and check out the other rooms? There is a lot going on in the dungeon room", he asked Vivian with his hand on her waist.

"Fuck yeah!" she said excitedly. "I want to watch people get whipped!"

"Let's go then", he said to her while looking at me and motioning with his head.

He took her by the hand and started to lead her toward the narrow hallway, with her following right behind him. She reached out with her other hand and took mine as the three of us made our way through the crowd in single file. Vivian was getting many looks from both men and women as she walked with two men. I imagined she must have felt like a mighty queen at that moment, which made me smile. We reached the dungeon room to find an extremely gorgeous naked woman bound to the cross getting flogged by a giant muscular man. That is where we headed, still all holding hands. As we watched the spectacular display before us, I let go of Vivian's hand and watched as the two of them got closer and closer to each other. It was my turn to use the bathroom, but I was unsure about leaving her alone with him until I remembered the club would not let her leave with anyone but me because of the numbered bracelets they give you at the door. They also take your IDs for the same reason. I knew she was safe, but I decided to check with her first.

I whispered in her ear that I needed to use the bathroom and asked if she was good with me leaving them alone. She smiled and said yes, so I kissed her and left the room. I took a piss as fast as I could because I did not want to leave her too long. I rushed back into the dungeon room and noticed they were not standing where I left them. A slight amount of panic set in as I scanned the room, still not being able to find them. I walked back to where I left them and looked around again, trying not to look worried, and then I finally spotted them. Mateo was sitting in a chair, Vivian was sitting on his lap with her legs across him sideways, and they were making out slowly and sensually. I instantly got hard. I decided to give them space as I was delighted that this was going so well and that she was this comfortable already.

I stood watching both shows now. My attention rotated from the naked whipping on the cross, to my wife's tongue in Mateo's mouth while his hands slowly rubbed her legs. While trying not to get caught watching them out of the corner of my eye, I saw her look up and notice me standing there. She got up, and they walked over to me.

"Why are you standing over here alone? I was wondering where you went and what was taking so long?" Vivian asked me, a bit agitated.

"I am sorry. I was just giving you guys some space. I didn't really want to interrupt", I responded.

"You are my husband, silly. You shouldn't be worried about interrupting anything", she countered back.

"Let's go check out the dance floor area", Mateo interjected and took Vivian's hand once again.

Vivian grabbed my hand, and the three of us went off once again. When we arrived at the dance floor, it was plain to see that the vibe was different, with no one dancing at all. I attributed that to the number of single men hunting for prey. The three of us stood around the cabana beds, not really talking. All three of us were sort of looking around, but I felt things had gotten uncomfortable, and I thought that it was my fault. I was not sure what I did wrong. Giving them space was better than standing next to them and forcing them to stop kissing each other.

"Sebastian, can you get me a drink, please?" Vivian asked, interrupting my self-blame session.

"Sure! Mateo?" I replied, trying to redeem myself.

"No, thank you. I am good, buddy", he retorted.

I returned from the bar with drinks for me and Vivian and found them sitting in a booth together, arranged precisely like they were in the dungeon room. I was a bit irritated that they would only wait for me to leave before making out with each other, but I knew I got in trouble for giving them space the last time, so this time, I walked right up to their table and put her drink on the table in front of her. She stopped kissing him and turned to me.

"Thank you, baby!" she said.

"You're welcome. You look hot as fuck right now, by the way", I told her as I leaned down to kiss her with his face right in front of ours.

I was going for a peck on the lips, but Vivian opened her mouth wide and slid her tongue into my mouth. Oh, yeah, she was feeling excited for sure! When we broke our kiss, I looked at them both and told them I would be standing against the cabana bed four feet behind them. She nodded and smiled, so that was where I went. They talked briefly before Vivian leaned her face to his and kissed him again. I stood against the cabana bed enjoying my time people-watching and wife-watching when suddenly, two girls walked past me. They both made eye contact with me as they passed when, unexpectedly, the second girl stopped and turned back to me.

"Hey there, handsome, do I know you?" the girl asked me.

"Hi, I do not think so", I replied.

"Are you sure? You look very familiar", she stated again.

"I'm sorry I don't know you, but my name is Sebastian", I said while I extended my hand to her.

"Misty", she retorted. "Are you here alone, handsome?"

"No, my wife is right there", pointing to Vivian.

Misty looked at her and turned back to me, "Wow, she is hot as fuck!"

"Thank you!" I laughed.

"Makes sense. You are hot as fuck too!" Misty said as she put her hand on my chest.

"Well, thank you, Misty", I said, giggling.

"Why are you laughing?" she asked, laughing now too.

"I am just shy, I guess, and not used to hearing that", I replied, smiling.

"Well, you are hot as fuck, and I really want to know if you are a good kisser. Can I kiss you?" Misty asked.

I laughed and peeked at Vivian, still kissing Mateo, "Sure!" I said as I put my hands on her waist and pulled her to me.

As soon as we started kissing, I noticed that she tasted like alcohol and cigarettes, which was a turn-off for me, but I indulged her anyhow. After kissing for a few minutes, she stopped and looked into my eyes.

"I have a reservation for a room in twenty minutes. Do you want to come with me?" Misty asked.

"Oh, thank you for that invite, but I can't leave my wife", I answered.

Misty turned her head to look at Vivian and Mateo again, which prompted me to also glance at them. Vivian had her head down, looking in the direction of his pant leg, while it appeared he was whispering in her ear. I could then see his prominent ten-inch bulge under his pants as Vivian slowly rubbed it with her hand. Misty turned back to me.

"She appears to be doing alright", she said sarcastically.

"Yeah, but this is the first time we have met him, and I am not comfortable leaving her alone that long", I told her.

"We will not be too long. I will make you cum fast", Misty said, smiling.

"This is our first time doing this. We agree that she can do what she pleases, but that is not the same for me. So, I really can't but thank you again", I said.

"That seems unfair. She is allowed to do what she is doing right now, and you are not? Do you want me to go ask her? I will introduce myself to her", she now said. I was starting to get irritated.

"No, please don't. She will say no, and it will cause a fight. As I said earlier, I really do not want to leave her alone with a guy we just met also."

"Ok, fine. Your loss. I will come back in twenty minutes to see if you changed your mind", Misty said, waiving and walking away. Fuck's sake. Just then, Vivian stood up off Mateo's lap. She started walking to me as he was walking to the bathrooms.

"Who was your friend?" Vivian asked me, smiling.

"Fuck! Just an annoying girl who kissed me and wants me to go to a room and fuck her in twenty minutes", I answered, a bit annoyed.

"Gosh! She was pretty, at least", she replied.

"Yeah, anyhow, things seem to be going very well with you two!" I said, changing the subject.

"Yeah, I like him, and he seems to really like me. He asked me if I wanted to feel his dick under his pants, and I am a bit scared. I think he has a huge dick!" she said and laughed.

"Fuck, really?" I asked, acting surprised.

"Yeah, I don't know how big, but it felt like it kept going down his pants. I took my hand away because it scared me", Vivian said.

"Poor Vivian", I joked and kissed her. "It is getting a bit late. I was thinking we should get going soon. Do you want to call it a night with him, or do you want to invite him back to our hotel room with us?" I added, nervously awaiting her answer.

She looked at the floor briefly before she looked back up at me.

"Sure. We can invite him back to our room."

CONCLUSION

In life, there is a saying that states if you are not growing, you are dying. It sounds a bit harsh, but there is a lot of truth in that statement. Growth comes in many forms and can sometimes be straightforward, while other times, it can be downright terrifying and complex. Adults generally know when they are not experiencing growth and can begin to feel a sense of stagnancy, ultimately leading them down a path of unhappiness and unworthiness. It is in our DNA that we make a change at that point, right? Whether it is pursuing a new career, relocating to a new region, earning a new educational degree, delving into a new hobby, or purchasing a mid-life crisis convertible, there is typically some change that occurs to spark some semblance of growth in our lives. This change evolves to make us feel useful again. It can make us feel smart again. It can make us feel inspired or vibrant again. Then there are some of us who are yearning for a bit more and need to feel seen again. That need to feel wanted again. That need to feel desired, pursued, excited, empowered, and sexy again.

Self-discovery, transformation, and growth are rugged enough for most adults in society, but what about two adults in a marriage bound by the sworn creed of 'in sickness and in health until death do us part'? How can two independent individuals grow together without growing apart? How do you achieve actual internal change without losing yourself, let alone without losing the love of your life? It takes a lot of work. It takes a lot of love. It takes a lot of trust, communication, and dedication to see it through. While it can be challenging, scary, and even ridiculous at times, we assure you that it is not impossible. We are living proof of that.

Transforming the sanctity of your marriage while empowering the woman you love to discover her sexual freedom and autonomy is not for the faint of heart. I can attest to that, and I think you can all agree now. I went through hell and back. We both did. There are hundreds upon thousands of couples that have opened up their marriage to swinging and swapping, which is not easy in its own right. Still, our finding is that there are not many men out there who are comfortable with their housewife transforming into a hotwife. It takes a special type of thinking. A special type of compassion. An extremely special type of connection.

This may be the end of our book, but it is certainly not the end of our adventure, and it may be the very beginning of your journey down the path less traveled. If we could offer you some advice on the matter, we would say communicate, communicate, and communicate. When you have done that, try to communicate some more! Communicate with one another with clarity and confidence and face your challenges head-on. Keeping feelings inside and hoping things will get better is not a sound strategy, and you will boil over eventually. Assuring each other that your relationship is strong and stable while confirming that your partner is supported is paramount for success and happiness.

Ensure that you are paying attention to your mental health, as it is your compass that guides you on this expedition together. It informs you who you are, who you want to become, what you want, and what you need. Listen to it and share it with your partner; when they share it with you, do not dismiss them. Actively listen to what they tell you, let it resonate with you, and act on it immediately. When you do this, there will be no limit to what you can achieve together.

There will be times on this voyage when, no matter how much you communicate and how much you try to compartmentalize your thoughts, you will feel hurt, angry, jealous, and insecure. You will feel that this was a colossal mistake that was all for nothing, and you will slip back into your old patterns and habits by lashing out with hurtful words or actions. It happens to us all. It is normal. You have not failed or wasted your time. You have not destroyed your marriage. Do not let one shitty day ruin or deprive you of all the good days you have experienced or that are yet to come. Believe in yourself. Believe in your partner.

When this occurs, and it will occur, come back to this book and remind yourself that you are not alone and that you absolutely can do it. You can unquestionably progress forward together by listening to each other, making simple adjustments, and maintaining a positive attitude that nothing bad is happening to you. Your feelings are your feelings, and you are allowed to have them. Your thoughts are your thoughts, and you are allowed to have them. The secret I am about to tell you is simple, but it is hard. Remember that your partner is allowed to have them as well. Practice compassion and active listening, and there is nothing you can't achieve together. Be honest with each other about what is working and what is not working, and make changes that work for you both. What was good last week is not necessarily good today. Check-in with each other. Remember, couples therapy is not the worst idea you could have.

Keep searching for ways to improve that will help you to continue to grow closer to each other. It can be a constant challenge not to be taken lightly, but we assure you that you can rise to the challenge and overcome the turmoil. If done correctly, this can strengthen the bond between you and lead to a rewarding and extraordinary life that you could never have imagined. Ironically, I just came to a stark realization while wrapping this book up. This story of self-discovery was not just about Vivian's transformation, growth, and awakening, but I can see clearly now that it was also about mine this entire time. Cheers!

VIVIAN GOT YOU INSPIRED?

Did Vivian's Awakening Leave You Feeling Inspired? Tell Us About It!

Vivian embarked on an intense sexual journey like no other that needed to be shared with the entire world, and now it is time for you to share your thoughts with the entire world! If you are still here reading this plea, then you obviously loved this story and treasured every moment that Vivian experienced of sexual exploration and self-discovery, that she was not even aware she needed. It is always the quiet and shy ones!

- Did you love how she started out as a self-conscious woman who had not discovered what a sexual being she truly was?
- Did you love how Sebastian would get so excited at the thought of sharing her with other men that kept you intrigued?

Page by page you salivated through the intense narrative of how this married couple braved the storm and began to enjoy sharing sexual experiences with others, and you can share your review with others!

Sharing a review will help us ensure that other individuals just like you will have a chance to read our book and have their lives positively impacted forever! Remember, like hot sexual experiences, the more reviews the merrier!

Scan the QR code to leave your inspiring review:

Or,

Click the link to leave your tantalizing review: https://bit.ly/VivianAwakened

Want Your Story in Our Next Book??

Do you have a story similar to ours that you want to share? Has Vivian inspired you to become a hotwife? We want to hear your story! Go to www.vivianawakened.com, click the Vivian Inspired tab, and send us your story to be featured in our next book!!!!

ABOUT THE AUTHOR

Sebastian Wolfe is an introspective 48-year-old husband and partner with a flair for storytelling and delving into the intricacies of relationships. Having navigated the fascinating journey of his wife's transformation, Sebastian became an outspoken advocate for relationship evolution, personal growth, and empowerment within committed partnerships.

His experiences, combined with his dedication to mutual respect, trust, and open communication, have uniquely positioned him to write about this personal and transformative journey. The narrative touches on love, trust, vulnerability, and the importance of breaking societal norms to find genuine happiness.

Sebastian's mission is to create a dialogue about modern relationship dynamics and challenge traditional marital expectations. He believes that every relationship has its unique path and seeks to inspire couples to find their own way towards mutual fulfillment.

His authenticity and raw honesty in sharing their journey make his book a compelling read for those interested in exploring new frontiers in their relationships. Through his narrative, Sebastian aims to spark discussions, eradicate judgments, and encourage couples to embrace change while fostering deep love and respect.

REFERENCES

Lehmiller, J. (2018, July). *Tell Me What You Want: The Science of Sexual Desire and How It Can Help You Improve Your Sex Life.*

https://medium.com/@manupriyankacpl/all-about-hotwifing-an-ultimate-guide-cc6e76a6ad6b

https://www.dictionary.com/e/slang/hotwife/

https://www.quoteambition.com/desire-quotes/

https://www.today.com/life/inspiration/quotes-about-change-rcna125491

https://www.blissquote.com/2019/10/comfort-zone-quotes.html

https://en.wikipedia.org/wiki/Conventional_sex

https://inspirationfeed.com/i-love-my-wife-quotes/

https://www.psychologytoday.com/us/blog/understanding-the-erotic-code/201910/the-complex-psychology-of-cuckolding

https://www.psychologytoday.com/us/blog/all-about-sex/201911/open-relationships-are-more-popular-you-might-think

https://www.psychologytoday.com/us/blog/women-who-stray/202201/why-cuckolding-has-become-more-mainstream

https://www.masterclass.com/articles/compersion

https://comparecamp.com/open-marriage-statistics/

https://medium.com/@manupriyankacpl/learn-the-joys-of-hotwifing-in-a-happy-marriage-e4417ceb30b2

https://www.psychologytoday.com/us/blog/the-myths-sex/201907/women-who-sleep-other-men-while-their-husbands-watch

https://mysteryvibe.com/blogs/learn/what-is-a-hotwife

https://www.bbc.com/future/article/20200320-why-people-can-love-more-than-one-person

https://www.wifewantstoplay.com/

https://hotwifecommunity.com/sessions/new

https://blog.swingtowns.com/hotwife-bull/

https://compersionclub.com/

https://adultfriendfinder.com/

https://www.tumblr.com/

https://www.reddit.com/r/HotWifeLifestyle/comments/iblna0/first_experience_hotwifing/?rdt=35572

https://www.marriage.com/advice/relationship/vulnerability-quotes/
https://www.1000minds.com/decision-making/decision-quotes
https://www.goodreads.com/quotes/tag/evolve
https://www.merriam-webster.com/dictionary/unicorn
https://en.wikipedia.org/wiki/DeLorean_Motor_Company
https://www.goalcast.com/butterfly-quotes/
https://www.brainyquote.com/authors/anatole-france-quotes
https://www.internationalwomensday.com/Missions/
    15539/Empowerment-quotes-from-women-leaders
https://dictionary.cambridge.org/dictionary/english/empowerment
https://www.swinglifestyle.com/

IMAGE REFERENCES

All images sourced on Shutterstock.

www.ingramcontent.com/pod-product-compliance
Lightning Source LLC
Chambersburg PA
CBHW070609030426
42337CB00020B/3724